Machine Learning with the Elastic Stack

Expert techniques to integrate machine learning with distributed search and analytics

Rich Collier
Bahaaldine Azarmi

BIRMINGHAM - MUMBAI

Machine Learning with the Elastic Stack

Commissioning Editor: Amey Varangaonkar
Acquisition Editor: Aditi Gour
Content Development Editor: Pratik Andrade
Technical Editor: Jovita Alva
Copy Editor: Safis Editing
Project Coordinator: Namrata Swetta
Proofreader: Safis Editing
Indexer: Priyanka Dhadke
Graphics: Jisha Chirayil
Production Coordinator: Arvindkumar Gupta

First published: January 2019

Production reference: 1300119

Published by Packt Publishing Ltd.
Livery Place
35 Livery Street
Birmingham
B3 2PB, UK.

ISBN 978-1-78847-754-3

www.packtpub.com

To the incredibly smart and talented development engineers of the Elastic Machine Learning team – thanks for making an incredible product that artfully balances complexity with simplicity.

– Rich and Baha

mapt.io

Mapt is an online digital library that gives you full access to over 5,000 books and videos, as well as industry leading tools to help you plan your personal development and advance your career. For more information, please visit our website.

Why subscribe?

- Spend less time learning and more time coding with practical eBooks and Videos from over 4,000 industry professionals

- Improve your learning with Skill Plans built especially for you

- Get a free eBook or video every month

- Mapt is fully searchable

- Copy and paste, print, and bookmark content

Packt.com

Did you know that Packt offers eBook versions of every book published, with PDF and ePub files available? You can upgrade to the eBook version at www.packt.com and as a print book customer, you are entitled to a discount on the eBook copy. Get in touch with us at customercare@packtpub.com for more details.

At www.packt.com, you can also read a collection of free technical articles, sign up for a range of free newsletters, and receive exclusive discounts and offers on Packt books and eBooks.

Contributors

About the authors

Rich Collier is a solutions architect at Elastic. Joining the Elastic team from the Prelert acquisition, Rich has over 20 years' experience as a solutions architect and pre-sales systems engineer for software, hardware, and service-based solutions. Rich's technical specialties include big data analytics, machine learning, anomaly detection, threat detection, security operations, application performance management, web applications, and contact center technologies. Rich is based in Boston, Massachusetts.

Bahaaldine Azarmi, or Baha for short, is a solutions architect at Elastic. Prior to this position, Baha co-founded ReachFive, a marketing data platform focused on user behavior and social analytics. Baha also worked for different software vendors such as Talend and Oracle, where he held solutions architect and architect positions. Before *Machine Learning with the Elastic Stack*, Baha authored books including *Learning Kibana 5.0, Scalable Big Data Architecture*, and *Talend for Big Data*. Baha is based in Paris and has an MSc in computer science from Polytech'Paris.

About the reviewers

Dan Noble is an accomplished full-stack web developer, data engineer, entrepreneur, and author with more than 12 years of industry experience and a passion for building novel software solutions that solve meaningful problems. Dan is the founder of Geofable, a software company that helps people tell stories with spatial data. He enjoys working with a variety of programming languages and tools, particularly Python, JavaScript, React, Elasticsearch, and Postgres.

Dan has been a user and advocate of Elasticsearch since 2011. He is the author of the book *Monitoring Elasticsearch*, and was a technical reviewer for several other books, including *The Elasticsearch Cookbook*, by Alberto Paro, and *Learning Elasticsearch*, by Abhishek Andhavarapu.

Matias Cascallares is a software engineer with more than 15 years of experience in software development in a variety of roles, with a deep focus on open source technologies and highly scalable environments. Having lived on three different continents, he has a wealth of experience in multicultural and distributed teams.

Nowadays, in the position of principal solutions architect at Elastic, he helps organizations to get value from their data and find success using the Elastic Stack. He has been involved in projects across multiple verticals, including finance and banking, transportation, e-commerce, and telecommunications.

Packt is searching for authors like you

If you're interested in becoming an author for Packt, please visit authors.packtpub.com and apply today. We have worked with thousands of developers and tech professionals, just like you, to help them share their insight with the global tech community. You can make a general application, apply for a specific hot topic that we are recruiting an author for, or submit your own idea.

Table of Contents

Preface

Data analysis, manual charting, thresholding, and alerting have been an inherent part of IT and security operations for decades. Until the advent of sophisticated machine learning algorithms and techniques, much of the burden of proactive insight, problem detection, and root cause analysis fell onto the shoulders of the analysts. As the complexity and scale of modern applications and infrastructure has grown exponentially, it is apparent that humans need help. Elastic **machine learning (ML)** is an effective, easy-to-use solution for anomaly detection and forecasting use cases in relation to time-series machine data. This definitive elastic ML guide will get the reader proficient in the operation and techniques of advanced analytics without the need to be well-versed in data science.

Who this book is for

If you are an IT professional eager to gain further insights into machine data within Elasticsearch without having to rely on an ML specialist or custom development, *ML with the Elastic Stack* is for you. Those looking to augment manual data analysis with automated, advanced anomaly detection and forecasting will find this book very useful. Prior experience with the Elastic Stack will be helpful in order to get the most out of this book.

What this book covers

Chapter 1, *Machine Learning for IT*, is an introductory and background primer on the historical challenges of manual data analysis in IT and security operations. This chapter provides a comprehensive overview of the theory of operation of Elastic ML in order to get an intrinsic understanding of what is happening under the hood.

Chapter 2, *Installing the Elastic Stack with Machine Learning*, walks you through the comprehensive and descriptive installation procedures for Elasticsearch, Kibana, Metricbeat, and the enabling of the ML feature. This is followed by several working examples of data analysis executed on Metricbeat data to introduce the basics of the mechanics of the ML analysis jobs.

Chapter 3, *Event Change Detection*, goes into detail regarding the count-based analysis techniques that are at the crux of effective log file analysis.

Chapter 4, *IT Operational Analytics and Root Cause Analysis*, explains how leveraging Elastic ML to holistically inspect and analyze data from disparate data sources into correlated views gives the analyst a leg up in terms of legacy approaches.

Chapter 5, *Security Analytics with Elastic Machine Learning*, explains how anomaly detection and behavioral analytics have become a must-have feature for assisting security experts in detecting and unraveling the advanced persistent threats posed by today's cyber adversaries. Elastic ML's approach of detecting behavioral outliers fits perfectly into the strategies of those analysts who use the Elastic Stack for security-based machine data.

Chapter 6, *Alerting on ML Analysis*, explains the different techniques for integrating the proactive notification capability of Elastic Alerting with the insights uncovered by ML in order to make anomaly detection even more actionable.

Chapter 7, *Using Elastic ML Data in Kibana Dashboards*, explains how to augment your traditional Kibana dashboard visualizations with information gleaned from ML.

Chapter 8, *Using Elastic ML with Kibana Canvas,* covers how to create pixel-perfect live reports with real-time data analysis from ML.

Chapter 9, *Forecasting*, explains how Elastic ML's sophisticated time-series models can be used for more than just anomaly detection. Forecasting capabilities enable users to extrapolate trends and behaviors into the future so as to assist with use cases such as capacity planning.

Chapter 10, *ML Tips and Tricks*, includes a variety of practical advice topics that didn't quite fit in other chapters. These useful tidbits will help you to get the most out of Elastic ML.

To get the most out of this book

While this book starts from the ground up in terms of instructions on installation and configuration of the Elastic Stack and the ML feature, it is helpful to have prior experience of setting up and using the Elastic Stack or a similar big data analysis platform.

While the majority of product installation and utilization can be managed by means of a personal computer/laptop (that meets the minimum specifications), the reader can also register for a free trial setup on `https://cloud.elastic.co/login?redirectTo=%2Fdeployments` if that is logistically easier.

No prior experience of IT and/or security operations is necessary to get the most out of this book, but many topics and concepts are written with a view to addressing the plight of an operations analyst.

Many examples shown in this book use demo data sets that are available on the GitHub repository for this book. However, some examples (in Chapter 3, *Event Change Detection* and Chapter 5, *Security Analytics with Elastic Machine Learning* for example) use datasets that could not be distributed publicly. In those cases, you can either replicate the examples using similar kinds of data sets (that is, web access logs) or just follow along conceptually.

Download the example code files

You can download the example code files for this book from your account at www.packt.com. If you purchased this book elsewhere, you can visit www.packt.com/support and register to have the files emailed directly to you.

You can download the code files by following these steps:

1. Log in or register at www.packt.com.
2. Select the **SUPPORT** tab.
3. Click on **Code Downloads & Errata**.
4. Enter the name of the book in the **Search** box and follow the onscreen instructions.

Once the file is downloaded, please make sure that you unzip or extract the folder using the latest version of:

- WinRAR/7-Zip for Windows
- Zipeg/iZip/UnRarX for Mac
- 7-Zip/PeaZip for Linux

The code bundle for the book is also hosted on GitHub at https://github.com/ PacktPublishing/Machine-Learning-with-the-Elastic-Stack. In case there's an update to the code, it will be updated on the existing GitHub repository.

We also have other code bundles from our rich catalog of books and videos available at https://github.com/PacktPublishing/. Check them out!

Download the color images

We also provide a PDF file that has color images of the screenshots/diagrams used in this book. You can download it here: https://www.packtpub.com/sites/default/files/ downloads/9781788477543_ColorImages.pdf.

Conventions used

There are a number of text conventions used throughout this book.

`CodeInText`: Indicates code words in text, database table names, folder names, filenames, file extensions, pathnames, dummy URLs, user input, and Twitter handles. Here is an example: "The `log` section will print a message to an output file, which by default is the Elasticsearch log file."

A block of code is set as follows:

```
GET _cat/indices/metricbeat*
```

Any command-line input or output is written as follows:

```
cd kibana-x.y.z-darwin-x86_64/
```

Bold: Indicates a new term, an important word, or words that you see on screen. For example, words in menus or dialog boxes appear in the text like this. Here is an example: "In the **Management** section of Kibana, click on the **Index Patterns** link."

Warnings or important notes appear like this.

Tips and tricks appear like this.

Get in touch

Feedback from our readers is always welcome.

General feedback: If you have questions about any aspect of this book, mention the book title in the subject of your message and email us at `customercare@packtpub.com`.

Errata: Although we have taken every care to ensure the accuracy of our content, mistakes do happen. If you have found a mistake in this book, we would be grateful if you would report this to us. Please visit `www.packt.com/submit-errata`, selecting your book, clicking on the Errata Submission Form link, and entering the details.

Piracy: If you come across any illegal copies of our works in any form on the internet, we would be grateful if you would provide us with the location address or website name. Please contact us at copyright@packt.com with a link to the material.

If you are interested in becoming an author: If there is a topic that you have expertise in, and you are interested in either writing or contributing to a book, please visit authors.packtpub.com.

Reviews

Please leave a review. Once you have read and used this book, why not leave a review on the site that you purchased it from? Potential readers can then see and use your unbiased opinion to make purchase decisions, we at Packt can understand what you think about our products, and our authors can see your feedback on their book. Thank you!

For more information about Packt, please visit packt.com.

Machine Learning for IT

A decade ago, the idea of using **machine learning** (ML)-based technology in IT operations or IT security seemed a little like science fiction. Today, however, it is one of the most common buzzwords used by software vendors. Clearly, there has been a major shift in both the perception of the need for the technology and the capabilities that the state-of-the-art implementations of the technology can bring to bear. This evolution is important to understand to fully appreciate how Elastic's ML came to be and what problems it was designed to solve.

This chapter is dedicated to reviewing the history and concepts behind how Elastic's ML works. If you are uninterested and want to jump right into the installation and usage of the product, feel free to skip to `Chapter 2`, *Installing the Elastic Stack with ML*.

Overcoming the historical challenges

IT application support specialists and application architects have a demanding job with high expectations. Not only are they tasked with moving new and innovative projects into place for the business, but they also have to also keep currently deployed applications up and running as smoothly as possible. Today's applications are significantly more complicated than ever before—they are highly componentized, distributed, and possibly virtualized. They could be developed using Agile, or by an outsourced team. Plus, they are most likely constantly changing. Some DevOps teams claim they can typically make more than a hundred changes per day to a live production system. Trying to understand a modern application's health and behavior is like a mechanic trying to inspect an automobile while it is moving.

IT security operations analysts have similar struggles in keeping up with day-to-day operations, but they obviously have a different focus of keeping the enterprise secure and mitigating emerging threats. Hackers, malware, and rogue insiders have become so ubiquitous and sophisticated that the prevailing wisdom is that there is no longer a question of *if* an organization will be compromised—it's more of a question of *when* they will find out about it. Clearly, knowing about it as early as possible (before too much damage is done) is much more preferable than learning about it for the first time from law enforcement or the evening news.

So, how can they be helped? Is the crux of the problem that application experts and security analysts lack access to data to help them do their job effectively? Actually, in most cases, it is the exact opposite. Many IT organizations are drowning in data.

The plethora of data

IT departments have invested in monitoring tools for decades and it is not uncommon to have a dozen or more tools actively collecting and archiving data that can be measured in terabytes, or even petabytes, per day. The data can range from rudimentary infrastructure- and network-level data to deep diagnostic data and/or system and application log files. Business-level **key performance indicators (KPIs)** could also be tracked, sometimes including data about the end user's experience. The sheer depth and breadth of data available, in some ways, is the most comprehensive that it has ever been.

To detect emerging problems or threats hidden in that data, there have traditionally been several main approaches to distilling the data into informational insights:

- **Filter/search**: Some tools allow the user to define searches to help trim down the data into a more manageable set. While extremely useful, this capability is most often used in an ad hoc fashion once a problem is suspected. Even then, the success of using this approach usually hinges on the ability for the user to know what they are looking for and their level of experience—both with prior knowledge of living through similar past situations and expertise in the search technology itself.

- **Visualizations**: Dashboards, charts, and widgets are also extremely useful to help us understand what data has been doing and where it is trending. However, visualizations are passive and require being *watched* for meaningful deviations to be detected. Once the number of metrics being collected and plotted surpasses the number of eyeballs available to watch them (or even the screen real estate to display them), visual-only analysis becomes less and less useful.
- **Thresholds/rules**: To get around the requirement of having data be physically watched in order for it to be proactive, many tools allow the user to define rules or conditions that get triggered upon known conditions or known dependencies between items. However, it is unlikely that you can realistically define all appropriate operating ranges or model all of the actual dependencies in today's complex and distributed applications. Plus, the amount and velocity of changes in the application or environment could quickly render any static rule set useless. Analysts found themselves chasing down many false positive alerts, setting up a *boy who cried wolf* paradigm that led to resentment of the tools generating the alerts and skepticism to the value that alerting could provide.

Ultimately, there needed to be a different approach—one that wasn't necessarily a complete repudiation of past techniques, but one that could bring a level of automation and empirical augmentation of the evaluation of data in a meaningful way. Let's face it, humans are imperfect—we have hidden biases, limitations of capacity for remembering information, and we are easily distracted and fatigued. Algorithms, if done correctly, can easily make up for these shortcomings.

The advent of automated anomaly detection

ML, while a very broad topic that encompasses everything from self-driving cars to game-winning computer programs, was a natural place to look for a solution. If you realize that the majority of the requirements of effective application monitoring or security threat hunting are merely variations on the theme of *find me something that is different than normal*, then the discipline of anomaly detection emerges as the natural place to begin using ML techniques to solve these problems for IT professionals.

The science of anomaly detection is certainly nothing new, however. Many very smart people have researched and employed a variety of algorithms and techniques for many years. However, the practical application of anomaly detection for IT data poses some interesting constraints that makes the otherwise academically-worthy algorithms inappropriate for the job. These include the following:

- **Timeliness**: Notification of an outage, breach, or other significant anomalous situation should be known as quickly as possible in order to mitigate it. The cost of downtime or the risk of a continued security compromise is minimized if remedied or contained quickly. Algorithms that cannot keep up with the real-time nature of today's IT data have limited value.

- **Scalability**: As mentioned earlier, the volume, velocity, and variation of IT data continues to explode in modern IT environments. Algorithms that inspect this vast data must be able to scale linearly with the data to be usable in a practical sense.

- **Efficiency**: IT budgets are often highly scrutinized for wasteful spending, and many organizations are constantly being asked to *do more with less*. Tacking on an additional fleet of super-computers to run algorithms is not practical. Rather, modest commodity hardware with typical specifications must be able to be employed as part of the solution.

- **Applicability**: While highly specialized data science is often the best way to solve a specific information problem, the diversity of data in IT environments drive a need for something that can be broadly applicable across the vast majority of use cases. Reusability of the same techniques is much more cost-effective in the long run.

- **Adaptability**: Ever-changing IT environments will quickly render a brittle algorithm useless in no time. Training and retraining the ML model would only introduce yet another time-wasting venture that cannot be afforded.

- **Accuracy**: We already know that alert fatigue from legacy threshold and rule-based systems is a real problem. Swapping one false alarm generator for another will not impress anyone.

- **Ease of use**: Even if all of the previously mentioned constraints could be satisfied, any solution that requires an army of data scientists to implement it would be too costly and would be disqualified immediately.

So, now we are getting to the real meat of the challenge—creating a fast, scalable, accurate, low-cost anomaly detection solution that everyone will use and love because it works flawlessly. No problem!

As daunting as that sounds, Prelert Founder and CTO Steve Dodson took on that challenge back in 2010. While Steve certainly brought his academic chops to the table, the technology that would eventually become Elastic's X-Pack ML had its genesis in the throes of trying to solve real IT application problems—the first being a pesky intermittent outage in a trading platform at a major London finance company. Steve, and a handful of engineers who joined the venture, helped the bank's team use the anomaly detection technology to automatically surface only the *needles in the haystacks* that allowed the analysts to focus on the small set of relevant metrics and log messages that were going awry. The identification of the root cause (a failing service whose recovery caused a cascade of subsequent network problems that wreaked havoc) ultimately brought stability to the application and prevented the need for the bank to spend lots of money on the prior solution, which was an unplanned, costly network upgrade.

As time passed, however, it became clear that even that initial success was only the beginning. A few years and a few thousand real-world use cases later, the marriage of Prelert and Elastic was a natural one—a combination of a platform making big data easily accessible with technology that helped overcome the limitations of human analysis.

What is described in this text is the theory and operation of the technology in Elastic ML as of version 6.5.

Theory of operation

To get a more intrinsic understanding of how the technology works, we will discuss the following:

- A rigorous definition of *unusual* with respect to the technology
- An intuitive example of learning in an unsupervised manner
- A description of how the technology models, de-trends, and scores the data

Defining unusual

Anomaly detection is something almost all of us have a basic intuition on. Humans are quite good at pattern recognition, so it should be of no surprise that if I asked a hundred people on the street "what's unusual?" in the following graph, a vast majority (including non-technical people) would identify the spike in the green line:

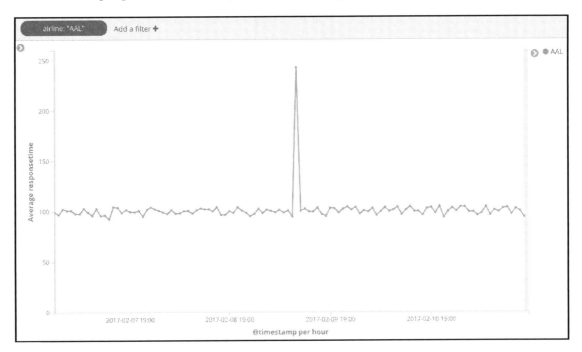

Similarly, let's say we asked "what's unusual?" using the following picture:

We will, again, likely get a majority that rightly claim that the seal is the unusual thing. But, people may struggle to articulate in salient terms the actual heuristics that are used in coming to those conclusions.

In the first case, the heuristic used to define the spike as unusual could be stated as follows:

- Something is unusual if its behavior has significantly deviated from an established pattern or range based upon its past history

In the second case, the heuristic takes the following form:

- Something is unusual if some characteristic of that entity is significantly different than the same characteristic of the other members of a set or population

These key definitions will be relevant to Elastic ML, as they form the two main fundamental modes of operation of the anomaly detection algorithms. As we will see, the user will have control over what mode of operation is employed for a particular use case.

Learning normal, unsupervised

ML—the discipline—has many variations and techniques of the process of learning. ML—the feature in the Elastic Stack—uses a specific type, called *unsupervised learning*. The main attribute of unsupervised learning is that the learning occurs *without anything being taught*. There is no human assistance to shape the decisions of the learning; it simply does so on its own via inspection of the data it is presented with. This is slightly analogous to the learning of a language via the process of immersion, as opposed to sitting down with books of vocabulary and rules of grammar.

To go from a completely naive state where nothing is known about a situation to one where predictions could be made with good certainty, a *model* of the situation needs to be constructed. How this model is created is extremely important, as the efficacy of all subsequent actions taken based upon this model will be highly dependent on the model's accuracy. The model will need to be flexible and continuously updated based upon new information, because that is all that it has to go on in this unsupervised paradigm.

Probability models

Probability distributions can serve this purpose quite well. There are many fundamental types of distributions, but the Poisson distribution is a good one to discuss first because it is appropriate in situations where there are discrete occurrences of things with respect to time:

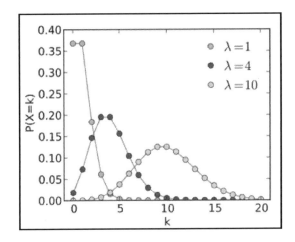

Source: https://en.wikipedia.org/wiki/Poisson_distribution#/media/File:Poisson_pmf.svg

There are three different variants of the distribution shown here, each with a different mean (λ), and the highest expected value of **k**. We can make an analogy that says that these distributions model the expected amount of postal mail that a person gets delivered to their home on a daily basis, represented by **k** on the x axis:

- For $\lambda = 1$, there is about a 37% chance that zero pieces or one piece of mail is delivered daily. Perhaps this is appropriate for a college student that doesn't receive much postal mail.
- For $\lambda = 4$, there is about a 20% chance that three or four pieces are received. Seemingly, this is a good model for a young professional.
- For $\lambda = 10$, there is about a 13% chance that 10 pieces are received per day—perhaps representing a larger family or at least a household that has somehow found themselves on many mailing lists!

The discrete points on each curve also give the likelihood (probability) of other values of **k**. As such, the model can be informative and answer questions such as "Is getting fifteen pieces of mail likely?". As we can see, it is not likely for the student ($\lambda = 1$) or the young professional ($\lambda = 4$), but it is somewhat likely for the large family ($\lambda = 10$).

Obviously, there was a simple declaration made here that the models shown were appropriate for the certain people described—but it should seem obvious that there needs to be a mechanism to learn that model for each individual situation, not just assert it. The process for learning it is intuitive.

Learning the models

Sticking with the postal mail analogy, it would be instinctive to realize that a method of determining what model is the best fit for a particular household could be ascertained simply by hanging out by the mailbox every day and recording what the postal carrier drops into the mailbox. It should also seem obvious that the more observations seen, the higher your confidence should be that your model is accurate. In other words, only spending 3 days by the mailbox would provide less complete information and confidence than spending 30 days, or 300 for that matter.

Algorithmically, a similar process could be designed to self-select the appropriate model based upon observations. Careful scrutiny of the algorithm's choices of the model type itself (that is, Poisson, Gaussian, log-normal, and so on) and the specific coefficients of that model type (as in the preceding example of λ) would also need to be part of this self-selection process. To do this, constant evaluation of the appropriateness of the model is done. Bayesian techniques are also employed to assess the model's likely parameter values, given the dataset as a whole, but allowing for tempering of those decisions based upon how much information has been seen prior to a particular point in time. The ML algorithms accomplish this automatically.

For those that want a deeper dive into some of the representative mathematics going on behind the scenes, please refer to the academic paper at `http://www.ijmlc.org/papers/398-LC018.pdf`.

Most importantly, the modeling that is done is *continuous*, so that new information is considered along with the old, with an exponential weighting to the information that is fresher. Such a model, after 60 observations, could resemble the following:

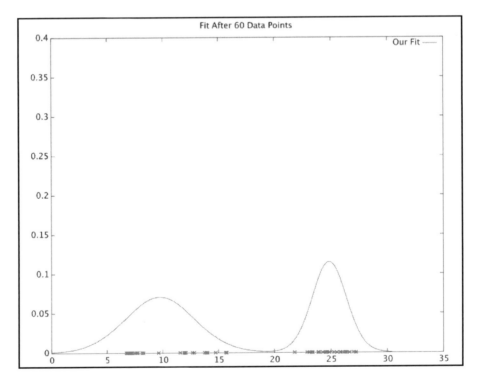

Sample model after 60 observations

It will then seem much different after 400 observations, as the data presents itself with a slew of new observations with values between **5** and **10**:

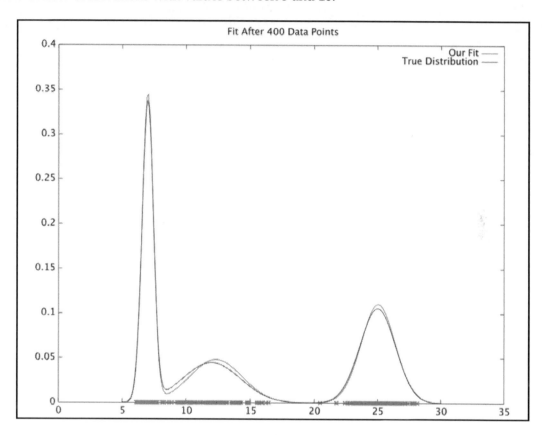

Sample model after 400 observations

Also notice that there is the potential for the model to have multiple *modes*, or areas/clusters of higher probability. The complexity and trueness of the fit of the learned model (shown as the blue curve) with the theoretically ideal model (in black) matters greatly. The more accurate the model, the better representation of the state of *normal* for that dataset, and thus ultimately, the more accurate the prediction of how future values comport with this model.

The continuous nature of the modeling also drives the requirement that this model be capable of *serialization* to long-term storage, so that if model creation/analysis is paused, it can be reinstated and resumed at a later time. As we will see, the operationalization of this process of model creation, storage, and utilization is a complex orchestration, which is fortunately handled automatically by ML.

De-trending

Another important aspect of faithfully modeling real-world data is to account for prominent overtone trends and patterns that naturally occur. Does the data ebb and flow hourly and/or daily with more activity during business hours or business days? If so, then this needs to be accounted for. ML automatically hunts for prominent trends in the data (linear growth, cyclical harmonics, and so on), and factors them out. Let's observe the following graph:

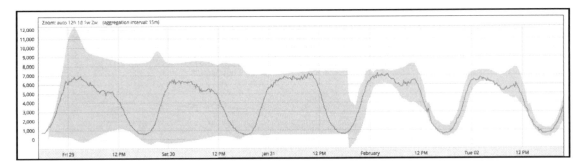

Periodicity de-trending in action after three cycles have been detected

Here, the periodic daily cycle is learned, then factored out. The model's prediction boundaries (represented in the light blue envelope around the dark blue signal) dramatically adjusts after automatically detecting three successive iterations of that cycle.

Therefore, as more data is observed over time, the models gain accuracy both from the perspective of the probability distribution function getting more mature, but also via the de-trending of other patterns that might not emerge for days or weeks.

Scoring of unusualness

Once a model has been constructed, the likelihood of any future observed value can be found within the probability distribution. As described earlier, we had asked the question, "Is getting fifteen pieces of mail likely?". This question can now be empirically answered, depending on the model, with a number between zero (no possibility) and one (absolute certainty). ML will use the model to calculate this fractional value out to approximately 300 significant figures (which can be helpful when dealing with very low probabilities). Let's observe the following graph:

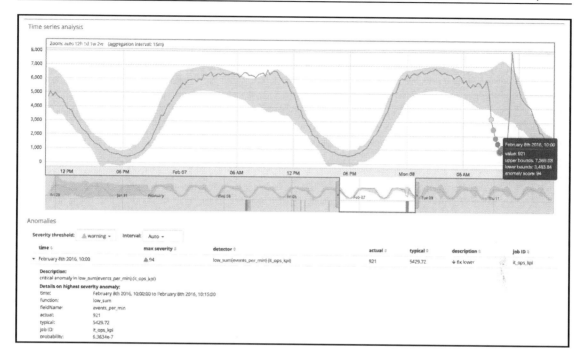

ML calculates the probability of the dip in value in this time series

Here, the probability of the observation of the actual value of **921** at this point in time was calculated to be **6.3634e-7** (or more commonly a mere 0.000063634% chance). This very small value is perhaps not that intuitive to most people. As such, ML will take this probability calculation, and via a process of quantile normalization, re-cast that observation on a severity scale between 0 and 100, where 100 is the highest level of unusualness possible for that particular dataset. In the preceding case, the probability calculation of **6.3634e-7** was normalized to a score of **94**. This normalized score will come in handy later as a means by which to assess the *severity* of the anomaly for purposes of alerting and/or triage.

Operationalization

While `Chapter 2`, *Installing the Elastic Stack with Machine Learning*, will focus on the installation and setup of the product itself, it is good to understand a few key concepts of how ML works from a logistical perspective—where things run and when—and which processes and indices are involved in this complex orchestration.

Jobs

In Elastic's ML, the *job* is the unit of work, similar to what a *watch* is for Elastic's alerting. As we will see in more depth later, the main configuration elements of a job are as follows:

- Job name/ID
- Analysis bucketization window (the **Bucket span**)
- The definition and settings for the query to obtain the raw data to be analyzed (the datafeed)
- The anomaly detection configuration recipe (the **Detector**)

ML jobs are independent and autonomous. Multiples can be running at once, doing independent things and analyzing data from different indices. Jobs can analyze historical data, real-time data, or a mixture of the two. Jobs can be created using the **Machine Learning** UI in Kibana, or programmatically via the API. They also require ML-enabled nodes.

ML nodes

First and foremost, since Elasticsearch is, by nature, a distributed multi-node solution, it is only natural that the ML feature of the Elastic Stack works as a native plugin that obeys many of the same operational concepts. As described in the documentation, ML can be enabled on any or all nodes, but it is a best practice in a production system to have dedicated ML nodes. This is helpful to optimize the types of resources specifically required by ML. Unlike data nodes that are involved in a fair amount of I/O load due to indexing and searching, ML nodes are more compute and memory intensive. With this knowledge, you can size the hardware appropriately for dedicated ML nodes.

One key thing to note—the ML algorithms do not run in the JVM. They are C++-based executables that will use the RAM that is *left over* from whatever is allocated for the **Java Virtual Machine (JVM)** heap. When running a job, the main process that invokes the analysis (called `autodetect`) can be seen in the process list:

```
top - 11:56:59 up 26 min,  1 user,  load average: 0.06, 0.18, 0.48
Tasks:  91 total,   1 running,  90 sleeping,   0 stopped,   0 zombie
Cpu0  :  0.0%us,  0.0%sy,  0.0%ni,100.0%id,  0.0%wa,  0.0%hi,  0.0%si,  0.0%st
Cpu1  :  0.3%us,  0.0%sy,  0.0%ni, 99.7%id,  0.0%wa,  0.0%hi,  0.0%si,  0.0%st
Cpu2  :  0.7%us,  0.0%sy,  0.0%ni, 99.3%id,  0.0%wa,  0.0%hi,  0.0%si,  0.0%st
Cpu3  :  0.3%us,  0.0%sy,  0.0%ni, 99.7%id,  0.0%wa,  0.0%hi,  0.0%si,  0.0%st
Mem:  15405348k total, 10182940k used,  5222408k free,    59148k buffers
Swap:        0k total,        0k used,        0k free,   813512k cached

  PID USER      PR  NI  VIRT  RES  SHR S %CPU %MEM    TIME+  COMMAND
 1835 ec2-user  20   0 15.1g 8.8g 214m S  1.0 59.9  6:39.09 /usr/lib/jvm/java/bin/java -Xms8g -Xmx8g -XX:+UseConcMarkSweepGC -XX:CMSInitiatingOcc
 1863 ec2-user  20   0 1276m 145m  20m S  1.0  1.0  0:25.73 /opt/elastic/ml/kibana/bin/../node/bin/node --no-warnings /opt/elastic/ml/kibana/bin/
 1958 ec2-user  20   0  138m 8224 7536 S  0.0  0.1  0:06.72 /opt/elastic/ml/elasticsearch/plugins/x-pack/platform/linux-x86_64/bin/controller
 2016 ec2-user  20   0  115m 3936 2840 S  0.0  0.0  0:00.06 sshd: ec2-user@pts/0
 2017 ec2-user  20   0  112m 3356 2876 S  0.0  0.0  0:00.01 -bash
 2060 ec2-user  20   0 15308 2132 1820 R  0.0  0.0  0:01.68 top
 2349 ec2-user  20   0 90388  26m  16m S  0.0  0.2  0:00.08 ./autodetect --jobid=weblogs --licenseValidation=846052866894315 --bucketspan=900 --l
```

View of top processes when a ML job is running

There will be one `autodetect` process for every actively running ML job. In multi-node setups, ML will distribute the jobs to each of the ML-enabled nodes to balance the load of the work.

Bucketization

Bucketing input data is an important concept to understand in ML. Set with a key parameter at the job level called `bucket_span`, the input data from the datafeed (described next) is collected into mini batches for processing. Think of the bucket span as a *pre-analysis aggregation interval*—the window of time in which a portion of the data is aggregated over for the purposes of analysis. The shorter the duration of the `bucket_span`, the more granular the analysis, but also the higher the potential for noisy artifacts in the data.

The following graph shows the same dataset aggregated over three different intervals:

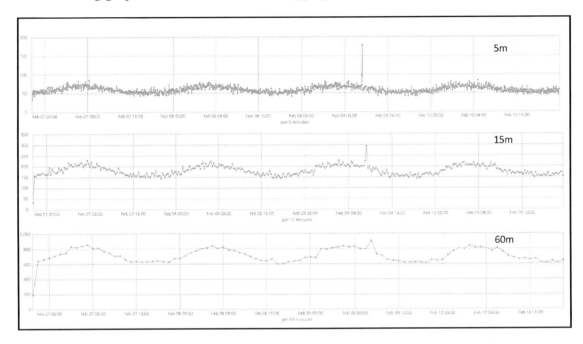

Aggregations of the same data over three different time intervals

Notice that the prominent anomalous spike seen in the version aggregated over the 5-minute interval becomes all but lost if the data is aggregated over a 60-minute interval due to the fact of the spike's short (<2 minute) duration. In fact, at this 60-minute interval, the spike doesn't even seem that anomalous anymore.

This is a practical consideration for the choice of `bucket_span`. On one hand, having a shorter aggregation period is helpful because it will increase the frequency of the analysis (and thus reduce the interval of notification on if there is something anomalous), but making it too short may highlight features in the data that you don't really care about. If the brief spike that's shown in the preceding data is a meaningful anomaly for you, then the 5-minute view of the data is sufficient. If, however, a perturbation of the data that's very brief seems like an unnecessary distraction, then avoid a low value of `bucket_span`.

 Some additional practical considerations can be found on Elastic's blog: `https://www.elastic.co/blog/explaining-the-bucket-span-in-machine-learning-for-elasticsearch`.

The datafeed

ML obviously needs data to analyze (and use to build and mature the statistical models). This data comes from your time series indices in Elasticsearch. The datafeed is the mechanism by which this data is retrieved (searched) on a routine basis and presented to the ML algorithms. Its configuration is mostly obscured from the user, except in the case of the creation of an advanced job in the UI (or by using the ML API). However, it is important to understand what the datafeed is doing behind the scenes.

Similar to the concept of a watch input in alerting, the datafeed will routinely query for data against the index, which contains the data to be analyzed. How often the data (and how much data at a time) the datafeed queries depends on a few factors:

- `bucket_span`: We have already established that `bucket_span` controls the width of the ongoing analysis window. Therefore, the job of the datafeed is to make sure that the buckets are full of chronologically ordered data. You can therefore see that the datafeed will make a date range query to Elasticsearch.
- `frequency`: A parameter that controls how often the raw data is physically queried. If this is between 2 and 20 minutes, `frequency` will equal `bucket_span` (as in, query every 5 minutes for the last 5 minutes' worth of data). If the `bucket_span` is longer, the `frequency`, by default, will be a smaller number (more frequent) so that the overall long interval is not expected to be queried all at once. This is helpful if the dataset is rather voluminous. In other words, the interval of a long `bucket_span` will be chopped up into smaller intervals simply for the purposes of querying.
- `query_delay`: This controls the amount of time "behind now" that the datafeed should query for a bucket span's worth of data. The default is 60s. Therefore, with a `bucket_span` value of 5m and a `query_delay` value of 60s at 12:01 PM, the datafeed will request data in the range of 11:55 AM to midnight. This extra little delay allows for delays in the ingest pipeline to ensure no data is excluded from the analysis if its ingestion is delayed for any reason.

- `scroll_size`: In most cases, the type of search that the datafeed executes to Elasticsearch uses the scroll API. Scroll size defines how much the datafeed queries to Elasticsearch at a time. For example, if the datafeed is set to query for log data every 5 minutes, but in a typical 5-minute window there are 1 million events, the idea of scrolling that data means that not all 1 million events will be expected to be fetched with one giant query. Rather, it will do it with many queries in increments of `scroll_size`. By default, this scroll size is set conservatively to 1,000. So, to get 1 million records returned to ML, the datafeed will ask Elasticsearch for 1,000 rows, a thousand times. Increasing `scroll_size` to 10,000 will make the number of scrolls be reduced to a hundred. In general, beefier clusters should be able to handle a larger `scroll_size` and thus be more efficient in the overall process.

There is an exception, however, in the case of a single metric job. The single metric job (described more later) is a simple ML job that allows only one time series metric to be analyzed. In this case, the scroll API is *not* used to obtain the raw data—rather, the datafeed will automatically create a query aggregation (using the `date_histogram` aggregation). This aggregation technique can also be used for an advanced job, but it currently requires direct editing of the job's JSON configuration and should be reserved for expert users.

Supporting indices

For Elastic's ML to function, there are several supporting indices that exist and serve specific purposes. We will look at the following indices and describe their roles:

- `.ml-state`
- `.ml-notifications`
- `.ml-anomalies-*`

.ml-state

The `.ml-state` index is the place where ML keeps the internal information about the statistical models that have been learned for a specific dataset, plus additional logistical information. This index is not meant to be understandable by a user—it is the backend algorithms of ML that will read and write entries in this index.

Information in the `.ml-state` index is compressed and is a small fraction of the size of the raw data that the ML jobs are analyzing.

.ml-notifications

The `.ml-notifications` index stores the audit messages for ML that appear in the **Job messages** section of the **Job Management** page of the UI:

Audit messages for a particular job in the ML UI

These messages convey the basic information about the job's creation and activity. Additionally, basic operational errors can be found here. Detailed information about the execution of ML jobs, however, is found in the `elasticsearch.log` file.

.ml-anomalies-*

The `.ml-anomalies-*` indices contain the detailed results of ML jobs. There is a single `.ml-anomalies-shared` index that can contain information from multiple jobs (keyed with the `job_id` field). If the user chooses to **Use a dedicated index** in the user interface when creating a job (or sets the `results_index_name` when using the API), then a dedicated results index for that job will be created.

These indices are instrumental in leveraging the output of the ML algorithms. All information displayed in the ML UI will be driven from this result data. Additionally, proactive alerting on anomalies will be accomplished by having watches configured against these indices. More information on this will be presented in `Chapter 6`, *Alerting on ML Analysis*.

The orchestration

ML sequences all of these pieces together when an ML job is configured to run. A simplified version of this process is shown in the following diagram:

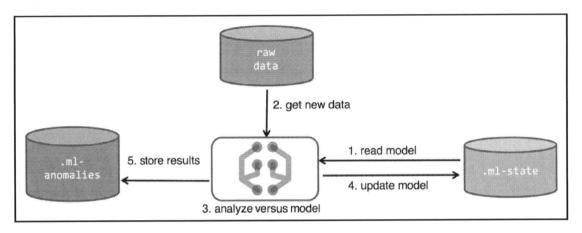

Simplified sequence of ML's procedures per bucket_span

In general, the preceding procedures are done once per `bucket_span`—however, additional optimizations are done to minimize I/O. Those details are beyond the scope of this book. The key takeaway, however, is that this orchestration enables ML to be *online* (that is, not offline/batch) and constantly learning on newly ingested data. This process is also automatically handled by ML so that the user doesn't have to worry about the complex logistics required to make it all happen.

Summary

Now that there is an understanding of both the theoretical and practical operation of Elastic's ML, we can now focus our efforts on getting it properly installed and applying it to different use cases. The following chapters will lead us on the journey of solving some real-world problems in IT operations and IT security with Elastic's state-of-the-art automated anomaly detection.

Installing the Elastic Stack with Machine Learning

2

In Chapter 1, *Machine Learning for IT*, we learned what anomaly detection for IT is by looking at the fundamental steps behind the theory. Most importantly, we learned that, thanks to the Elastic Stack, Elastic **machine learning** (**ML**) allows us to operationalize anomaly detection, from analysis to visualization. Now, in this chapter, we'll roll up our sleeves and get to work installing the entire Elastic Stack. By doing so, we'll have a better understanding of the anatomy of Elastic ML. In this chapter, we will be covering the following topics:

- Installing Elasticsearch
- Installing Kibana
- Enabling ML features
- Elastic ML features

Installing the Elastic Stack

Installing the Elastic Stack is a pretty straightforward process. We first need to download and install Elasticsearch and Kibana. Once installed, there are a few configurations that are necessary to fully enable Elastic ML.

Downloading the software

The Elastic software can be downloaded from `https://elastic.co/guide`. In this book, we'll use version 6.5, which is the latest version at the time of writing. Obviously, it is possible that a more recent version may exist by the time you are reading this book—keep that in mind. Software can change quickly!

To download Elasticsearch, browse `https://www.elastic.co/downloads/elasticsearch`, and choose the appropriate download distribution. Do the same for Kibana at `https://www.elastic.co/downloads/kibana`.

Once downloaded, we are ready to begin the installation process.

 As an alternative to downloading the software, you can request a free trial at `http://cloud.elastic.co`.

Installing Elasticsearch

If, like us, you downloaded the TAR file, start by extracting the content on your filesystem (where x, y, and z are the current version numbers):

```
tar -xvf elasticsearch-x.y.z.tar.gz
```

Otherwise, you could refer to the installation documentation at `https://www.elastic.co/guide/en/elasticsearch/reference/current/_installation.html` if you prefer to use another type of installation.

Once extracted, go into the extracted folder with your favorite Terminal tool and run the following command to start Elasticsearch:

```
cd elasticsearch-x.y.z/bin
./elasticsearch
```

Elasticsearch will start an empty cluster with the default configuration located in the `config` folder of the installation directory, as the following example listing of the directory shows:

```
%> pwd
/Users/yourusername/elasticsearch-6.5.1
%> ls -lF
total 848
-rw-r--r--@  1  yourusername staff 13675 Nov 15 21:20 LICENSE.txt
-rw-r--r--@  1  yourusername staff 403816 Nov 15 21:26 NOTICE.txt
-rw-r--r--@  1  yourusername staff 8519 Nov 15 21:19 README.textile
drwxr-xr-x@ 45 yourusername staff 1440 Nov 15 21:26 bin/
drwxr-xr-x@  9 yourusername staff 288 Nov 15 21:26 config/
drwxr-xr-x@ 42 yourusername staff 1344 Nov 15 21:26 lib/
drwxr-xr-x@  2 yourusername staff 64 Nov 15 21:26 logs/
drwxr-xr-x@ 28 yourusername staff 896 Nov 15 21:26 modules/
drwxr-xr-x@  2 yourusername staff 64 Nov 15 21:26 plugins/
```

For simplicity, we won't change anything in the configuration of Elasticsearch, and we will only use a single node cluster installation.

When Elasticsearch has started, you should see something like the following log in your console:

```
%> bin/elasticsearch
[2018-11-25T09:12:51,181][INFO ][o.e.e.NodeEnvironment ] [1RGCSTv] using
[1] data paths, mounts [[/ (/dev/disk1s1)]], net usable_space [47.1gb], net
total_space [233.4gb], types [apfs]
[2018-11-25T09:12:51,183][INFO ][o.e.e.NodeEnvironment ] [1RGCSTv] heap
size [990.7mb], compressed ordinary object pointers [true]
[2018-11-25T09:12:51,187][INFO ][o.e.n.Node ] [1RGCSTv] node name derived
from node ID [1RGCSTvXQZODVPq8gp2LUw]; set [node.name] to override
[2018-11-25T09:12:51,187][INFO ][o.e.n.Node ] [1RGCSTv] version[6.5.1],
pid[22781], build[default/tar/8c58350/2018-11-16T02:22:42.182257Z], OS[Mac
OS X/10.14.1/x86_64], JVM[Oracle Corporation/Java HotSpot(TM) 64-Bit Server
VM/1.8.0_171/25.171-b11]
[2018-11-25T09:12:51,188][INFO ][o.e.n.Node ] [1RGCSTv] JVM arguments [-
Xms1g, -Xmx1g, -XX:+UseConcMarkSweepGC, -
XX:CMSInitiatingOccupancyFraction=75, -XX:+UseCMSInitiatingOccupancyOnly, -
XX:+AlwaysPreTouch, -Xss1m, -Djava.awt.headless=true, -
Dfile.encoding=UTF-8, -Djna.nosys=true, -XX:-OmitStackTraceInFastThrow, -
Dio.netty.noUnsafe=true, -Dio.netty.noKeySetOptimization=true, -
Dio.netty.recycler.maxCapacityPerThread=0, -
Dlog4j.shutdownHookEnabled=false, -Dlog4j2.disable.jmx=true, -
Djava.io.tmpdir=/var/folders/df/g2gdg5r509d49mv0t7mnft8h0000gn/T/elasticsea
rch.yNPajKl3, -XX:+HeapDumpOnOutOfMemoryError, -XX:HeapDumpPath=data, -
XX:ErrorFile=logs/hs_err_pid%p.log, -XX:+PrintGCDetails, -
XX:+PrintGCDateStamps, -XX:+PrintTenuringDistribution, -
XX:+PrintGCApplicationStoppedTime, -Xloggc:logs/gc.log, -
XX:+UseGCLogFileRotation, -XX:NumberOfGCLogFiles=32, -XX:GCLogFileSize=64m,
-Des.path.home=/Users/yourusername/elastic/v6.5/elasticsearch-6.5.1, -
Des.path.conf=/Users/yourusername/elastic/v6.5/elasticsearch-6.5.1/config,
-Des.distribution.flavor=default, -Des.distribution.type=tar]
...
[2018-11-25T09:13:04,168][INFO ][o.e.l.LicenseService ] [1RGCSTv] license
[f33e8be3-7742-4390-80dd-35275611de75] mode [basic] - valid
```

We can see that the node has properly started, bound to the `9200` port, and that a license of the `basic` type has been applied and is valid. From there, the easiest way to check whether Elasticsearch is properly running is to check through the API. On the Linux/macOS X command line, you could invoke the following:

```
%> curl -X GET "localhost:9200/"
{
 "name" : "1RGCSTv",
```

```
"cluster_name" : "elasticsearch",
"cluster_uuid" : "xV8D0pBdSUS-1LU2OLYmlg",
"version" : {
"number" : "6.5.1",
"build_flavor" : "default",
"build_type" : "tar",
"build_hash" : "8c58350",
"build_date" : "2018-11-16T02:22:42.182257Z",
"build_snapshot" : false,
"lucene_version" : "7.5.0",
"minimum_wire_compatibility_version" : "5.6.0",
"minimum_index_compatibility_version" : "5.0.0"
},
"tagline" : "You Know, for Search"
}
```

Alternatively, you could load the URL directly in your favorite browser or could use PowerShell if you are on Windows. Regardless of the platform, Elasticsearch gives the same basic information—the name of the node that is servicing the request (here, called 1RGCSTv), and the version of Elasticsearch that is running (here, 6.5.1).

Installing Kibana

The Kibana installation process is as simple as Elasticsearch, if you are using the TAR for macOS, extract the archive shown as follows:

```
tar -xvf kibana-x.y.z-darwin-x86_64.tar.gz
```

 You can also refer to the installation process documentation here:
https://www.elastic.co/guide/en/kibana/current/install.html.

As our previously installed Elasticsearch cluster uses the default configuration, we don't need to change the Kibana configuration, so we just need to get into the installation folder and run the following command:

```
cd kibana-x.y.z-darwin-x86_64/
bin/kibana
```

This should produce an output similar to the following:

```
%> bin/kibana
 log [14:27:00.947] [info][status][plugin:kibana@6.5.1] Status changed from
uninitialized to green - Ready
```

```
 log [14:27:01.026] [info][status][plugin:elasticsearch@6.5.1] Status
changed from uninitialized to yellow - Waiting for Elasticsearch
 ...
 log [14:27:08.057] [info][migrations] Finished in 1027ms.
 log [14:27:08.059] [info][listening] Server running at
http://localhost:5601
 log [14:27:08.300] [info][status][plugin:spaces@6.5.1] Status changed from
yellow to green - Ready
```

The important lines are the last two—where you can see that the Kibana server is properly running (with a status of green) on the 5601 port. To visually check whether Kibana is properly running, connect to http://localhost:5601/status and see if you get the following status screen:

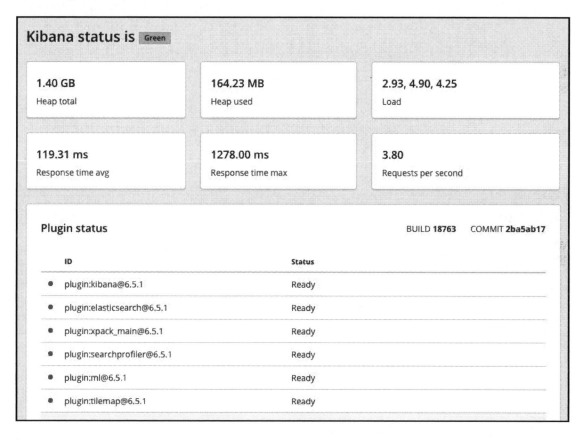

This shows Kibana's status (here **Green**) and the status of each of the core plugins—including the plugin to connect to Elasticsearch and the plugin that ML needs.

Enabling Platinum features

At this point, we have an up-and-running Elasticsearch and Kibana installation, which also has the basic feature set enabled. These basic features (described here: `https://elastic.co/subscriptions`) are value-added features that enhance the operation and functionality of the Elastic Stack over and above the open source version of the Stack or versions found on third-party services (such as the Amazon Elasticsearch service).

Platinum features, however, provide ever more enterprise-class functionality, such as:

- **Security**: Allows you to secure the data indexed in the cluster, encrypt the data at the transport level, and audit all access to the cluster
- **Alerting**: Triggers actions based on condition sets of data or events in the Elasticsearch cluster and beyond
- **Monitoring**: Provides a complete vision of the operational health of Elasticsearch, Kibana, and Logstash
- **Canvas**: Allows pixel-perfect infographics driven by dynamic data
- **ML**: Is of course, the topic of this book

Platinum features can be evaluated out of the box by enabling a trial license. In Kibana, click on **Management**, then **License Management** in the **Elasticsearch** section to reveal the place where a trial license can be enabled:

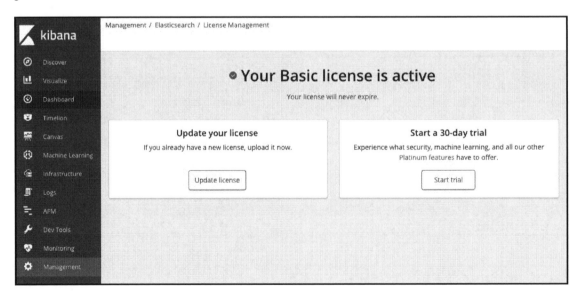

Simply click the **Start trial** button to enable ML and the other Platinum features and to agree to the license terms and conditions:

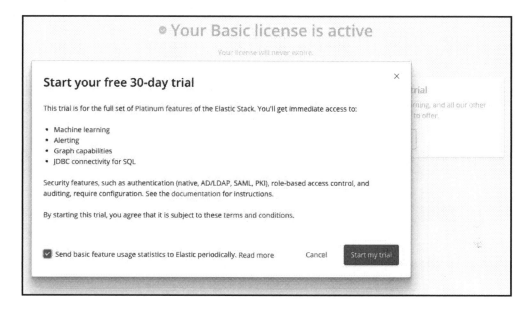

Once this is complete, the licensing screen will indicate that you are in the middle of an active trial of the Platinum features:

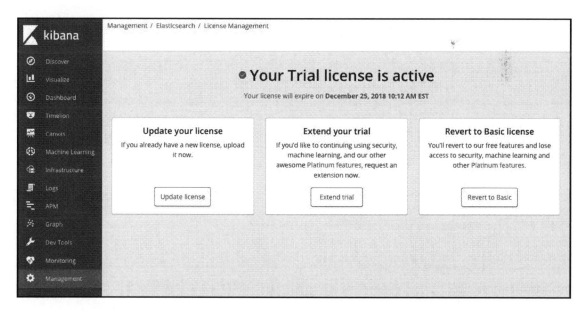

An astute observer will notice the following lines being printed to the Elasticsearch log file upon enabling the `trial` license:

```
[2018-11-25T10:12:13,175][INFO ][o.e.l.LicenseService     ] [1RGCSTv]
license [c1300014-2522-41cb-a0f3-7c5a2bd17f36] mode [trial] - valid
```

Similar messages occur in the Kibana log:

```
 log [15:12:13.230] [info][license][xpack] Imported changed license
information from Elasticsearch for the [data] cluster: mode: trial |
status: active | expiry date: 2018-12-25T10:12:13-05:00
 log [15:12:13.231] [info][kibana-monitoring][monitoring-ui] Starting
monitoring stats collection
 log [15:12:38.937] [info][license][xpack] Imported changed license
information from Elasticsearch for the [monitoring] cluster: mode: trial |
status: active | expiry date: 2018-12-25T10:12:13-05:00
```

Once this is done, you can start to use Elastic ML right away. Additional configuration steps are needed to take advantage of the other Platinum features (such as **Security** and **Monitoring**), but those steps are outside the scope of this book. Consult the Elastic documentation for further assistance on configuring those features.

A guided tour of Elastic ML features

Now that we have Elastic ML enabled, we will use the remainder of this chapter to take a cursory overview of ML capabilities by using the data collected by Metricbeat (which collects and ships system performance metrics to Elasticsearch) as a mechanism to help us manifest some use cases. We will create a variety of ML analysis jobs via the Kibana plugin for ML, and will also learn how to interact with ML via its API.

Getting data for analysis

ML is not very exciting without data in Elasticsearch to analyze. So, let's get some using Metricbeat! Metricbeat is easy to install and configure. It serves as a great source of raw telemetry data that is perfect for ML. Follow along—we'll assume you haven't yet installed Metricbeat, so we can do this together now.

Start by downloading Metricbeat from this page:
`https://www.elastic.co/downloads/beats/metricbeat`. We will run through the installation on macOS X, but if you want to install on a different platform, please refer to the installation documentation
at `https://www.elastic.co/guide/en/beats/metricbeat/current/metricbeat-installation.html`.

After extracting Metricbeat to the directory of your choice, you will notice the following folder structure:

```
%> ls -lF
total 102296
-rw-r--r--@ 1  yourusername staff 13675 Nov 15 20:24 LICENSE.txt
-rw-r--r--@ 1  yourusername staff 163067 Nov 15 20:24 NOTICE.txt
-rw-r--r--@ 1  yourusername staff 808 Nov 15 20:39 README.md
-rw-r--r--@ 1  yourusername staff 373373 Nov 15 20:35 fields.yml
drwxr-xr-x@ 4  yourusername staff 128 Nov 15 20:35 kibana/
-rwxr-xr-x@ 1  yourusername staff 51739288 Nov 15 20:39 metricbeat*
-rw-r--r--@ 1  yourusername staff 61538 Nov 15 20:35
metricbeat.reference.yml
-rw-------@ 1  yourusername staff 5549 Nov 15 20:35 metricbeat.yml
drwxr-xr-x@ 37 yourusername staff 1184 Nov 15 20:35 modules.d/
```

Metricbeat uses modules to collect metrics. Each module defines the basic logic for collecting data from a specific service, such as Redis or MySQL. A module consists of metricsets that fetch and structure the data. The definitions of these modules are in the `modules.d` subdirectory. By default, only the `system` module is enabled—and this is enough for us to use as example data for ML. However, all kinds of data that Metricbeat collects can be analyzed with ML.

Because Metricbeat's default configuration is everything that we need to get started (and because we haven't fully enabled other Platinum features such as security, which would require Metricbeat to know how to authenticate with Elasticsearch, we can simply just start Metricbeat using this default configuration:

```
%> ./metricbeat
```

After starting Metricbeat, go to the Kibana
DevTools console (`http://localhost:5601/app/kibana#/d ev_tools/console`) in order to check whether newly indexed data can be found in the expected `metricbeat` index. In the console, execute the following command:

```
GET _cat/indices/metricbeat*
```

This leverages the `_cat/indices` API to display the summary information about any `metricbeat` index that may exist in your Elasticsearch cluster. If, like me, you've executed this command relatively recently after starting Metricbeat, you will only have a small number of documents in a single index whose name is appended with the date of the index's creation. In our example setup, the return from the preceding call is the following:

```
yellow open metricbeat-6.5.1-2018.11.25 k4tKS42hSJCER9kV8wkP4g 1 1 930 0
532.9kb 532.9kb
```

We can see here that our newly created `metricbeat` index contains 930 documents.

One last thing before we go any further, we need to create a Kibana index pattern in order to visualize and use our Metricbeat data in Kibana. In the **Management** section of Kibana, click on the **Index Patterns** link.

Again, if you're following this installation sequence as we've documented, starting completely from scratch, you won't have any Kibana index patterns yet. As such, you will immediately get the following screenshot:

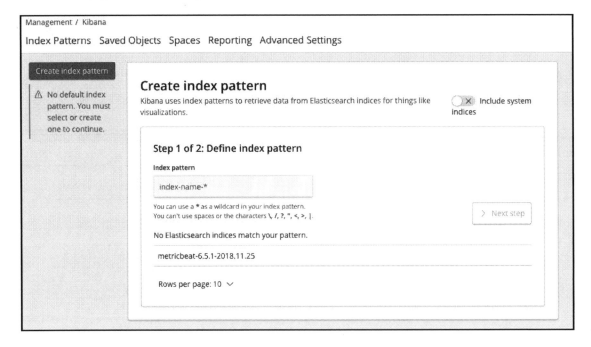

Create an index pattern for the current `metricbeat-*` index (and those that will be created in the future) by defining a pattern that uses a wildcard for the mutable part of the index names:

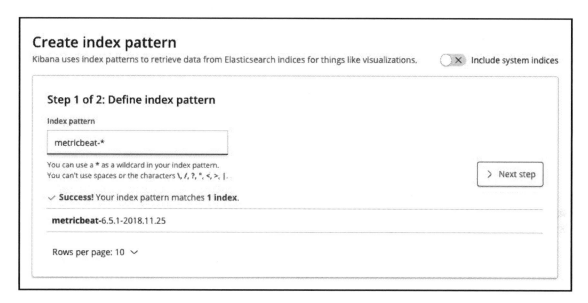

After clicking **Next step**, enter `@timestamp` for the **Time Filter field name**:

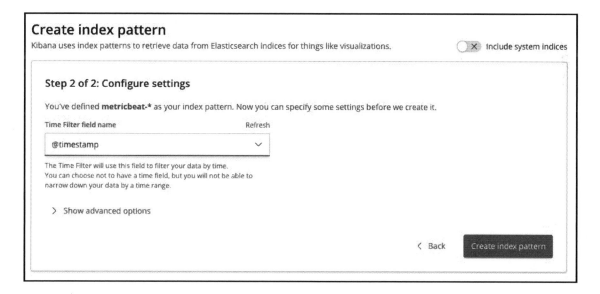

Then click **Create index pattern** to see the completed index pattern definition:

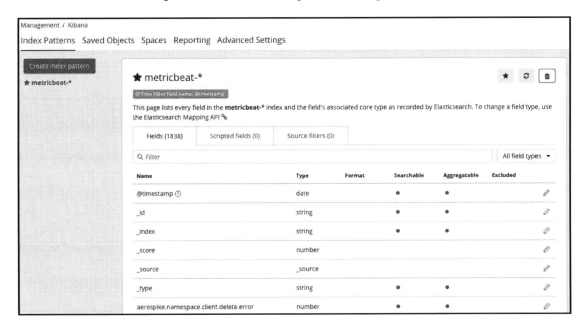

Notice that the creation of the index pattern includes the definition of over 1,800 fields—most of which are not being collected, since we only have the system module enabled. This fact will not affect the ML ability to analyze data that is populated in some of the fields, however.

With Metricbeat running in the background, we now have a process that continuously pushes data to our cluster. This lays the groundwork on which we will rely for the ML walk-through in this chapter. It should be noted that you should let Metricbeat run for at least a few hours, if not longer, before proceeding so that there's a good amount of data for ML to work with.

ML job types in Kibana

As described earlier, using Elastic ML starts with creating and starting a job, the essential unit of work that executes a given analysis based on its configuration.

There are different ways to create a job—either through the UI or through the API. The latter will be discussed later in this chapter, and we'll focus on the UI approach here. In Kibana, in the left-hand menu, you will see a button to access **Machine Learning**. Clicking on it will bring you to the **Job Management** page (you should not have any jobs yet):

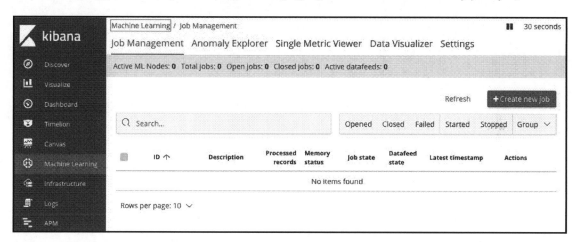

There are other tabs in the UI (namely, the **Anomaly Explorer** and the **Single Metric Viewer** tabs), but we'll discuss those after creating some jobs. If you click on the **+Create new job** button, you will get the following choices:

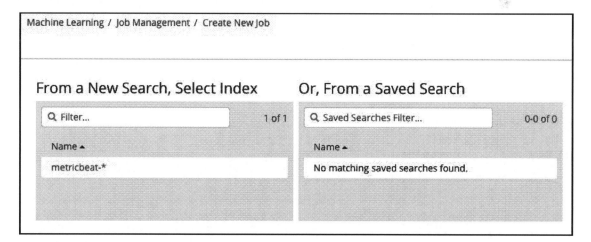

This is asking which data should be considered for analysis. On the left, we can select which index of raw data the ML job should analyze. At the moment, this assumes that no special searching or filtering of the data is required. If we had already created a **Saved Search** in Kibana that filters the data in an index using certain criteria, then the names of of these saved searches would show up on the right-hand side. Since we haven't created any yet, let's just click and choose the `metricbeat-*` index pattern.

The following screenshot shows the available options:

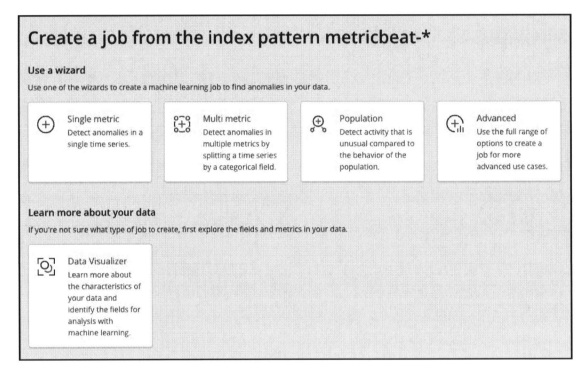

Let's take the time to go through each one of them.

Data Visualizer

Data Visualizer is a handy tool to explore what a dataset contains if you're unfamiliar with it. Because this is probably the first time that you have installed Metricbeat, **Data Visualizer** could be a nice place to visit first, to see the contents of this index:

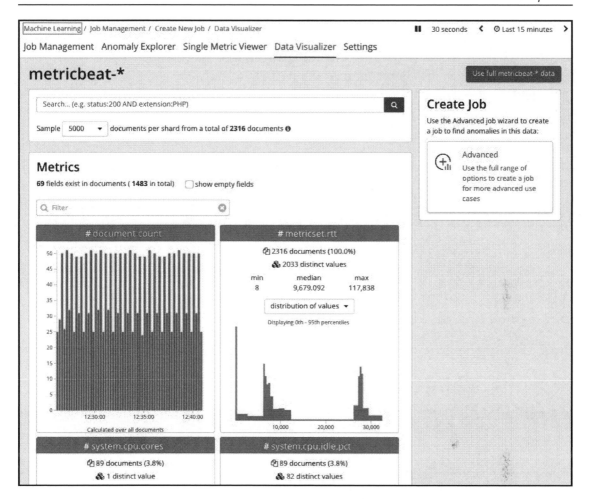

We can see that the immediate benefits of using **Data Visualizer** is that it automatically identifies which fields of the index are *actually* populated (not empty) and also gives the user the ability to see the top values (or a distribution of values) of each field. These will come in handy when deciding which fields to analyze with Elastic ML and which ones to potentially avoid. For example, it is unlikely that the # **system.cpu.cores** field is useful to analyze with ML because it only has **1 distinct value** for all time. Conversely, the # **system.cpu.idle.pct** field may be useful to analyze with ML.

The Single metric job

The Single metric job allows the analysis of a single time series metric at a time. With Metricbeat running in the background, grabbing all the data relative to resource utilization on my laptop, it should be easy to find a good single metric candidate for analysis. In fact, as discussed previously, the **system.cpu.idle.pct** field may be a great place to start.

Let's go back to start the ML job creation again, after clicking on the **Single metric** icon:

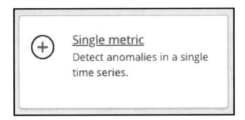

We are now presented with a screen that looks like the following:

Basically, the user has to make a few choices as to how to configure the analysis:

- Pick an **Aggregation** function
- Pick the **Field** to operate that **Aggregation** function on
- Pick the **Bucket span** or time resolution for the analysis
- Pick the duration of history over which the ML job should run

Since we want to operate on the **system.cpu.idle.pct** field, we will pick that, and we will pick the **Min** aggregation function to spot possible anomalies on the low side of the data (since, the longer the CPU is idle, the "worse" it is). Because the data is sampled once per minute, a **Bucket span** of 1m can be fine, but clicking on the **Estimate bucket span** button might yield a more conservative suggestion. Ultimately, choose a **Bucket span** that is the balance between running the analysis frequently enough (to spot anomalies in timeframes that you care about) without running them too frequently. Refer back to Chapter 1, *Machine Learning for IT*, for a review of the discussion on bucketization for more information. Lastly, since we probably haven't been running Metricbeat for too long, it would be useful to leverage all historical data for this metric as part of the ML job. Selecting the **Use full metricbeat-* data** button at the top right will modify Kibana's time/data picker to show the entire history of the metric that is stored in Elasticsearch. The resulting screen after these modifications could look something like the following:

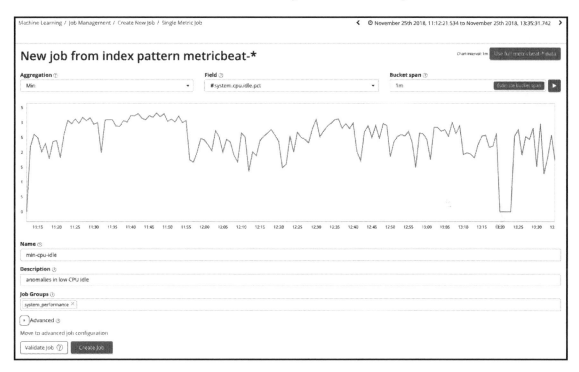

After naming the job and, optionally, giving it a plain text description and putting it into a job group (which could be useful later), clicking on the **Create Job** button will show a view of the ML in action:

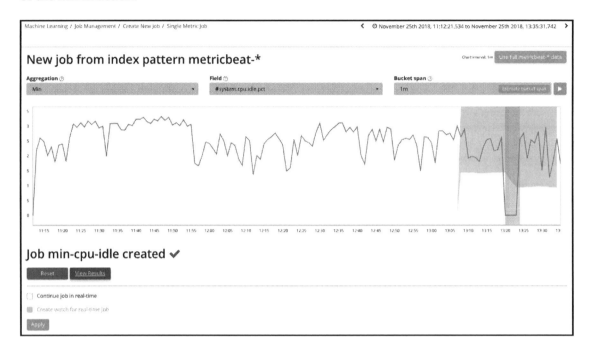

Notice that you will start to see a blue area appearing in the chart, surrounding the actual data values: this is a visual representation of the ML model for this dataset. In this specific example, the model doesn't start to be colorized until the last part of the dataset—this is because, in reality, there's not really enough history on this dataset yet (we could have let Metricbeat collect more data first). But despite that, ML did properly identify (with a vertical yellow bar) the moment when the CPU idle percentage dropped.

Just as a side note for this chapter, after running the job, you will be asked if you want to continue to run the job in real-time or create a watch (an alert) for the real-time job, as the following screen shows:

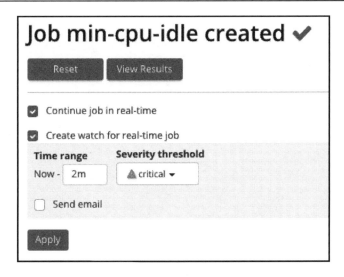

You can enable both options. The first option keeps our ML analysis running in the background in order to detect anomalies in our CPU utilization in real time. The second option relates to ML integration with alerting—a topic we will come back to later in this book.

Click on the **View Results** button to be brought to the **Single Metric Viewer**.

As you will see on the chart, the model is learning as it sees data. If you don't have much data to learn yet, the model may only make a conservative, rough fit around the actual dataset:

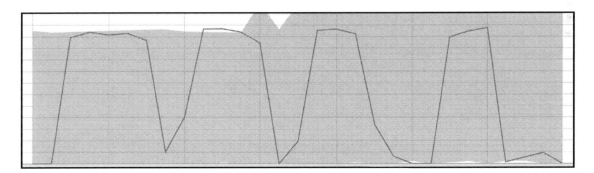

This is typical. As more data is collected by Metricbeat, and more data is seen by ML, the model will get more mature and will more accurately identify the dynamic behavioral patterns in the data, as the following chart shows:

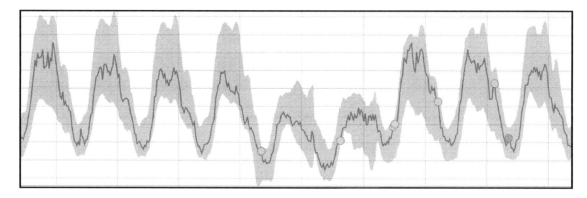

The ML model will automatically detect any periodicity in the data. A metric may behave differently during the day than at night, or differently during the week than it does over the weekend. Therefore, the more data you feed Elastic ML, the more steady and accurate the model gets. Having a large corpus of historical data helps you quickly build a model that is ready for real-time data, without the long wait.

Even though your model isn't that mature yet, you may see in the analysis that anomalies start appearing in the form of dots on the data source in different colors:

- **Warning (blue)**: Scores less than 25
- **Minor (yellow)**: Scores between 25 and 50
- **Major (orange)**: Scores between 50 and 75
- **Critical (red)**: Scores from 75 to 100

In my case, I have one minor anomaly, as the following screenshot shows:

This anomaly shows a higher-than-normal utilization of the CPU (because of the low idle), based on past observations of this metric. I can get more detail from the table located at the bottom of the **Single Metric Viewer**, as seen in the following screenshot:

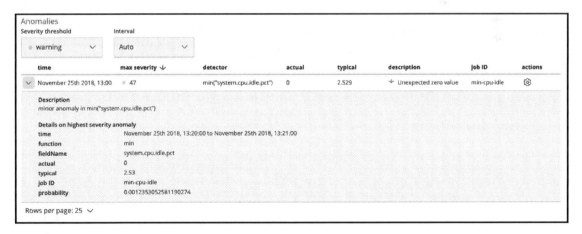

Notice that this anomaly was given a score of **47**, a normalized version of the probability assessment of the actual value of the CPU measurement against the ML model of expected values at the time of occurrence—cast onto a scale from 0 to 100. The probability calculation itself was slightly low: **0.001235**; the normalized anomaly score is inversely proportional and evaluates to **47**, a minor anomaly. Keep in mind that the anomaly scoring is dynamic, depending on the data and its history. In other words, there is no rule that says a probability calculation of a certain value must equal a certain anomaly score.

Note that this analysis doesn't show any details of which process is using the CPU at this time; the way that we choose to aggregate all of the CPU measurements together into a single number has, by design, lost this level of detail. If we'd like to have this detail, we would need to separate or split the CPU measurements on a per-process basis. This is the exact situation where a multi-metric job comes in handy.

Multi-metric job

As explained, a multi-metric job is very helpful for splitting an analysis across many individual metrics at the same time. In our example, we are looking to understand the CPU utilization on a per- process basis. This will lead us to a more accurate analysis of what, if anything, is wrong on our machine, and to immediately understand which process is the cause.

To do that, create a new multi-metric job, in which the first thing to choose is the field or numeric feature of your data to include in the analysis, as the following screenshot shows:

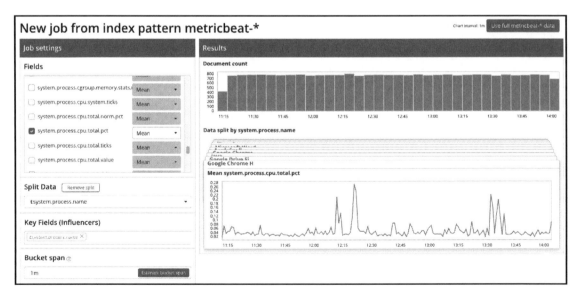

In this case, we've chosen a new metric to model, **system.process.cpu.total.pct**, and have split the analysis by the **tsystem.process.name** field in order to get an individual analysis baselined for every unique process name.

 You should only use relatively low cardinality categorical fields to split an analysis.

You can also pick **Key Fields (Influencers)** that you think might be useful to know whether they impact on the creation of an anomaly. By default, at least the field used to split the data is automatically selected, but you can also choose other fields.

I'm not using any other influencers here, and we'll run the analysis as it is. If you click on the **View Results** button, you will be redirected to the **Anomaly Explorer** page. This is different than the previous visualization, because now we're able to view anomalies across multiple entities at once:

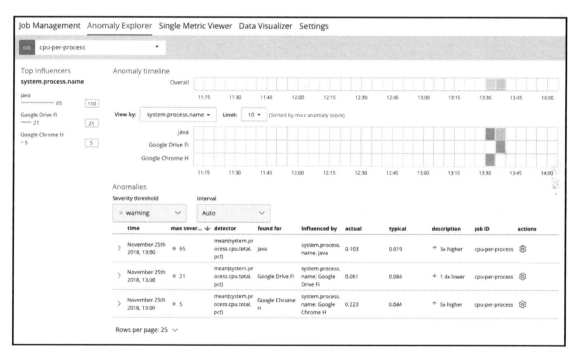

The **Anomaly Explorer** page is comprised of a heat map in the center-right of the preceding screenshot, an influencer list on the left, and a details table, as in the **Single Metric Viewer**.

The heat map in my example contains a line per partition found in the source data; there is a selector to limit the number of rows in the heat map—each of which here represents the most anomalous processes (those with the highest anomaly scores) during the viewed time frame.

If I click on a given square in the heat map to get the detail of the anomaly, I'll get pretty much the same experience as in the **Single Metric Viewer**, except for the fact that the model boundaries will not be drawn, as seen in the following screenshot:

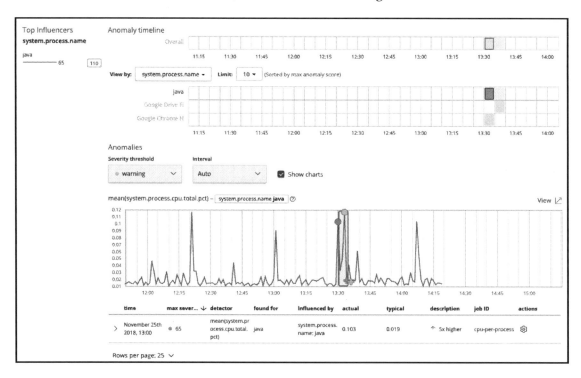

In my example, the Java process is apparently using more CPU than it has in the past (five times more). The **Anomaly Explorer** page is very convenient for getting a sneak peek of the anomalies across the top *n* entities, but if I want to see the analysis for a given process, I can click the **View series** menu item off of the **actions** gear:

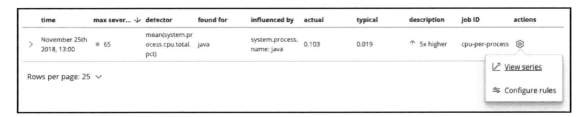

This will bring us back to the **Single Metric Viewer** for the process of interest (in this case, `java`):

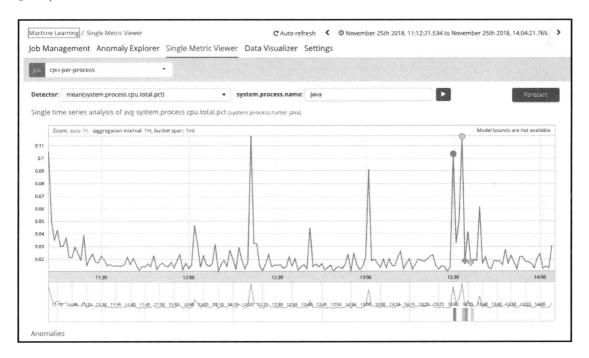

The multi-metric job allows us to split the analysis into multiple parallel analyses. But what if we want to analyze entities compared to each other, not compared to their own history? To accomplish this, we will leverage the **Population** job type.

Population job

Selecting the **Population** job wizard will enable us to compare entities against each other. This can be especially useful if we expect most entities to behave similarly, and we want to find cases of outlier behavior. It is also handy when it is impractical to individually model every entity over all time, because either the entity's behavior is sparse (comes and goes) or the total number of entities is so large that modeling them individually is impractical given a finite amount of compute space.

As such, we could imagine a use case in which we want to find processes that use more CPU than the *typical* process on our system. To create this job, choose the **Population** job wizard and select something as shown in the following screenshot:

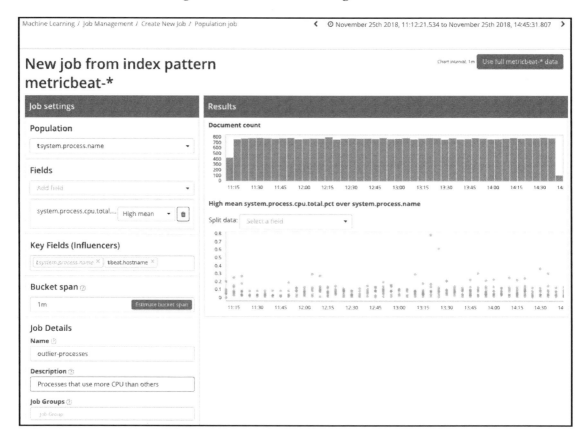

Here, we have specified that **tsystem.process.name** is the field that defines the population; all processes running on the system will be pitted against each other for their behavior—specifically, in terms of the amount of CPU utilized (here, we select the **High mean** of the **system.process.cpu.total.pct** field. Notice that **tbeat.hostname** was also chosen as a candidate influencer. We will see how that worked out in the results.

Running this job gives the following example results:

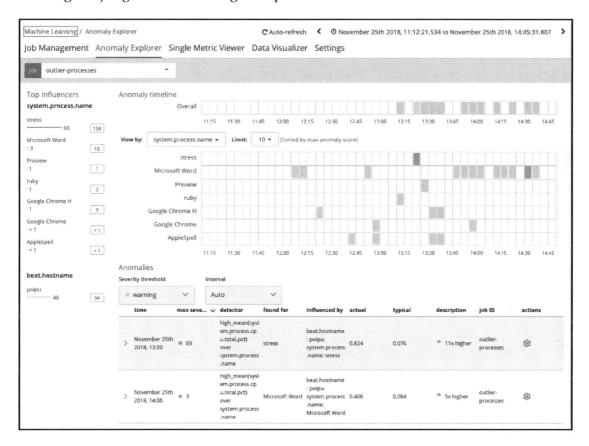

We can see that the process **stress** was found to be hogging the CPU unusually (at 11 times higher than the typical process). Additionally, we are shown that the **poipu** hostname was influential to this anomaly. In other words, this is the machine name running the process called **stress**—pretty handy that it was found despite not being part of the actual anomaly detection itself!

The stress process is a free utility that can be used to exert stress on a system. It was manually used in this example to contrive an anomaly in the data.

If we click on the square in the heat map associated with our anomalous process, we can see the details:

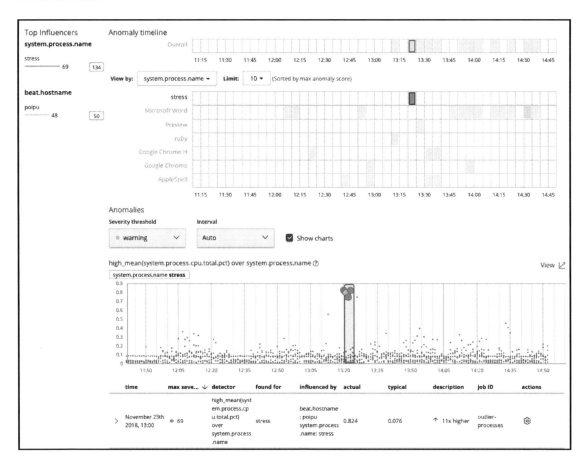

Notice that this visualization is slightly different than seen for multi-metric jobs. It shows the samples of the entity in the context of a sample of the behavior of other entities so that we can more intuitively judge the reason why an entity was unusual compared to its peers.

Advanced job

Advanced jobs allow us to have more control over how they run the analysis. They are not, however, a new kind of job. All ML jobs, regardless of which wizard is used to create them, result in a common job configuration definition. It is just that some wizards are optimized for specific job applications. Configuring a job using the **Advanced** job wizard does, however, give you the ability to control almost every aspect (using the API, discussed in the next section, gives access to every possible aspect).

As a result, we won't discuss much about the **Advanced** job wizard now, but we will leverage it in other examples later in the book.

Controlling ML via the API

As with just about everything in the Elastic Stack, ML can also be completely automated via API calls—including job configuration, execution, and result gathering. Actually, all interactions you have in the Kibana UI leverage the ML API behind the scenes. You could, for example, completely write your own UI if there were specific workflows or visualizations that you wanted.

For more in-depth information about the APIs, please refer to https://www.elastic.co/ guide/en/elasticsearch/reference/current/ml-apis.html. We won't go into each one of them in this part, but we would like to highlight some parts that are worth a detour.

The first API is the job creation API, which allows for the creation of the ML job configuration. For example, if you wanted to recreate the population analysis job shown in the previous example, the following JSON describes the configuration to create a job called my_cpu_job:

```
PUT _xpack/ml/anomaly_detectors/my_cpu_job
{
"description":"Processes that use more CPU than others",
"analysis_config":{
    "bucket_span":"15m",
    "detectors":[
        {
            "detector_description":"high mean CPU",
            "function":"high_mean",
            "field_name":"system.process.cpu.total.pct",
            "over_field_name":"system.process.name"
        }
    ],
    "influencers":[
      "system.process.name",
```

```
            "beat.hostname"
        ]
    },
    "data_description":{
        "time_field":"@timestamp",
        "time_format":"epoch_ms"
    }
}
```

The preceding JSON contains all the configuration we passed through a click experience to Kibana, so it's completely equivalent to what we created in the UI. If you send this to the endpoint, you will get the following JSON response:

```
{
  "job_id" : "my_cpu_job",
  "job_type" : "anomaly_detector",
  "job_version" : "6.5.1",
  "description" : "Processes that use more CPU than others",
  "create_time" : 1543197011209,
  "analysis_config" : {
    "bucket_span" : "15m",
    "detectors" : [
      {
        "detector_description" : "high mean CPU",
        "function" : "high_mean",
        "field_name" : "system.process.cpu.total.pct",
        "over_field_name" : "system.process.name",
        "detector_index" : 0
      }
    ],
    "influencers" : [
      "system.process.name",
      "beat.hostname"
    ]
  },
  "analysis_limits" : {
    "model_memory_limit" : "1024mb",
    "categorization_examples_limit" : 4
  },
  "data_description" : {
    "time_field" : "@timestamp",
    "time_format" : "epoch_ms"
  },
  "model_snapshot_retention_days" : 1,
  "results_index_name" : "shared"
}
```

Note that the `job_id` field needs to be unique when creating the job.

It's important to note that the job also needs to be configured to know which index of raw data to analyze and which query needs to be executed against that index. This is part of the `datafeed` configuration and is set via the documentation found at: `https://www.elastic.co/guide/en/elasticsearch/reference/current/ml-put-datafeed.html`.

An example request to configure the `datafeed` for a job called `my_cpu_job` would be the following:

```
PUT _xpack/ml/datafeeds/datafeed-my_cpu_job
{
        "job_id" : "my_cpu_job",
        "indexes" : [
          "metricbeat-*"
        ]
}
```

The response would be as follows:

```
{
 "datafeed_id" : "datafeed-my_cpu_job",
 "job_id" : "my_cpu_job",
 "query_delay" : "106392ms",
 "indices" : [
 "metricbeat-*"
 ],
 "types" : [ ],
 "query" : {
 "match_all" : {
 "boost" : 1.0
 }
 },
 "scroll_size" : 1000,
 "chunking_config" : {
 "mode" : "auto"
 }
}
```

Notice that the default query to the index is `match_all`, which means that no filtering will take place. We could, of course, insert any valid Elasticsearch DSL in the query block to perform custom filters or aggregations. This concept will be covered later in the book.

There are other APIs that can be used to extract results or modify other operational aspects of the ML job. Consult the online documentation for more information.

Summary

At this point, you should have installed Elastic ML and have a decent understanding of how to use it to analyze data in real time in Elasticsearch. In the next chapter, Chapter 3, *Event Change Detection* you will start learning additional ways to effectively use ML to solve a variety of new use cases.

3
Event Change Detection

As shown in the previous chapter, Chapter 2, *Installing the Elastic Stack with Machine Learning,* tracking metrics and their potential abnormalities over time is certainly an extremely important application of anomaly detection to IT data. This affords a broad, proactive coverage of many key indicators of performance and availability.

However, there are many important use cases that revolve around the idea of event change detection. These include the following:

- Discovering a flood of error messages suddenly cropping up in a log file
- Detecting a sudden drop in the amount of orders processed by an online system
- Determining a sudden excessive number of attempts at accessing something (for example, brute-force authentication or reconnaissance scanning)

In this chapter, we'll discuss the concepts of determining anomalies based on the occurrence rates of things, and we will go through several practical examples such as the following:

- Count functions
- Counting in population analysis
- Detecting things that rarely occur
- Counting message-based logs via categorization

How to understand the normal rate of occurrence

Imagine that you're troubleshooting a problem by looking at a particular log file. You see a line in the log that looks like the following:

```
18/05/2017 15:16:00 DB Not Updated [Master] Table
```

Unless you have some intimate knowledge about the inner workings of the application that created this log, you may not know whether the message is important. Having the database be `Not Updated` possibly sounds like a negative situation. However, if you knew that the application routinely writes this message, day in and day out, several hundred times per hour, then you would naturally realize that this message is benign and should possibly be ignored, because clearly the application works fine every day despite this message being written to the log file.

The problem, obviously, is one of human interpretation. Inspection of the text of the message and the reading of a negative phrase (`Not Updated`) potentially biases a person toward thinking that the message is noteworthy because of a possible problem. However, the frequency of the message (it happens routinely) should inform the person that the message must not be that important because the application is working (that is, there are no reported outages) despite these messages being written to the log.

It can be hard for a human to process that information (assess the message content/relevance and also the frequency over time) for just a few types of messages in a log file. Imagine if there were thousands of unique message types occurring at a total rate of millions of log lines per day. Even the most seasoned expert in both the application content and search/visualizations will find this impractical, if not impossible, to wrangle.

ML comes to the rescue with capabilities that allow empirical assessment of both the uniqueness of the content of the messages and the relative frequency of occurrence. Let's first focus on the frequency aspect of things with an introduction to counting functions.

Exploring count functions

As seen in Chapter 2, *Installing the Elastic Stack with Machine Learning*, Elastic ML jobs contain detectors for a combination of a function applied to some aspect of the data (for example, a field). The example jobs shown in Chapter 2, *Installing the Elastic Stack with Machine Learning*, have detectors using metric-based functions operating on metric-based fields (such as CPU utilization). However, the detectors we will be exploring in this chapter will be those that simply count occurrences of things over time.

The three main functions to get familiar with are as follows:

- **Count**: Counts the number of documents in the bucket resulting from a query of the raw data index
- **High Count**: The same as **Count**, but will only flag an anomaly if the count is higher than expected
- **Low Count**: The same as **Count**, but will only flag an anomaly if the count is lower than expected

You will see that there are a variety of one-sided functions in ML (to only detect anomalies in a certain direction). Additionally, it is important to know that this function is not counting a field or even the existence of fields within a document, it is merely counting the documents.

To get a more intuitive feeling for what the **Count** function does, let's see what a standard (non-ML) Kibana visualization shows us for a particular dataset when that dataset is viewed with a **Count** aggregation on the **Y-Axis** and a 10-minute resolution of the **Date Histogram** aggregation on the **X-Axis**:

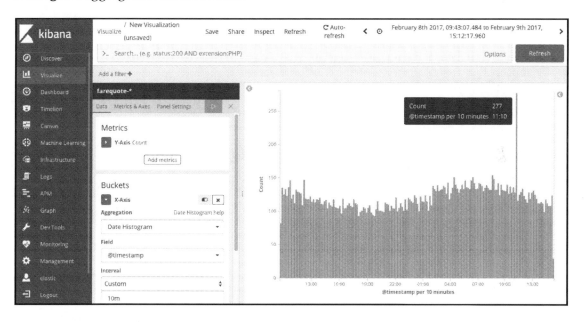

From the preceding screenshot, we can make a few observations:

- This vertical bar visualization counts the number of documents in the index for each 10-minute bucket of time and displays the resulting view. We can see, for example, that the number of documents at the 11:10 AM mark on February 9 has a spike in documents/events that seems much higher than the *typical* rate (the points of time excluding the spike); in this case, the count is 277.
- To automate the analysis of this data, we plotted it with an ML job. We can use a **Single Metric Job** since there is only one time series (a count of all docs in this index). Configuring the job will look like the following, after the initial steps of the **Single Metric Job** wizard are completed (as described in `Chapter 2`, *Installing the Elastic Stack with Machine Learning*):

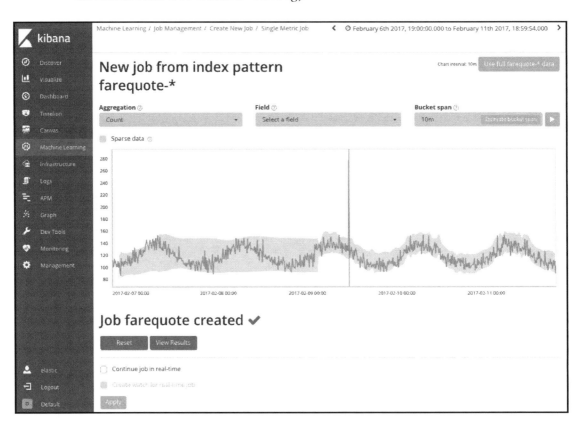

We can see that the **Count** aggregation function is used (although **High Count** would also have been appropriate), and the **Bucket span** is set to the same value we have when we build our Kibana visualization. After running the job, the resulting anomaly is found:

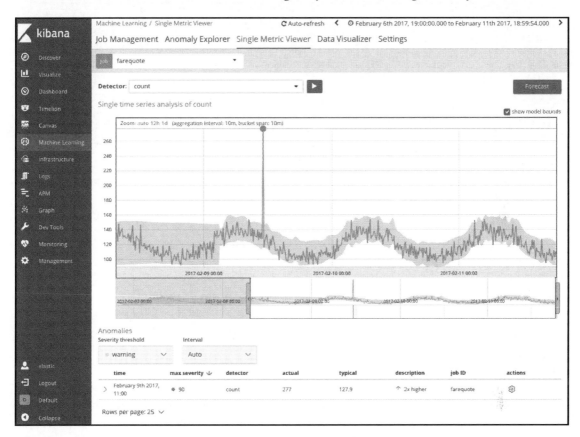

Of course, the anomaly of **277** documents/events is exactly what we had hoped would be found, since this is exactly what we saw when we manually analyzed the data in the vertical bar visualization earlier.

Notice what happens, however, if the same data is analyzed with a 60m bucket span instead of a 10m one:

Note that because the rate spike that occurred was so short, when the event count aggregates over the span of an hour, the spike doesn't look anomalous anymore, and as such ML doesn't even consider it anomalous. This is similar to the situation pointed out in Chapter 1, *Machine Learning for IT*, where the value of the bucket span has a direct effect on the resulting analysis.

As mentioned earlier, the *one-sided* functions of **Low Count** and **High Count** are especially useful when trying to find deviations only in one direction. Perhaps you only want to find a drop of orders on your e-commerce site (because a spike in orders would be good news!), or perhaps you only want to spot a spike in errors (because a drop in errors is a good thing too!).

Remember, the **Count** functions count documents, not fields. If you have a field that represents a summarized count of something, then that will need special treatment as described in the next section.

Summarized counts

We clearly stated that the **Count** functions simply tally the number of documents per unit of time. But what if the data that you are using actually has a field value that contains a summarized count already? For example, in the following data, the events_per_min field represents a summarized number of occurrences of something (online purchases in this case) that occurred in the last minute:

```
{
    "metrictype": "kpi",
    "@timestamp": "2016-02-12T23:11:09.000Z",
    "events_per_min": 22,
    "@version": "1",
    "type": "it_ops_kpi",
    "metricname": "online_purchases",
    "metricvalue": "22",
    "kpi_indicator": "online_purchases"
}
```

To get the ML job to recognize that the events_per_min field is the thing that needs to be tallied (and not the documents themselves), we need to set a **summary_count_field_name** directive (which is only settable in the UI in **Advanced** jobs):

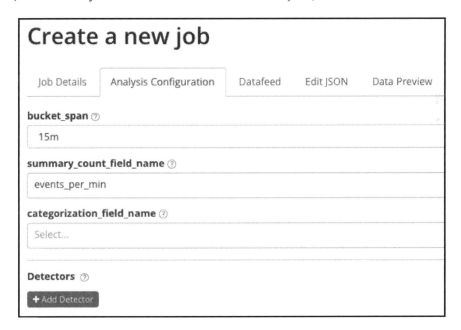

After specifying `events_per_min` as **summary_count_field_name**, then the appropriate detector configuration in this case simply employs the **low_count** function:

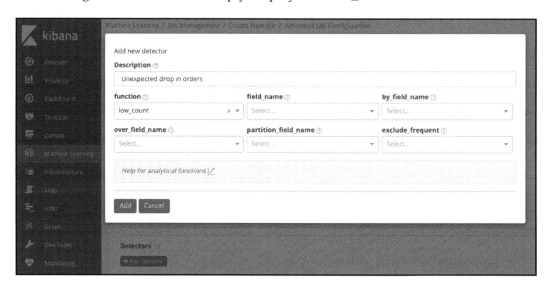

The results of running the job give exactly what we expect—a detection of some cases when my customer online purchases were lower than they should have been, including times when the orders dropped completely to zero, as well as a partial loss of orders on one midday:

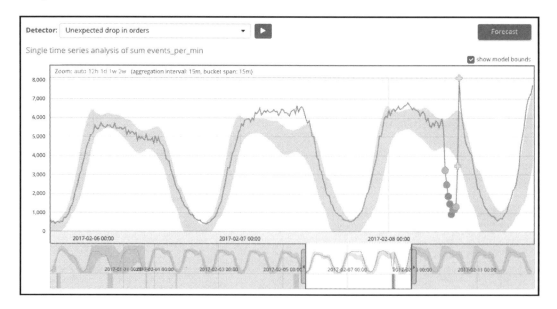

Splitting the counts

In a similar approach to one shown in previous chapters with respect to splitting and/or partitioning the analysis along categorical fields, this can be done with the **Count** functions. This makes it handy to get many simultaneous event rate analyses at once, accomplished with either the **Multi Metric job** or the **Advanced** job UI wizards.

Some common use cases for this are as follows:

- Finding an increase in error messages in a log by error ID or type
- Finding a change in log volume by host; perhaps some configuration was changed
- Determining whether certain products suddenly are selling better or worse than they used to

To accomplish this, the same mechanisms are used. For example, in a **Multi Metric job**, one can choose a categorical field by which to split the data while using a **Count** (**event rate**) function:

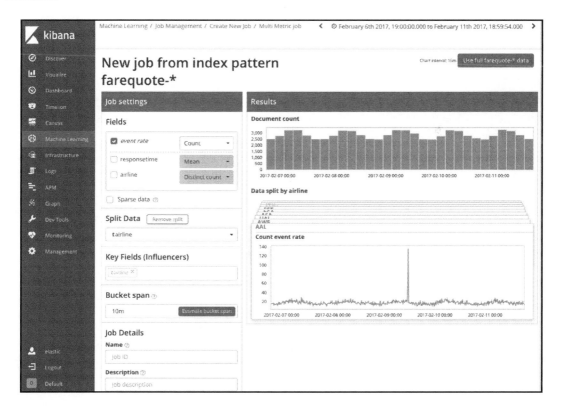

This results in the following, where it was determined that only one of the many entities being modeled was actually unusual (the spike in the volume of requests for the airline **AAL**):

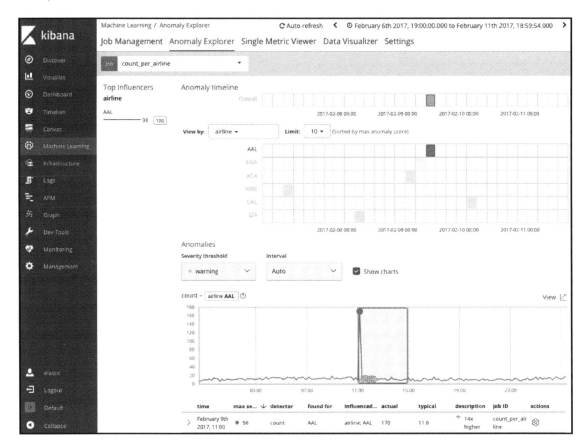

As you can see, it is extremely easy to see volume-based variations across a wide number of unique instances of a categorical field in the data. We can see at a glance which entities are unusual and which are not.

Other counting functions

In addition to the functions we've described so far, there are several other counting functions that enable a broader set of use cases.

Non-zero count

The non-zero count functions (`non_zero_count`, `low_non_zero_count`, and `high_non_zero_count`) allow the handling of count-based analysis, but also allow for accurate modeling in cases where the data may be sparse and you would not want the non-existence of data to be explicitly treated as zero, but rather as null. In other words, a dataset in time, which looks like the following:

    4,3,0,0,2,0,5,3,2,0,2,0,0,1,0,4

Data with the `non_zero_count` functions will be interpreted as the following:

    4,3,2,5,3,2,2,1,4

The act of treating zeros as null can be useful in cases where the non-existence of measurements at regular intervals is expected. Some practical examples of this are as follows:

- The number of airline tickets purchased per month by an individual
- The number of times a server reboots in a day
- The number of login attempts on a system per hour

Distinct count

The distinct count functions (distinct_count, low_distinct_count, and high_distinct_count) measure the uniqueness (cardinality) of values for a particular field. There are many possible uses of this function, particularly when used in the context of population analysis (see next) to uncover entities that are logging an overly diverse set of field values. A good classic example is looking for IP addresses that are engaged in port scanning, accessing an unusually large number of distinct destination port numbers on remote machines:

```
{
    "function" : "high_distinct_count",
    "field_name" : "dest_port",
    "over_field_name": "src_ip"
}
```

Notice that the src_ip field is defined as the over field, thus invoking population analysis and comparing the activity of source IPs against each other. An additional discussion on population analysis follows next.

Counting in population analysis

The execution of anomaly detection on counting the occurrence of things with respect to an entity's own history is clearly useful. But, as we introduced conceptually in Chapter 1, *Machine Learning for IT*, the idea of comparing the behavior of something against its peers is also informative, especially in cases where we assess the number of times something happens. Counting the occurrence of things across a population to find individual outliers has a variety of important use cases. Some of these use cases include the following:

- Finding machines that are logging more (or less) than similarly configured machines. Here are some example scenarios:
  - Incorrect configuration changes that have caused more errors to suddenly occur in the log file for the system or application.
  - A system that might be compromised by malware may actually be instructed to suppress logging in certain situations, thus drastically decreasing the log volume.
  - A system that has lost connectivity or has operationally failed, thus having its log volume diminished.
  - An otherwise harmless change to a logging-level setting (debug instead of normal), now annoyingly making your logs take up more disk space.

- Finding a behavior that differs from that of most *normal* users. A nod in the direction of user-behavioral analytics, a comparison of the rate of activity of users against their peers can be useful in the following cases:
    - **Automated users**: Instead of the typical human behavior or usage pattern, an automated script may exhibit behavioral patterns that look quite different in terms of the speed, duration, and diversity of events they create. Whether it is finding a crawler trying to harvest the products and prices of an online catalog or detecting a bot that might be engaged in the spread of misinformation on social media, the automatic identification of automated users can be helpful.
    - **Snooping users**: Whether it is a real human testing the boundaries of what they can get away with or an intelligent piece of malware doing some reconnaissance, a snooper may execute a wide variety of things, hoping for a match or to find a way in (such as by port scanning). Often, using the `distinct_count` function can help find a snooper.
    - **Malicious/abusive users**: After the reconnaissance phase, a malicious user or malware is now actively wreaking havoc and is involved in active measures such as denial of service, brute forcing, or stealing valuable information. Again, compared with typical users, malicious and abusive users have stark contrasts in their behavior regarding volume, diversity, and intensity of activity per unit of time.

A practical example of exposing behavioral anomalies would involve the analysis of a log that tracks usage, such as a web access log. We could set up a job looking for unusual client IP addresses, those that are acting like automated bots and not like humans (since bots often make requests with higher volumes, frequency, and diversity than humans). The configuration compares the count of web requests per unit of time, split by the HTTP status code (since bots will also often make random access patterns that result in a diverse set of response codes), against a population of client IPs:

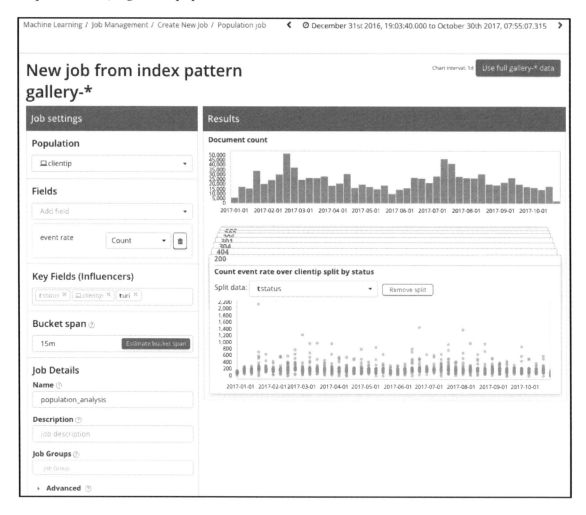

When executed, the job nicely identifies some rogue IP addresses:

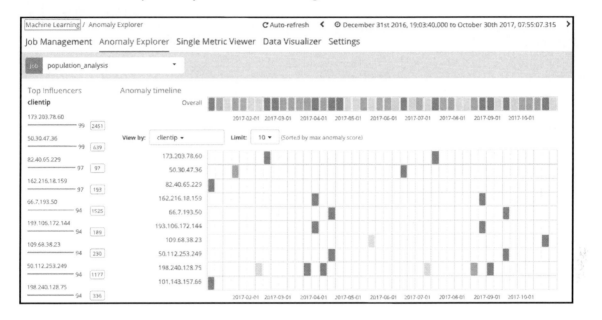

The heatmap shows the top 10 most unusual client IP addresses, again based on the volume of requests per unit of time. Focusing on the top offender, `173.203.78.60`, we can see the details when clicking on the red tile in its swim lane:

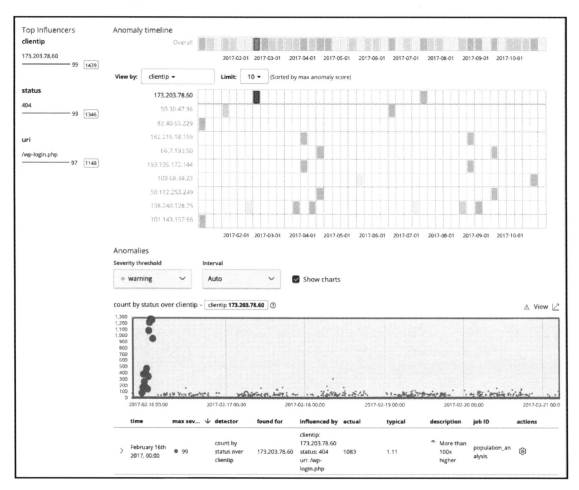

We can see that this rogue IP address was executing literally thousands of requests for a URI of `/wp-login.php`, which fortunately doesn't exist on this web server (thus resulting in the status code of 404). It seems like this was a rather unsophisticated brute-force login attempt, but an interesting find nonetheless.

As a point of comparison, if the analysis of the web logs had instead leveraged `distinct_count` of the URL field instead of the standard **Count** function, then the preceding rogue IP address would not have been highlighted as anomalous. This is simply because the thousands of requests made were all made for the same URL (`wp-login.php`). Thus, the diversity of the requests was really low. However, in a job that looks for IP addresses with an unusually high diversity of URL requests, using `distinct_count` will find different situations, such as this IP:

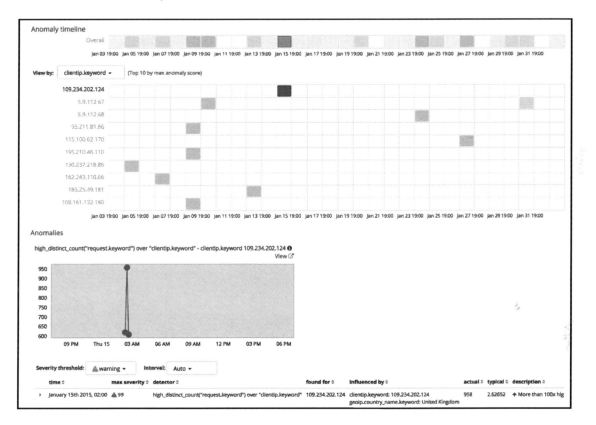

This IP (`109.234.202.124`) was making hundreds of requests for unique URLs (whereas a human does not make that many different ones in the same amount of time). If you were to use Kibana's **Discover** panel to look at the raw requests in the web logs, filtered for this IP address, it would reveal that this IP was trying all sorts of requests for different PHP pages, each time passing an odd-looking argument in the query string:

It seems as if this traffic is driven by a bot that is hoping to find an exploit in a site's PHP code. It is blindly testing a variety of presumably well-known PHP filenames, and passing the contents of an established text file (that's always hosted on Google) may indicate to the bot that a vulnerability exists for that PHP page. If found, it is likely that some malicious subsequent actions will be taken against that PHP page.

Detecting things that rarely occur

In the context of a stream of temporal information (such as a log file), the notion of something being statistically rare (occurs at a low frequency) is paradoxically both intuitive and hard to understand. If I were asked, for example, to trawl through a log file and find a rare message, I might be tempted to label the first novel message that I saw as a rare one. But what if practically every message was novel? Are they all rare? Or is nothing rare?

In order to define *rarity* to be useful in the context of a stream of events in time, we need to agree that the declaration of something as being rare must take into account the context in which it exists. If there are lots of other routine things and a small number of unique things, then we can deem the unique things rare. If there are many unique things, then we will deem that nothing is rare.

When applying the **rare** function in an ML job, there is a requirement to declare which field the **rare** function is focusing on. This field is then defined in the **by_field_name** box. So, for example, to find log entries that reference a rare country name, structure your detector similar to this:

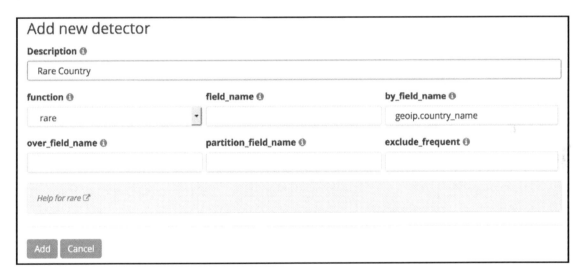

This could be handy for finding unexpected geographical access (as in *our admins usually log in from the New York and London office almost daily, but never from Moscow!*).

When looking at the results from a rarity analysis (such as rare process names running on hosts), you will see the **Anomaly Explorer** has a little different look to it. For more details, you can refer to the link at `https://discuss.elastic.co/t/dec-4th-2018-en-ml-rarity-analysis-with-machine-learning/158979`.

Counting message-based logs via categorization

If you have log entries that are message-based, but are machine-generated, then before they can be useful for anomaly detection, they first need to be organized into similar message types. This process is called categorization and Elastic ML can help with that process.

Types of messages that can be categorized by ML

We need to be a little rigorous in our definition of the kinds of message-based log lines that are being considered here. What we are *not* considering are log lines/events/documents that are completely free-form and likely the result of human creation (emails, tweets, comments, and so on). These kinds of messages are too arbitrary and variable in their construction and content.

Instead, we are focused on machine-generated messages that are obviously emitted when an application encounters different situations or exceptions, thus constraining their construction and content to a relatively discrete set of possibilities (understanding that there may indeed be some variable aspects of the message). For example, let's look at the following few lines of an application log:

```
18/05/2016 15:16:00 S ACME6 DB Not Updated [Master] Table 18/05/2016
15:16:00 S ACME6 REC Not INSERTED [DB TRAN] Table 18/05/2016 15:16:07 S
ACME6 Using: 10.16.1.63!svc_prod#uid=demo;pwd=demo 18/05/2016 15:16:07 S
ACME6 Opening Database = DRIVER={SQL
Server};SERVER=10.16.1.63;network=dbmssocn;address=10.16.1.63,1433;DATABASE
=svc_prod;uid=demo;pwd=demo;AnsiNPW=No 18/05/2016 15:16:29 S ACME6 DBMS
ERROR : db=10.16.1.63!svc_prod#uid=demo;pwd=demo Err=-11 [Microsoft][ODBC
SQL Server Driver][TCP/IP Sockets]General network error. Check your network
documentation.
```

Here, we can see that there is a variety of messages with different text in each, but there is some structure here. After the date/time stamp and the server name from which the message originates (here ACME 6), there is the actual meat of the message, where the application is informing the outside world what is happening at that moment—whether something is being tried or errors are occurring.

The categorization process

In order to bring some order to the otherwise disorderly flow of the messages in the log file, Elastic ML will employ a technique of grouping similar messages together by using a string-similarity clustering algorithm. The heuristics behind this algorithm are roughly as follows:

- Focus on the (English) dictionary words more than mutables (that is, *network* and *address* are dictionary words, but dbmssocn is likely a mutable/variable string)
- Pass the immutable dictionary words through a string-similarity algorithm (similar to Levenshtein distance) to determine how similar the log line is to past log lines
- If the difference between the current log line and an existing category is small, then group the existing log line into that category
- Otherwise, create a new category for the current log line

As a simple example, consider these three messages:

```
Error writing file "foo" on host "acme6"
Error writing file "bar" on host "acme5"
Opening database on host "acme7"
```

The algorithm would cluster the first two messages together in the same category, as they would be deemed as Error writing file on types of messages, whereas the third message would be given its own (new) category.

The naming of these categories is simple: ML will just call them mlcategory N where N is an incrementing integer. Therefore, in this example, the first two lines will be associated with mlcategory 1, and the third line will be associated with mlcategory 2. In a realistic machine log, there may be thousands (or even tens of thousands) of categories that are generated due to the diversity of the log messages, but the set of possible categories should be finite. However, if the number of categories starts to get into the hundreds of thousands, it may become obvious that the log messages are not a constrained set of possible message types and will not be a good candidate for this type of analysis.

Counting the categories

Now that the messages are going to be categorized by the algorithm described previously, the next part of the process is to do the counting. In this case, we're not going to be counting the log lines (and thus the documents of an Elasticsearch index) themselves; instead, we're going to be counting the occurrence rate of the different categories that are the output of the algorithm. So, for example, given the example log lines in the previous section, if they occurred within the same bucket span, we would have the following output of the categorization algorithm:

```
mlcategory 1: 2
mlcategory 2: 1
```

In other words, there were two occurrences of the `Error writing file on` types of messages and one occurrence of the `Opening database on host` type in the last bucket span interval. It is this information that will ultimately get modeled and determined if found unusual by the ML job, as shown in next section.

Putting it all together

The two-step process of first categorizing then counting the message-based log lines is implemented as a single configuration step in the ML job. However, two key pieces of the ML job configuration need to exist:

- The definition of **categorization_field_name** as the field within the Elasticsearch document that contains the text to be categorized by ML
- The use of the `mlcategory` field as part of the detector configuration

Note that the `mlcategory` field is not part of the actual document of the raw data being analyzed; it is similar to a scripted field that only comes into existence if **categorization_field_name** is defined as part of the job configuration.

Let's have a look at the following steps:

1. Given a set of example log lines ingested into Elasticsearch that look like the following (in JSON format, only showing the relevant fields):

   ```
   {
     "@timestamp": "2016-02-08T15:21:06.000Z",
     "message": "REC Not INSERTED [DB TRAN] Table",
   }
    {
     "@timestamp": "2016-02-08T15:21:06.000Z",
   ```

```
        "message": "Fail To Connect Database   ReActivate Application /
Check Connection String",
        }
        {
        "@timestamp": "2016-02-08T15:21:06.000Z",
        "message": "Opening Database = DRIVER={SQL
Server};SERVER=127.0.0.1;network=dbmssocn;address=127.0.0.1
1433;DATABASE=svc_prod;;Trusted_Connection=Yes;AnsiNPW=No",
        }
        {
        "@timestamp": "2016-02-08T15:21:23.000Z",
        "message": "REC Not INSERTED [DB TRAN] Table",
        }
        {
        "@timestamp": "2016-02-02T07:36:00.000Z",
        "message": "012 Head Office Link Active 127.0.0.1",
        }
        {
        "@timestamp": "2016-02-02T10:52:00.000Z",
        "message": "Transaction Match In DB / Duplicate Transaction",
        }
```

2. We will leverage the `message` field as the **categorization_field_name** in an
    Advanced job:

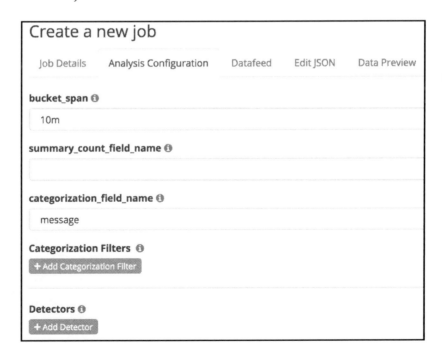

Then, in the detector configuration, we can split the **count** detector using **by_field_name** of `mlcategory`:

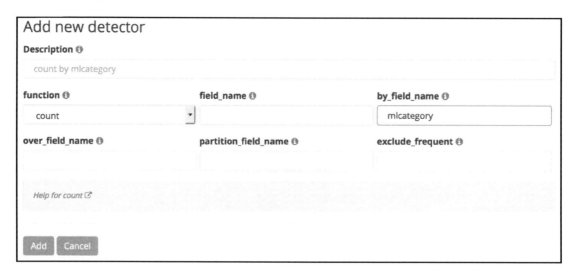

3. The end result is that the ML job will look for unusual counts of documents split using this dynamic categorization. The output may look like the following screenshot:

Here, we see that the ML job has identified a few categories of messages that have increased volume of occurrence during this time frame. An uptick in messages relating to database problems (**Fail to Connect Database**, **DBMS ERROR**, and so on) is evident.

Additionally, notice the **category examples** column in the table. In it, ML will show you (by default) up to four example log messages that have matched and were grouped into that category. In some cases, there's only one example (because subsequent messages were exactly the same), whereas if there are multiple, then there are subtle differences (such as a host name or IP address). The storing of these samples is the only time ML will store a copy of a log message that was analyzed as part of the execution of the ML job. In all other cases, only summarized information about the data is stored.

More information on parameters that control how categorization works and how to view the results of categorization can be found in the *Documentation* section of the Elastic website at `https://www.elastic.co/guide/en/elastic-stack-overview/current/ml-configuring-categories.html`, and the *Get categories API* documentation at `https://www.elastic.co/guide/en/elasticsearch/reference/current/ml-get-category.html`.

When not to use categorization

Despite categorization being quite useful, it's not without its limitations. Specifically, here are some cases where attempting to use categorization will likely return poor results:

- Fields of text that are free-form, likely created by humans. Examples include tweets, comments, emails, and notes.
- Log lines that should actually be parsed into proper name/value pairs, such as a web access log.
- Documents that contain a lot of multi-line text, XML, and so on.

Summary

We've seen that ML can highlight variations in volume, diversity, and uniqueness in log lines, including those that need some categorization first. These techniques help solve the challenges we described in the first part of this chapter, where a human must both recognize the uniqueness of the content and the relative frequency of occurrence of each raw log message.

The skills learned in this chapter will be helpful in the next chapter, Chapter 4, *IT Operational Analytics and Root Cause Analysis*, where we will use ML to assist in the process of getting to the root cause of a complex problem that spans multiple datasets, including log files and performance metrics. The analysis will most certainly include the detection of unusually occurring log events.

4
IT Operational Analytics and Root Cause Analysis

Up until this point, we have extensively explained the value of detecting anomalies across metrics and logs separately. This is extremely valuable, of course. In some cases, however, the knowledge that a particular metric or log file has gone awry may not tell the whole story of what is going on. It may, for example, be pointing at a symptom and not the cause of the problem. To have a better understanding of the full scope of an emerging problem, it is often helpful to look holistically at many aspects of a system or situation. This involves smartly analyzing multiple kinds of related datasets together.

In this chapter, we will cover the following topics:

- Understanding the roles and importance of **key performance indicators (KPIs)** and other supporting metrics
- Learning methods to organize, filter, and enrich the data to supply context
- Exploiting that contextual information via ML jobs that employ data splitting and statistical influencers
- Combining the anomalies that are created by ML into one common view that enables better triage, collaboration, and resolution

Holistic application visibility

IT operations and IT security organizations are collecting massive amounts of data. Some of that data is collected and/or stored in specialized tools, but some may be collected in general-purpose data platforms such as the Elastic Stack. But the question still remains: what percentage of that data is being paid attention to? By this, we mean the percentage of collected data that is actively inspected by humans, or being *watched* by some type of automated means (defined alarms based on rules, thresholds, and so on). Even generous estimates might put the percentage in the range of single digits. So, with 90% or more data being collected going *unwatched*, what's being missed? The proper answer might be that we don't actually know.

Before we admonish IT organizations for the sin of collecting piles of data, but not *watching it*, we need to understand the magnitude of the challenge associated with such an operation. A typical user-facing application may do the following:

- Span hundreds of physical servers
- Have dozens (if not hundreds) of microservices, each of which may have dozens or hundreds of operational metrics or log entries that describe its operation

The combinatorics of this can easily rise to a six or seven figure range of unique measurement points. Additionally, there may be dozens or even hundreds of such applications under the umbrella of management by the IT organization. It's no wonder that the amount of data being collected by these systems per day can easily be measured in terabytes.

Accordingly, it is incredibly daunting to jump head-first into a strategy of bringing proactive coverage to all (or at least a significant portion) of this data to get holistic application visibility. Where you should start and what data to prioritize is not a trivial task, but it usually starts with a focus on the KPIs of the application.

The importance and limitations of KPIs

Because of the problem of scale and the desire to make some amount of progress in making the collected data actionable, it is natural that some of the first metrics to be tackled for active inspection are those that are the best indicators of performance or operation. The KPIs that an IT organization chooses for measurement, tracking, and flagging can span diverse indicators, including the following:

- **Customer**: Impacting metrics such as application response times or error counts
- **Availability**: Oriented metrics such as uptime or **mean time to repair (MTTR)**
- **Business**: Oriented metrics such as orders per minute, revenue, or number of active users

As such, these types of metrics are usually displayed, front and center, on most high-level operational dashboards or on staff reports for employees ranging from technicians to executives. A quick Google image search for `KPI dashboard` will return countless examples of charts, gauges, dials, maps, and other eye candy.

While there is great value in such displays of information that can be consumed with a mere glance, there are still fundamental challenges with manual inspection:

- **Interpretation**: Difficulty in understanding the difference between *normal* operation and *abnormal*, unless that difference is already intrinsically understood by the human.
- **Challenges of scale**: Despite the fact that KPIs are already a distillation of all metrics down to a set of *important* ones, there still may be more KPIs to display than is feasible given the real estate of the screen that the dashboard is displayed upon. The end result may be crowded visualizations or lengthy dashboards that require scrolling/paging.
- **Lack of proactivity**: Many dashboards like this do not have their metrics also tied to alerts, thus requiring constant supervision if it's proactively known that a KPI that is faltering is important.

The bottom line is that KPIs are an extremely important step in the process of identifying and tracking meaningful indicators of health and behavior of an IT system. However, it should be obvious that the mere act of identifying and tracking a set of KPIs with a visual-only paradigm is going to leave some significant deficiencies in the strategy of a successful IT operations plan.

To assist with this, it should be obvious that KPIs are a great candidate for metrics that can be tracked by Elastic's ML. We saw an example of this in `Chapter 3`, *Event Change Detection*, with the following data:

```
{
    "metrictype": "kpi",
    "@timestamp": "2016-02-12T23:11:09.000Z",
    "events_per_min": 22,
    "@version": "1",
    "type": "it_ops_kpi",
    "metricname": "online_purchases",
    "metricvalue": "22",
    "kpi_indicator": "online_purchases"
}
```

In this case, kpi represents the summarized total number of purchases per minute for some online transaction processing system. We also saw that tracking this KPI over time was extremely easy with ML, and that an unexpected dip in online sales (to a value of **921**) is detected and flagged as anomalous:

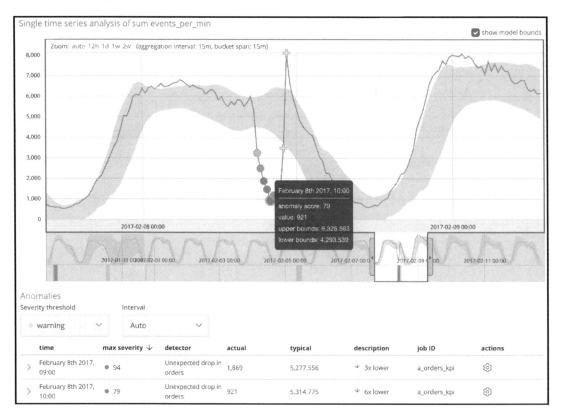

We also saw in Chapter 3, *Event Change Detection*, that if there was another categorical field in the data that allowed it to be segmented (for example, sales by product ID, product category, geographical region, and so on), then ML could easily split the analysis along that field to expand the analysis in a parallel fashion (in Chapter 6, *Alerting on ML Analysis*, we'll see how we can easily tie the detected anomalies to proactive alerts). But with all of that, let's not lose sight of what we're accomplishing here: a proactive analysis of a key metric that someone likely cares about. The amount of online sales per unit of time is directly tied to incoming revenue and thus is an obvious KPI.

However, despite the importance of knowing that something unusual is happening with our KPI, there is still no insight as to why it is happening. Is there an operational problem with one of the backend systems that supports this customer-facing application? Was there a user interface coding error in the latest release that makes it harder for users to complete the transaction? Is there a problem with the third-party payment processing provider that is relied upon? None of these questions can be answered merely by scrutinizing the KPI.

To get that kind of insight, we will need to broaden our analysis to include other sets of relevant and related information.

Beyond the KPIs

The process of selecting KPIs, in general, should be relatively easy, as it is likely obvious what metrics are the best indicators (if online sales are down, then the application is likely not working). But if we want to get a more holistic view of what may be contributing to an operational problem, we must expand our analysis beyond the KPIs to indicators that emanate from the underlying systems and technology that support the application.

Fortunately, there are a plethora of tools that allow for the collection of all kinds of data for centralization in the Elastic Stack. Some examples from within the portfolio of Elastic's free and open source tools are as follows:

- **Elastic Metricbeat**: An easy-to-use lightweight data shipper that can gather performance metrics from systems and forward them to Elasticsearch
- **Elastic Filebeat**: Another member of the Beat family that forwards log lines from any application or system log to Elasticsearch
- **Elastic application performance monitoring (APM)**: Allows for the instrumentation and measurement of detailed application performance metrics at the code level

Regardless of what tools you use to gather the underlying application and system data, one thing is likely true: there will be a lot of data when all is said and done.

Remember that our ultimate goal is to proactively and holistically pay attention to a larger percentage of the overall dataset. To do that, we must first organize this data so that we can effectively analyze it with ML.

Data organization

Before we can effectively wrangle all of this underlying data, we need to smartly segment it, possibly enrich it, and leverage the contextual information contained within it. First, we will focus on segmentation and enrichment.

Effective data segmentation

Simply by virtue of collecting some types of data (system performance metrics, log files, and so on) from underlying servers/hosts, there is likely already a natural segmentation of the data by server/host. Let's look at a sample measurement from Metricbeat:

```
{
    "_index":"metricbeat-6.0.0-2018.01.01",
    "_type":"doc",
    "_id":"ZQtas2ABB_sNnq-vMrgR",
    "_score":1,
    "_source":{
        "@timestamp":"2018-01-01T20:10:19.227Z",
        "system":{
            "memory":{
                "swap":{
                    "used":{
                        "bytes":0,
                        "pct":0
                    },
                    "free":0,
                    "total":0
                },
                "total":15464677376,
                "used":{
                    "bytes":9050693632,
                    "pct":0.5852
                },
                "free":6158319616,
                "actual":{
                    "free":6413983744,
                    "used":{
                        "pct":0.5852,
```

```
                    "bytes":9050693632
                }
            }
        }
    },
    "metricset":{
        "rtt":214,
        "module":"system",
        "name":"memory"
    },
    "beat":{
        "name":"demo",
        "hostname":"demo",
        "version":"6.0.0"
    }
  }
}
```

In the document, we can see the beat.name nested object field (and/or beat.hostname, both having a value of demo in this example). This is the name of the system that the data originates in. By default, all data from all instances of Metricbeat will be collated into a single, daily index of documents with a name similar to metricbeat-6.0.0.2018-01.01, where the date is the particular day in which the data was recorded. Time-based index names are a common practice in the Elastic Stack for this kind of time series data, primarily because it is easy to manage historical data based upon a certain retention policy (dropping data older than X days old is accomplished by deleting the appropriate indices).

Perhaps some of our hosts in our environment support one application (that is, online purchases), but other hosts support a different application (that is, invoice processing). With all hosts reporting their Metricbeat data into a single index, if we are interested in orienting our reporting and analysis of the data for one or both of these applications, it is obviously inappropriate to orient the analysis based solely on the index. And, as we've seen in previous chapters with respect to setting up ML jobs, the job configurations are very index-centric: you need to specify the index of the data to be analyzed in the first step of the configuration.

Despite it seeming like a conundrum, with our desire for our analysis to be application-centric but our data to not be application-centric, we have a few options:

- Modifying the base query of the ML job so that it filters the data for the hosts associated with the application of interest
- Modify the data on ingest to insert additional contextual information into each document, which is later used to filter the query made by the ML job

Both require the customization of the data query that the ML job makes to the raw data. However, the first option usually requires a more complex query and the second option requires an interstitial step of data enrichment using something like Logstash. Let's briefly discuss each.

Custom queries for ML jobs

While somewhat obscured from the user when configuring anything but an **Advanced** job (or configuring a job via the API), the user does indeed have complete control over the query being made to the raw data index to feed the ML job. This is the **Query** parameter of the ML job config:

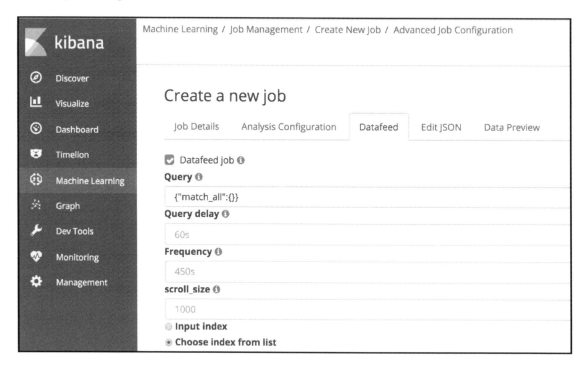

The default is {"match_all":{}} (return every record in the index), but just about any valid Elasticsearch DSL is supported for filtering the data. Free-form composing Elasticsearch DSL into this text field is a little error-prone. Therefore, a more intuitive way would be to approach this from Kibana via saved searches.

For example, let's say that we have an index pattern called `operational-analytics-metricbeat-*` and the appropriate hosts associated with the application we'd like to monitor and analyze consists of three servers, **site-search-es1**, **site-search-es2**, and **site-search-es3**. In Kibana's **Discover** option, we can build a **Filter** that specifies that we would like to select data only for these hosts by choosing to filter on `beat.name` to be one of a sublist of all of the hosts available in the index:

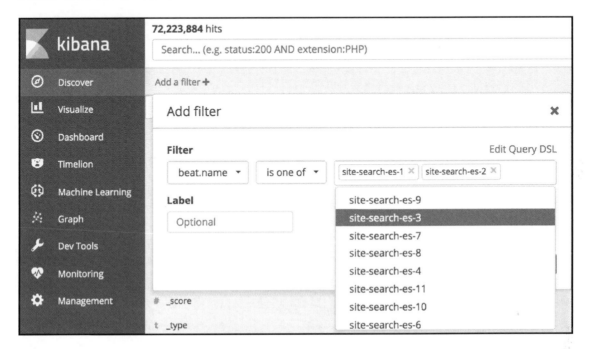

After creating the filter, Kibana will apply it to the original data (now, you can see that the returned filtered set of data is smaller, containing 21 million records instead of the original 72 M records):

Under the hood, this filter, when built with the Kibana UI, ultimately manifests itself as Elasticsearch DSL of the following form:

```
{
  "query": {
    "bool": {
      "should": [
        {
          "match_phrase": {
            "beat.name": "site-search-es-1"
          }
        },
        {
          "match_phrase": {
            "beat.name": "site-search-es-2"
          }
        },
        {
          "match_phrase": {
            "beat.name": "site-search-es-3"
          }
        }
      ],
      "minimum_should_match": 1
    }
  }
}
```

Kibana has done the work for us. Kibana also offers us the ability to make this a **Saved Search**, meaning that we can name it and refer to it later. By clicking on the **Save** menu item, we can give our search a name of `only_es1_es2_es3`:

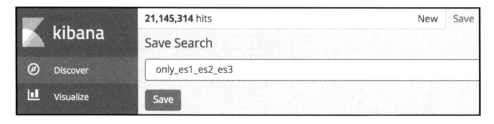

Now that the search has been saved, when we create an ML job, we can choose this **Saved Search** as the basis of our job:

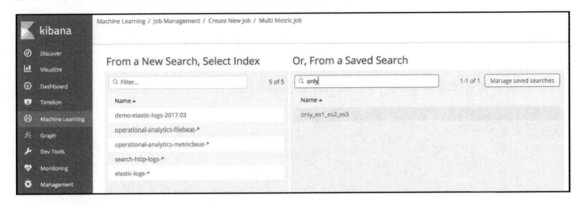

As such, our ML job will now only run for the hosts of interest for this specific application. We can also see that if we split the data along the `beat.name` field, that only the three hosts of interest will have their data analyzed by the ML job, as indicated by following the visual representation of the split on the right-hand side:

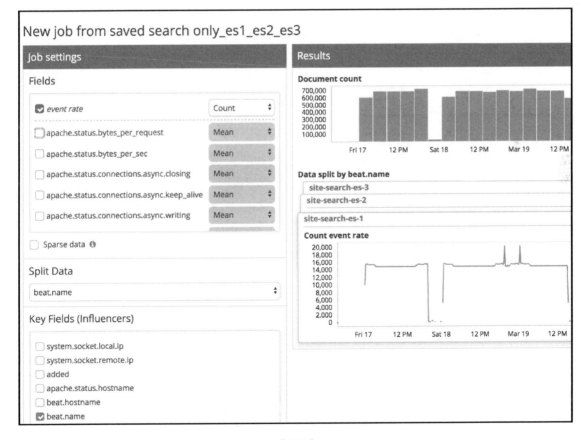

Thus, we have been able to effectively limit and segment the data analysis to the hosts that we've defined to have made a contribution to this application.

Data enrichment on ingest

Another option is to move the decision making about which hosts belong to which applications further upstream to the time of ingest. One way to do this would be to direct your data through Logstash, and use a filter plugin to add additional fields to the data based upon a lookup against an asset list (file, database, and so on). Consult the Logstash documentation at `https://www.elastic.co/guide/en/logstash/current/lookup-enrichment.html`, which shows you how to dynamically enrich the indexed documents with additional fields to provide context.

For example, you could have Logstash add an `application_name` field and dynamically populate the value of this field with the appropriate name of the application, for example (truncated JSON here):

```
"host": "wasinv2.acme.com",
"application_name": "invoice_processing",
```

Alternatively, you could do the following:

```
"host": "www3.acme.com",
"application_name": "online_purchases",
```

Once the value of this field is set and inserted into the indexed documents, then you would use the `application_name` field, along with the ability of filtering the query for the ML job (as previously described) to limit your data analysis to the pertinent application of interest. The addition of the data enrichment step may seem like a little more up-front effort, but it should pay dividends in the long term as it will be easier to maintain as asset names change or evolve, since the first method requires hardcoding the asset names into the searches of the ML jobs.

Leveraging the contextual information

Now that we have effectively organized, and perhaps enriched our data with additional information, we should take full advantage of it. The two primary ways to do this are via analysis splits and statistical influencers.

Analysis splits

We have already seen that an ML job can be split based on any categorical field. As such, we can individually model behavior separately for each instance of that field. This could be extremely valuable, especially in the case where each instance needs its own separate model.

Take, for example, the case where we have data for different regions of the world:

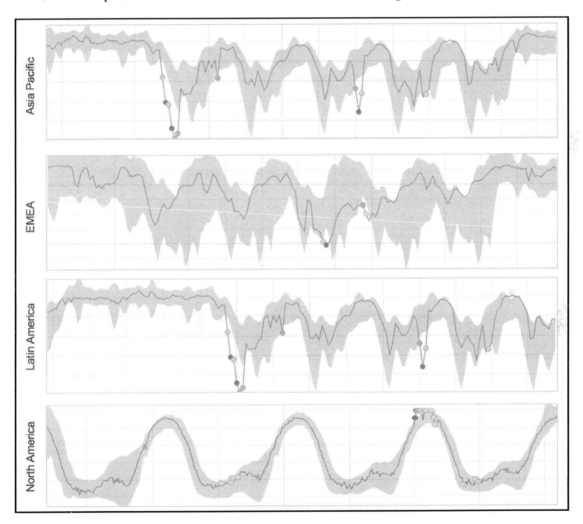

Whatever data this is (sales KPIs, utilization metrics, and so on), clearly it has very distinctive patterns that are unique to each region. In this case, it makes sense to split any analysis we do with ML for each region to capitalize on this uniqueness. We would be able to detect anomalies in the behavior that's specific to each region.

Let's also imagine that, within each region, a fleet of servers support the application and transaction processing, but they are load balanced and contribute equally to the performance/operation. In that way, there's nothing unique about each server's contribution with a region. As such, it probably doesn't make sense to split the analysis per server.

We've naturally come to the conclusion that splitting by region is more effective than splitting by server. But what if a particular server within a region is having problems contributing to the anomalies that are being detected? Wouldn't we want to have this information available immediately, instead of having to manually diagnose further? This is possible to know via an implementation in ML called influencers.

Statistical influencers

Within the ML job configuration, there is the ability to define fields as **Influencers** (also sometimes called **Key Fields** in the user interface). The concept of an influencer is a field that describes an entity that you'd like to know is to blame for the existence of the anomaly, or at least had a significant contribution. Note that any field chosen as a candidate to be an influencer doesn't need to be part of the detection logic, although it is natural to pick fields that are used as splits to also be influencers. To see how influencers work, let's discuss an example.

Imagine we have data that describes financial transactions at merchants for a family's monthly credit card bill. The data includes the following fields:

- timestamp
- merchant
- purchase_amount
- location
- user (the name of the person who invokes the transaction)

 Note that the actual purchasing user isn't tracked in a credit card bill for a shared account, but let's assume this for the sake of the example.

Let's also assume that our desire is to find *unusually high purchases per merchant*. As such, we would likely create an ML job that focused on high_sum(purchase_amount) by merchant (where we are splitting the analysis on the merchant field). In this case, what fields could be interesting to choose as influencers? Ideally, they would be the following ones:

- merchant: Because this is the field the analysis is split on, and naturally we'd like to know which merchant was the most influential
- location: Was there a specific location in which all (or most) of the anomalous transactions occurred?
- user: What person, if any, invoked the majority of the transactions that caused the anomaly?

Notice that we purposely did not choose to use purchase_amount as a candidate for an influencer. Hopefully, it is obvious that the numerical value of purchases is more likely to be random and that any particular value of a purchase amount is not likely to dominate.

Given the choice of these three influencers, let's now imagine that we've detected an anomaly of a large amount of money spent at Starbucks for the current billing period. Here's a partial anomaly record for this fictitious example:

```
. . .
            "timestamp": 1514764800000,
            "partition_field_name": "merchant",
            "partition_field_value": "Starbucks",
            "function": "high_sum",
            "function_description": "high_sum",
            "typical": [
              10.21
            ],
            "actual": [
              104.52
            ],
            "field_name": "purchase_amount",
            "influencers": [
              {
                "influencer_field_name": "merchant",
                "influencer_field_values": [
                  "Starbucks"
                ]
              },
              {
                "influencer_field_name": "user",
                "influencer_field_values": [
                  "Rich"
                ]
```

```
        }
    ],
  . . .
```

 See `Chapter 6`, *Alerting on ML Analysis*, for information on how to query the anomaly results indices to get anomaly record results.

We can see that over a hundred dollars was spent this month, when usually only about ten dollars is spent. Who is to blame? Who/what are the influencers? They seem to be as follows:

- `merchant=Starbucks`: Again, this one is obvious because that's how the analysis was split. It is a bit of a tautology to say that Starbucks is the influencer of this anomaly because the anomaly is already for the merchant `Starbucks`.
- `user=Rich`: In this case, the bulk of the transactions for `Starbucks` were invoked by `Rich`. Other family members also may have purchased items from `Starbucks` during the month, but Rich's transactions highly dominate for the feature that we are analyzing, the amount of money spent.
- `location`: In our fictitious example, location did not emerge as an influencer. This is because Rich's transactions at `Starbucks` occurred in many different locations throughout the month, due to his heavy business travel. As such, no one location of transactions dominated. Therefore, location does not emerge as an influencer and is not listed in the results.

To summarize, two out of the three fields that were candidates for being influencers were identified as being influencers. Despite `location` not being an influencer in this scenario, the choice of `location` as a candidate still makes sense and may be useful on some other future anomaly.

It is also key to understand that the process of finding potential influencers happens after ML finds the anomaly. In other words, it does not affect any of the probability calculations that are made as part of the detection. Once the anomaly has been determined, ML will systematically go through all instances of each candidate influencer field and remove that instance's contribution to the data in that time bucket. If, once removed, the remaining data is no longer anomalous, then via counterfactual reasoning, that instance's contribution must have been influential and is scored accordingly (with an `influencer_score` in the results).

More importantly, it is how we're going to leverage these influencers when viewing the results of not just a single ML job, but potentially several related jobs. Let's move on and discuss the process of grouping and viewing jobs together to assist with root cause analysis.

Bringing it all together for root cause analysis

We are at the point now where we can now discuss how we can bring everything together. In our desire to increase our effectiveness in IT operations and look more holistically at application health, we now need to operationalize what we've prepared in the prior sections and configure our ML jobs accordingly. To that end, let's work through a real-life scenario in which ML helped us get to the root cause of an operational problem.

Outage background

This scenario is loosely based on a real application outage, although the data was somewhat simplified and sanitized to obfuscate the original user. The problem was with a retail application that processed gift card transactions. Occasionally, the app would stop working and transactions could not be processed. This would only be discovered when the individual stores called headquarters to complain. The root cause of the issue was unknown and couldn't be ascertained easily by the customer. Because they never got to the root cause, and because the problem could be fixed by simply rebooting the application servers, the problem would randomly recur and plagued them for months.

The following data was collected and included in the analysis to help understand the origins of the problem. This data included the following:

- A summarized (1-minute) count of transaction volume (the main KPI)
- Application logs (semi-structured text based messages) from the transaction processing engine
- SQL Server performance metrics from the database that backed the transaction processing engine
- Network utilization performance metrics from the network the transaction processing engine operates on

As such, four ML jobs were configured against the data. They were as follows:

- `it_ops_kpi`: Using `low_sum` on the number of transactions processed per minute
- `it_ops_logs`: Using a `count` by the `mlcategory` detector to count the number of log messages by type, but using dynamic ML-based categorization to delineate different message types
- `it_ops_sql`: Simple mean analysis of every SQL Server metric in the index
- `it_ops_network`: Simple mean analysis of every network performance metric in the index

These four jobs were configured and run on the data when the problem occurred in the application. Anomalies were found, especially in the KPI that tracked the number of transactions being processed. In fact, this is the same KPI that we saw at the beginning of this chapter, where an unexpected dip in order processing was the main indicator that a problem was occurring:

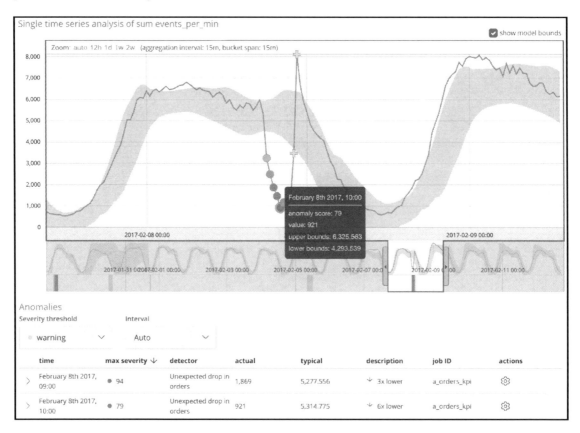

However, the root cause wasn't understood until this KPI's anomaly was correlated with the anomalies in the other three ML jobs that were looking at the data in the underlying technology and infrastructure. Let's see how the power of visual correlation and shared influencers allowed the underlying cause to be discovered.

Visual correlation and shared influencers

In addition to the anomaly in the transactions processed KPI (in which an unexpected dip occurs), the other three ML jobs (for the network metrics, the application logs, and the SQL database metrics) were superimposed on the same time frame in the **Anomaly Explorer**. The following screenshot shows the results of this:

Notice that during the time the KPI was exhibiting problems on **February 8th 2017**, the three other jobs also showed correlated anomalies (see the vertical stripe of significant anomalies in the annotated red circle across all four jobs). Upon closer inspection (by clicking on the red tile for the `it_ops_sql` job), you can see that there were issues with several of the SQL Server metrics going haywire at the same time:

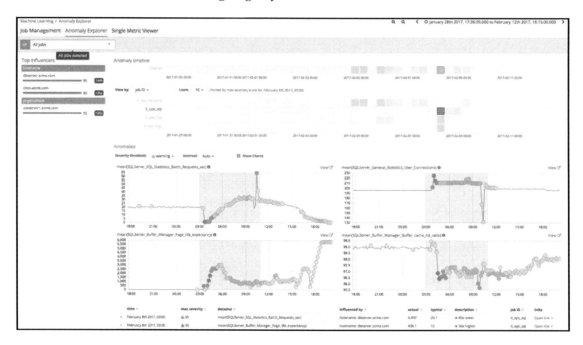

 Notice that the gray-shaded area of the thumbnail charts is highlighting the window of time associated with the width of the selected red tile in the preceding swim lane. This window of time might be larger than the bucket span of the analysis (as is the case here) and therefore the gray-shaded area can contain many individual anomalies during that time frame.

If we look at the anomalies in the ML job for the application log, there is an influx of errors all referencing the database (further corroborating an unstable SQL Server):

However, interesting things were also happening on the network:

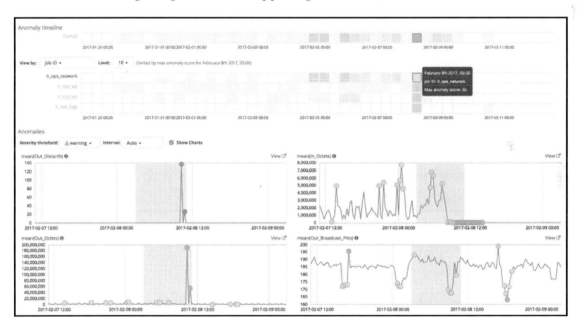

Specifically, there was a large spike in network traffic (shown by the **Out_Octets** metric), and a high spike in packets getting dropped at the network interface (shown by the **Out_Discards** metric).

At this point, there was clear suspicion that this network spike might have something to do with the database problem. And, while correlation is not always causation, it was enough of a clue to entice the operations team to look back over some historical data from prior outages. In every other occasion of the outage, this large network spike and packet drops pattern also existed.

The ultimate cause of the network spike was VMware's action of moving VMs to new ESX servers. Someone had misconfigured the network switch and VMware was sending this massive burst of traffic over the application VLAN instead of the management VLAN. When this occurred (randomly, of course), the transaction processing app would temporarily lose connection to the database and attempt to reconnect. However, there was a critical flaw in this reconnection code in that it would not attempt the reconnection to the database at the remote IP address that belonged to SQL Server. Instead, it attempted the reconnection to `localhost` (IP address **127.0.01**), where, of course, there was no such database. The clue to this bug was seen in one of the example log lines that ML displayed in the examples column (circled in the following screenshot):

Once the problem occurred, the connection to the SQL Server was therefore only possible if the application server was completely rebooted, the startup configuration files were re-read, and the IP address of SQL Server was relearned. This was why a full reboot always fixed the problem.

One key thing to notice is how the influencers in the UI also assist with narrowing down the scope of *who's at fault* for the anomalies:

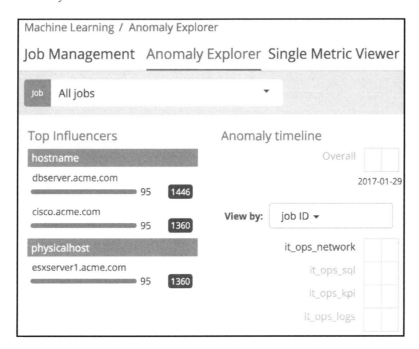

The top scoring influencers over the time span selected in the dashboard are listed in the **Top Influencers** section on the left. For each influencer, the maximum influencer score (in any bucket) is displayed, together with the total influencer score over the dashboard time range (summed across all buckets). And, if multiple jobs are being displayed together, then those influencers that are common across jobs have higher sums, thus pushing their ranking higher.

This is a very key point because now it is very easy to see commonalities in offending entities across jobs. If esxserver1.acme.com is the only physical host that surfaces as an influencer when viewing multiple jobs, then we immediately know which machine to focus on; we know it is not a widespread problem.

Summary

ML can certainly boost the amount of data that IT organizations *pay attention to*, and thus get more insight and proactive value out of their data. The ability to organize, correlate, and holistically view related anomalies across data types is critical to problem isolation and root cause identification. It reduces application downtime and limits the possibility of problem recurrence.

In the next chapter, Chapter 5, *Security Analytics with Elastic Machine Learning*, we will see how ML can benefit those that have more of a more security operations focus by allowing us to distill out bad behaviors and anomalous activities that might be indicators of compromise or malice.

Security Analytics with Elastic Machine Learning

5

It may sound clichéd to say that managing security threats inside an enterprise environment isn't like it used to be, but this is the honest truth. It's no longer a question of whether portions of your environment are compromised, but rather now it is a question of when you will figure it out.

In other words, most security professionals currently take the posture that assets within their control have already been compromised and that active measures must be taken on a daily basis to find any occurrences of these **Indicators of Compromise (IoC)**.

This is not to say that you should give up on perimeter security because the effort is moot; security teams still need a solid set of rules and policies that will safeguard internal assets from the outside threats that are trying to get into an environment. Firewalls and other perimeter defense techniques are just as relevant as ever. However, it's not always the case that the threat is outside looking to get in; you must obviously try to prevent someone on the inside from reaching out and facilitating a compromise, such as an email phishing scenario or a drive-by attack when visiting a compromised website that may allow for the installation of malware. Certainly, some conservative organizations mitigate this by being very selective as to which outside websites are even visible from within the company network.

Even though your perimeter rules and corporate policies seem to be prudent, they will not suffice on their own. Security professionals now orient their daily tasks around threat intelligence programs to help them understand this better:

- Which most recent types of attacks and adversaries are prominent
- What goals and objectives attackers would look for in the organization
- What methodologies malicious actors are employing to infiltrate organizations

These key concepts allow security teams to clearly understand the motivation of their adversary, perform threat hunting, and mitigate risk.

Then, it all comes down to being able to anticipate attacks that become more and more sophisticated over time. In other words, the challenge of IT security professionals is making the data actionable to be able to do the following:

- Detect IoCs existing in near-real time
- Prioritize these incidents based on the risk for the organization
- Proactively contain and/or resolve the incident

There's no doubt that the most critical part of the preceding points is how to scale the technical infrastructure with regards to the massive amount of information and how to scale the human understanding of the data, all while fighting an ever-changing landscape of attacks.

In this chapter, we will cover the following topics:

- How to use Elastic ML to detect behavioral-based anomalies
- Understanding the details of a long vector attack
- Threat hunting for those details of an attack
- Taking actions based on the analytics results

Security in the field

The Elastic Stack wasn't originally designed with the security analytics use case in mind; remember, it was designed to be an efficient data store and search engine. However, it has become apparent that—similar to the logging/metrics/performance use case in IT operations—the Elastic Stack is also a very good platform to use for Security Analytics because of its ability to allow real-time access to high volumes of a variety of data. Let's see why and how the evolution of the Elastic Stack into a viable platform for security analytics has taken place.

The volume and variety of data

Before diving into how to operate against security threats with Elastic ML, let's provide a bit of context about the challenges that security teams face in terms of the volume and variety of data.

Even modestly sized enterprises can collect over a terabyte of data per day and keep that data for a 6-month retention period. This is an ingest rate of about 25,000 events per second if we consider that an event's size, on average, is 800 bytes. Bigger enterprises may collect 100,000 or more events per second.

For a security professional, the daunting challenge is not just simply coping with this amount of data and looking for the known bad behaviors that may exist, it is also challenging to spot what is anomalous compared to normal behaviors and being able to correlate multiple anomalies together to understand the entire life cycle of an emerging threat. Plus, you have to do all of this while simultaneously assessing the potential impact for the organization. Thus, it's not just about taking action on a single IoC, but rather tracing back from IoC to IoC to understand the source of an attack and take action from there to prevent any further similar events.

Timing is very important from the point where the IoC has been identified, because the more time it takes to find the source, the more vulnerable the organization assets are. This means that security teams can't wait to get an answer; real time, or near-real time to stay realistic, is mandatory for threat hunting from ingestion to anomaly detection and analytics.

We went through most of these requirements in the previous chapter, `Chapter 4`, *IT Operational Analytics and Root Cause Analysis*, but security analytics brings another level of expectations from the use profile standpoint that could not fit in a traditional security solution, such as **Security Information and Event Management (SIEM)**, which is not scalable by nature.

In the field, we can see more and more legacy SIEM projects adopting the SIEM augmentation pattern, allowing the security team to combine the benefits of SIEM in terms of data collection, compliance reporting, and incident handling process, but also the benefits of the Elastic Stack in terms of being able to have all the data in one place, detect anomalies, and threat hunt in real time. Eventually, those SIEM solutions are replaced by Elastic when the functional needs are slowly implemented with features within the stack.

This migration path becomes even more natural with the help of Elastic ML, whose configuration and operation are agnostic of the type of time series or use case implemented. In other words, it can cope with versatility and a variety of data to analyze in real time, leaving the heavy lifting of data management to Elasticsearch.

Two key points stand out here:

- Having all of the data easily accessible in one place makes it possible to search, analyze, correlate, and gain insight with less time and effort
- The process of that analysis should be agnostic of the data types, offering flexibility over use cases, including ones that have yet to be conceived

In many legacy security projects, this is not the case: data is spread across multiple systems or datastores, which severely hinders the process of finding threats in the first place, but also relating detected threats to a potential overall attack. Legacy security solutions, such as **intrusion detection system (IDS)** platforms, are extremely efficient in detecting known threats based on a knowledge base of existing rules. However, being too specific limits the flexibility of detection, potentially missing events when the variety of data grows. Even worse, being too specific with a set of known detection rules enables the adversaries to know what types of behaviors are being looked for in advance, allowing the modification of behaviors to stay *under the radar* and avoid detection. We will see how the Elastic Stack enables the security team to operate flexibly and face complex and versatile attacks later.

The geometry of an attack

Attacks can be manifested in different forms: a single, discrete action or a complex, connected set of actions over time, spanning different parts of the infrastructure and thus different datasets. The shape or the geometry of an attack is very variable and will depend on the goal of the attack, plus the structure of the IT environment.

Let's take the example of a DNS tunneling attack, which consists of a **Compromised Server** exfiltrating data from the organization using encrypted messages disguised as a series of legitimate-looking **DNS** requests. This behavior, which is described in the following diagram, shows that **Compromised Server** emits a series (thousands, even millions) of **DNS** requests over time, with a small payload of data encrypted into the subdomain part of the request to an unconventional domain name. On the other side, a compromised **DNS** server, run by a hacker, accepts and re-assembles the encrypted data:

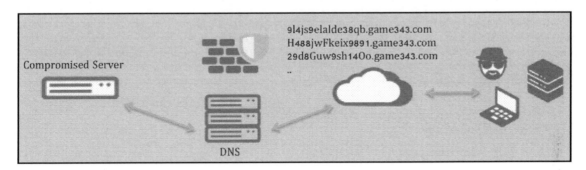

This exfiltration technique often goes undetected because of the following points:

- **DNS** traffic from inside an organization to the outside world is not blocked or restricted by security policies; **DNS** is too fundamental to the operation of the internet.
- **DNS** traffic is often incredibly voluminous, so the collection, storage, and analysis of the data isn't possible or practical with non-big data platforms. Therefore, the data is often not collected and is unwatched, making it the perfect place to hide malicious behaviors.
- The actual technique that's employed in **DNS** tunneling is inefficient and painstakingly slow; it can take weeks or months to exfiltrate a significant amount of data. So, this low and slow approach is an asset when being covert.

Clearly, it should be obvious that if you do not collect and analyze this kind of data due to a lack of capability in your legacy security tools, then you've just admitted that not only are you vulnerable to this attack vector, you would never even know if it were occurring right now.

This **DNS** tunneling activity is a discrete, malicious behavior that surely any security analyst would love to be able to detect and thwart. However, this activity could be at or near the end of a long chain of related malicious activities; it could have started with a user's machine getting compromised days, weeks, or months earlier.

To get the full picture of how this threat morphs over time from the point of initial compromise to the point of data exfiltration, the security analyst would have to have a vast set of diverse data, and have weeks or months of it on hand. The evidence of the threat's activity could manifest itself in various ways in network data, authentication logs, endpoint logs, or other data.

To illustrate this, the following diagram represents the life cycle of this kind of **advanced persistent threat (APT)**:

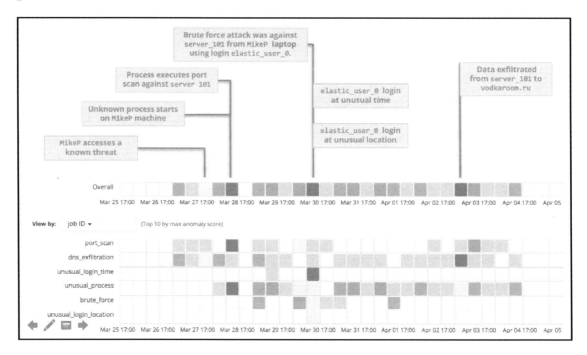

We'll use this scenario throughout this chapter and will see how Elastic ML helps to uncover the details of such an attack.

But first, a couple of words on the preceding diagram in terms of how the kill-chain is articulated:

- The first step (the initial compromise) occurs when a machine within the organization accesses a known threat via a malicious external website
- Right after the threat was touched and the machine was infected, an unusual process starts running on the same machine
- Port scanning activity is then invoked from that machine as the APT enters its reconnaissance phase
- Suspicious login activity later occurs against a server that we know hosts some valuable assets
- Those valuable assets are then exfiltrated via DNS to the outside world

ML can help us detect each of these different IoCs occurring over time and would allow the alerting of the security team to investigate and take action.

Because the attack is broken down in different steps, and because the evidence of each step exists in different parts of the IT system, different datasets such as Windows machine logs, network logs, and others must be indexed and searchable. Therefore, building the proper data acquisition architecture is fundamental for being able to retrace all of those events.

Threat hunting architecture

In this section, we'll go through the basic building blocks of a threat hunting architecture structure. These include a multiple ingestion layer starting with Beats to collect the data from different sources and Logstash to enrich the data for threat intelligence. Once the data has been properly prepared, the next step will be to focus on the investigation analytics.

Layer-based ingestion

A threat hunting architecture relies on rich and reliable data ingestion that will allow you to detect and investigate anomalous behaviors. In our scenario, we need to use both data coming from end user workstations and data coming from the network. Luckily, we have Packetbeat and Winlogbeat, which capture the network activity and ingest logs generated on Windows machines, respectively. These can be downloaded from `https://www.elastic.co/downloads/beats`, where all the Beats are listed:

As you can see, they are not the only Beats available to ingest data from; there are different Beats for different purposes. Each Beat can have a set of modules or metrics set that can be enabled, based on the data that you desire to ingest. For example, here is the one that's available for **Packetbeat**:

- *AMQP fields*
- *Beat fields*
- *Cassandra fields*
- *Cloud provider metadata fields*
- *Common fields*
- *DNS fields*
- *Docker fields*
- *Flow Event fields*
- *HTTP fields*
- *ICMP fields*
- *Kubernetes fields*
- *Memcache fields*
- *MongoDb fields*
- *MySQL fields*
- *NFS fields*
- *PostgreSQL fields*
- *Raw fields*
- *Redis fields*
- *Thrift-RPC fields*
- *TLS fields*
- *Transaction Event fields*
- *Measurements (Transactions) fields*

In our example of detecting DNS tunneling, we will need to enable the collection of DNS data to see and detect the unusual outbound DNS queries.

In general, for data not originating from the Beats framework, it is advisable to enrich that data as much as possible before ingestion. This allows the data to be better understood and will ultimately allow for the data to be more comprehensively analyzed. Fortunately, the data that's originating from Beats is already rich with context.

Another aspect to think about is the index pattern naming convention; that is, if you desire to correlate the data across indices. In our example, our environment is made of three index patterns, as shown in the following screenshot:

This hierarchy-based index structure is laid out so that every time you add a layer of infrastructure, the index name follows the same naming pattern. As a consequence, if you need to see a specific layer of data (such as the network data), you just select the **Packetbeat** index. If you want to see all of the data, you can easily choose the top-level index. This approach is applicable for every view in Kibana: **Discover**, **Visualize**, and **Machine Learning**.

Elastic ML needs a minimum amount of data to be able to build an effective model for anomaly detection. Essentially, it's based on how quickly ML can get the first estimates of the various model parameters. For sampled metrics such as mean, min, max, and median, the minimum data amount is either eight non-empty bucket spans or two hours, whichever is greater. For all other non-zero/null metrics and count-based quantities, it's four non-empty bucket spans or two hours, whichever is greater. For the count and sum functions, empty buckets matter and therefore it is the same as sampled metrics (eight buckets or two hours). For the rare function, it'll typically be around 20 bucket spans. It can be faster for population models, but it depends on the number of people that interact per bucket.

So, in our scenario, as shown as following screenshot, we have about a month's worth of data, which represents about 7 million documents for Packetbeat:

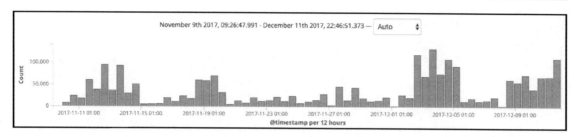

This index will help us to understand what's happening on the network, such as which DNS requests have been made, as the following example shows:

```
{
    "server": "",
    "dns": { ... },
    "method": "QUERY",
    "proc": "",
    "source": { ... },
    "dns_ips": "...",
    "client_port": 63446,
    "host": "localhost",
    "tags": [],
    "subdomain": "elastic.",
    "bytes_out": 51,
    "query": "class IN, type A, elastic.slack.com.",
    "resource": "elastic.slack.com.",
    "client_proc": "",
    "ip": "...",
    "port": 53,
    "type": "dns",
    "data_source": "elastic",
    "client_server": "",
    "geoip": { ... },
    "@version": "1",
    "geo_ip_dns": { ... },
    "client_ip": "...",
    "bytes_in": 35,
    "highest_registered_domain": "slack.com",
    "beat": {
        "version": "5.1.1",
        "hostname": "HR08",
        "name": "HR08"
    },
    "status": "OK",
    "dest": { ... },
    "transport": "udp",
    "domain": "slack.com.",
    "@timestamp": "2017-12-12T23:59:58.153Z",
```

```
    "responsetime": 22
  }
```

The preceding document describes a normal DNS request. Remember that in the case of DNS tunneling, the important bit is the subdomain field, which is where the exfiltrated data will be hidden as an encrypted payload. We will see how this subdomain field will be leveraged in the ML job that we will use in our investigation.

Threat intelligence

As part of a threat hunting architecture and best practice, enriching the ingested data can add insightful information (such as the geolocation of IP addresses), but it can also identify at a glance if an IP address is on a known threat list. This is part of threat intelligence. Enhancing threat information is a process that consists of using a threat database and tagging data that has been ingested or already indexed data as a threat if it exists in the given database.

There are many threat intelligence databases and data feeds that can be used out there. But whichever you are using, make sure that the threat information is embedded into each document you index into Elasticsearch, whether you doing either of the following:

- Using your own enrichment process to tag the data once in Elasticsearch
- Using Logstash at ingestion time to tag the data

The second strategy can be easily built using either the translate plugin or the lookup features in Logstash. The translate feature can be used for use cases where the data being used for enrichment can be stored in a file and is fairly static. This method is explained in a blog post (https://www.elastic.co/blog/bro-ids-elastic-stack) as an example and consists of creating a dictionary against which the data is compared over time. The following configuration gives an idea of what it consists of in Logstash:

```
filter {
  translate {
  field => "evt_dstip"
  destination => "tor_exit_ip"
  dictionary_path => "/path/to/yaml"
  }
}
```

The preceding configuration shows an example of a lookup for the `evt_dstip` field against a dictionary. If a match is found in the dictionary, the `tor_exit_ip` field is populated with the content of the dictionary. You can set whatever content you need in the dictionary as long as you keep in mind that this will be the content that's used to do reporting and also to be leveraged by ML.

While this is a very handy feature, its scalability is limited by the fact that it relies on a dictionary file. This is where the `memcahed` plugin brings more value as it relies on a scalable cache that can hold millions of records that can change over time. For the purpose of this book, we will not dig too much into the details here, but you can find a comprehensive description of how to set this up in the Elastic blog at https://www. elastic.co/blog/elasticsearch-data-enrichment-with-logstash-a-few-security-examples.

The important bit for us is to understand how it is done in Logstash, as the following example shows:

```
input {
  stdin {
    codec => json
  }
}
filter {
  memcached {
      hosts => ["localhost:11211"]
      get => {
         "%{ip}" => "threat_src"
      }
  }
}
output {
  stdout {
     codec => rubydebug
  }
}
```

As explained in the blog, for any input message, the `ip` field will be looked up in `memcached` and populate the `threat_src` field accordingly if the IP exists. So, even if Beats uses an out-of-the-box data model, we could still use a Logstash instance to enrich the data and add more value to our ingestion architecture, and have the following type of architecture:

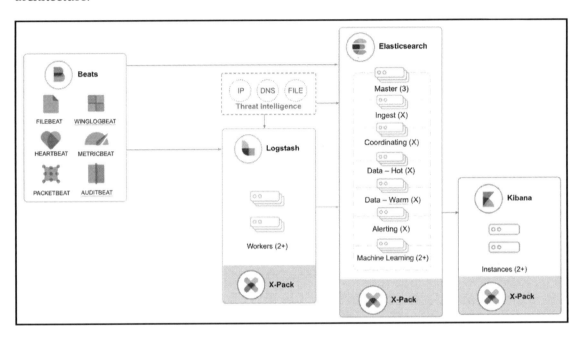

Investigation analytics

Preparing the data as we described previously was fundamental to being able to properly analyze the data with Elastic ML and reveal the steps of an attack. In this section, we will go through an investigation scenario of a DNS exfiltration attack and leveraging the anomalies that are detected by using Elastic ML to guide the analyst in the process.

Assessment of compromise

It all starts with an email, as a consequence of abnormal behavior in the IT system. This time, it appears that an Elastic ML node has spotted a potential DNS exfiltration attack. The following screenshot shows that there were unusual activities against a given domain, originating from a server called **server_101**:

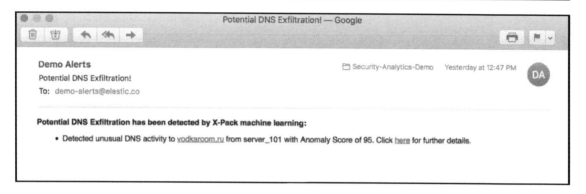

The alert shows a high anomaly score, **95**, signifying a very unusual situation. Elastic Alerting can send emails like the preceding one based on conditions such as the anomaly score value. The creation of such an alert based upon the anomaly score is quite simple, and in Chapter 6, *Alerting on ML Analysis*, we will discuss Alerting in more depth. For now, you can see that the Alerting configuration can easily allow the user to create a threshold-based alert using that field:

This configured alert will run every minute and will check the last 5 seconds to see whether there are documents where the **max()** of the **anomaly_score** field, which is self-explanatory, is above **70**.

The email contains a link to Kibana, which is contextualized to the period of time where the anomaly occurs. Clicking on the link will bring you directly to the Elastic ML **Anomaly Explorer** view:

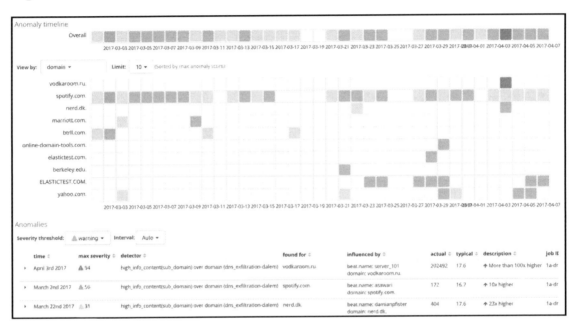

In the context of our use case, the preceding **Anomaly Explorer** view shows some abnormal activities for some domains such as **vodkaroom.ru**, which besides the name, displays suspicious activities (see the red tile in its swim lane). In the table at the bottom, you can see that this domain has an anomaly with a score of **94**. The job that detected this anomaly has been configured to inspect DNS data for evidence of exfiltration/tunneling, in which the **high_info_content** function is aimed at the **sub_domain** field. The configuration in the **Advanced** job wizard looks as follows:

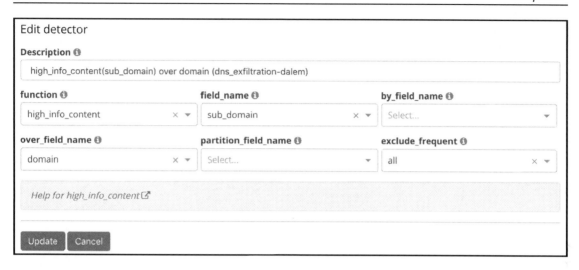

Edit detector

Description ⓘ

high_info_content(sub_domain) over domain (dns_exfiltration-dalem)

function ⓘ	**field_name** ⓘ	**by_field_name** ⓘ
high_info_content × ▾	sub_domain × ▾	Select... ▾

over_field_name ⓘ	**partition_field_name** ⓘ	**exclude_frequent** ⓘ
domain × ▾	Select... ▾	all × ▾

Help for high_info_content ☒

Update   Cancel

Functions such as **info_content** and others are listed and described in the online ML documentation at `https://www.elastic.co/guide/en/elastic-stack-overview/current/ml-functions.html`.

As stated earlier, the DNS tunneling technique encrypts data into that **sub_domain** field, thus giving the field a high amount of information content in the string itself. The ML job is configured as a population analysis where the population is defined by all high-level domains. Therefore, the job finds cases of high information content in the subdomain of the DNS requests across all domains, comparing each high-level domain against its peers, surfacing the most unusual domains.

From there, we know that an exfiltration happened, and we also know from which system it originated. If you look at the **Influenced by** column, you will notice that **server_101** is spotted as a significant influencer of the anomaly.

In fact, looking at the **Top Influencers** list on the left-hand side of the **Anomaly Explorer** also corroborates that **vodkaroom.ru** and **server_101** are the most unusual domain and hostname during this time period:

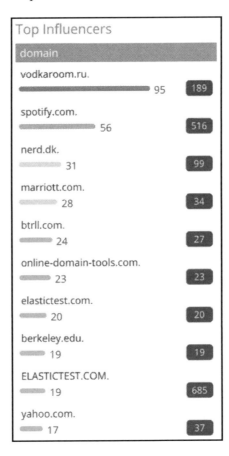

The following screenshot shows the **Top Influencers server_101**:

They are both the highest ranked influencers in the lists.

We need to investigate this machine and domain, and if we look at the detail of the anomaly, we can see that the amount of information in the **sub_domain** field is 100 times higher than usual:

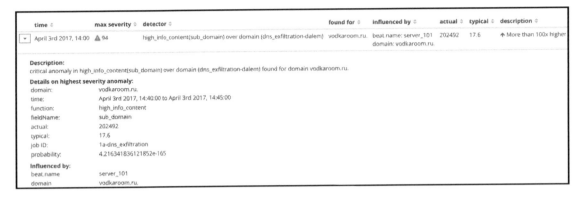

 Remember: Because this is a population analysis, what is typical is defined by surveying the domain's behavior over time to obtain a collective model.

Elastic ML allows for the creation of a dynamic link to any URL, such as a Kibana dashboard. This is described in the documentation, which can be found at `https://www.elastic.co/guide/en/elastic-stack-overview/current/ml-configuring-url.html`.

This has been implemented in this case; an **Open link** button exposes a list of user-defined custom links. In our case, we defined a link called **Explore Server**:

Our custom link, **Explore Server**, passes the name of the server (the appropriate `beat.hostname`) to a subsequent dashboard so that it can be filtered to only show the hostname that was an influencer on this anomaly (in our case, `beat.hostname:server_101`):

It filters the dashboard to the machine that is the source of the exfiltration. Because this dashboard also contains visualizations of other data types as well, we can also see that server_101 has a visually interesting pattern of SSH login attempts:

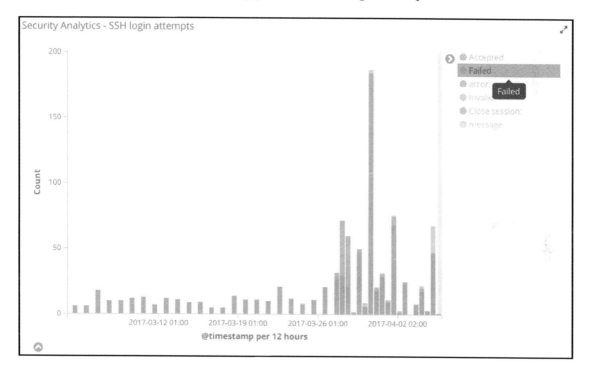

This visually interesting anomalous pattern can, of course, also be automated in its own ML job, which will monitor login attempts.

Another section of our custom dashboard shows a data table highlighting the details of those login attempts. Inspection of the data shows that a user finally manages to connect:

	Time ⌄	system.auth.ssh.event	system.auth.ssh.method	system.auth.user	s
▸	April 5th 2017, 13:13:44.000	Accepted	publickey	ubuntu	8
▸	April 5th 2017, 09:45:38.000	error:	maximum authentication attempts exceeded	webconfig	6
▸	April 5th 2017, 09:45:38.000	Failed	password	webconfig	6
▸	April 5th 2017, 09:45:36.000	Failed	password	webconfig	6
▸	April 5th 2017, 09:45:34.000	Failed	password	webconfig	6
▸	April 5th 2017, 09:45:31.000	Failed	password	webconfig	6
▸	April 5th 2017, 09:45:29.000	Failed	password	webconfig	6
▸	April 5th 2017, 09:45:27.000	Failed	password	webconfig	6
▸	April 5th 2017, 09:45:25.000	Invalid	.	webconfig	6

Security Analytics - SSH login attempts

1–50 of 934

Since we have also made geolocation enrichment at the time of ingest, the authentication document contains information about the physical location of the user that is authenticating. This is very useful to understand the location of those login attempts, and if the location of the attempt is unusual as well:

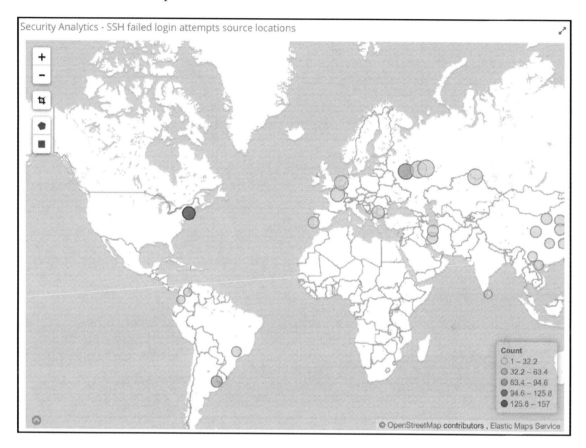

In addition to enriching the data with geolocation, we can also track whether any machine in our environment had been in contact with a potential threat. As mentioned earlier, a threat database is cross-referenced during ingestion, and any interaction with an IP address on a known threat list will be tagged and visible in this visualization of our dashboard:

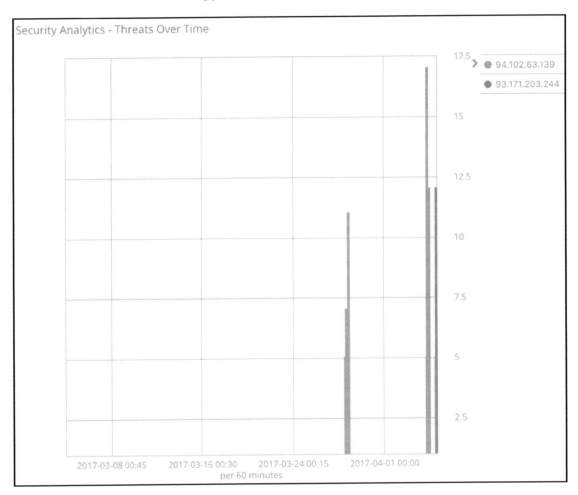

The preceding screenshot shows that our machine of interest (**server_101**) has touched two IPs on a threat list multiple times over time.

With a growing list of suspicious activities relating to this machine, we are led to create a job to detect a brute-force attack, specifically because a high amount of login attempts have been made on this machine:

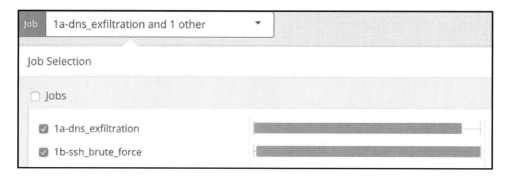

Once the job has been created to automate this part of the investigation, you can display it alongside the other job to make a correlation with the previous one and confirm the attack scenario.

The following screenshot shows the anomaly timeline for the two jobs (the brute-force job being a simple high count over the **system.auth.ssh.ip** configuration):

What we see in the preceding screenshot is very interesting, both in terms of the scenario and also in terms of the attack itself. Clearly, we had a brute-force attack (orange square) that happened before the exfiltration, indicating that once the machine was accessed, some sensitive information was exfiltrated.

If we were to analyze this in greater detail, we will see the source IP of the brute-force attack in the influencers (**24.151.103.17**), the target machine (**server_101**), and the user ID used to authenticate (`elastic_user_0`), as shown in the following screenshot:

But what is even more interesting is the fact that the brute-force attack wasn't intense from the connection rate standpoint. We can theorize that the adversary did this on purpose to stay under the radar of a classic security solution that would use a static threshold.

Here, even if the rate is low, we still get an anomaly with an average score, but we are able to detect it anyway:

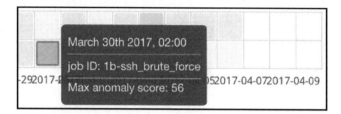

Moreover, since we have made a population analysis with ML, we are not analyzing the IP independently, but rather comparing the behavior of the different IPs against each other. So, even if an IP address appears in the data just for a short period of time—which wouldn't be enough to build a model out of it—if the behavior is significantly different from the normal IP profile, then it is spotted, as illustrated in the following screenshot:

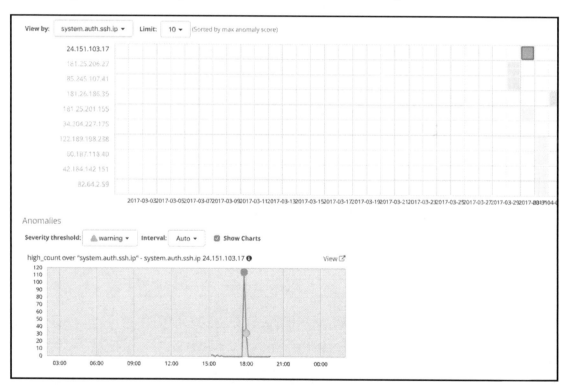

Here, you can see that the IP produced a connection spike that couldn't have been captured if we had partitioned the analysis, since the lack of substantial history wouldn't have given ML a chance to build a proper model.

Looking at the details of the anomaly, our suspicions are confirmed about the brute-force attack. Again, this is an activity that's hundreds of times higher than the norm:

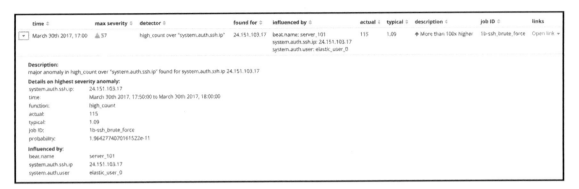

Now, knowing that we did have a brute-force attack, and the fact that we have geolocation data, it is interesting to enrich our investigation with other insights such as the login time and location.

Here, we created two more jobs to confirm what we think. `elastic_user_0` has been used during the usual time of day and an unusual location, as shown in the following screenshot:

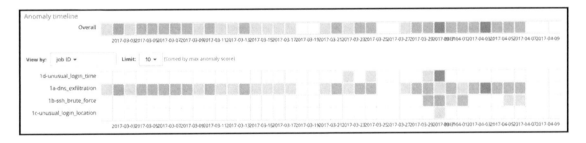

We can see that all of this unusual behavior has happened in relatively the same time frame as the brute-force attack. We can dig into the traffic by using a custom link to the **Discover** tab (via a custom link):

In the resulting **Discover** view, we can see a very interesting indication; the connection has been made from a laptop named **mikep**:

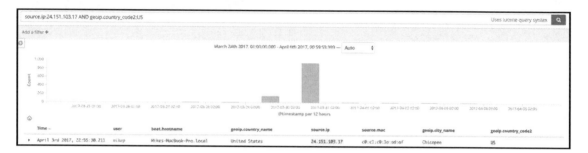

To confirm that the suspect behavior is coming from the **mikep** laptop, we can leverage yet another Kibana dashboard that describes the domain traffic, ports, and also the processes that have been executed. We can clearly see a high amount of outbound port usage from **mikep**:

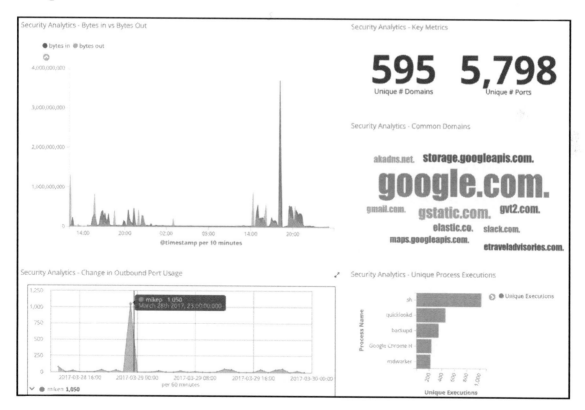

This is yet another step in the investigation that could be automated with ML, as scanning the ports was required for the adversary to understand how to intrude **server_101** through a brute force authentication. This is illustrated with the anomaly timeline, which now includes the port scan jobs and shows two interesting aspects:

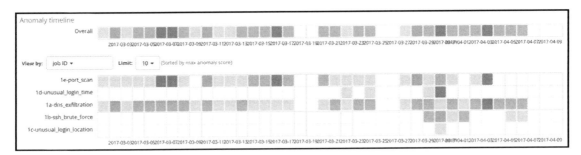

The first thing we notice is that we had a port scan not very long before the brute-force attack. If we click on one of the port scan anomalies, we can see that the port scan comes from the **mikep** laptop and targets server_101's IP address:

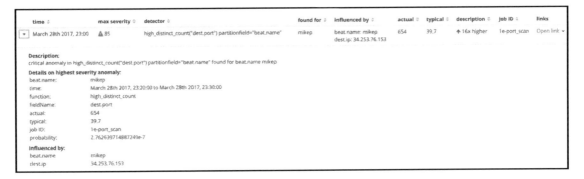

The second thing we can notice in the anomaly timeline is the fact that the port scan happened multiple times before the actual attack, so the adversary has been doing reconnaissance for a long time:

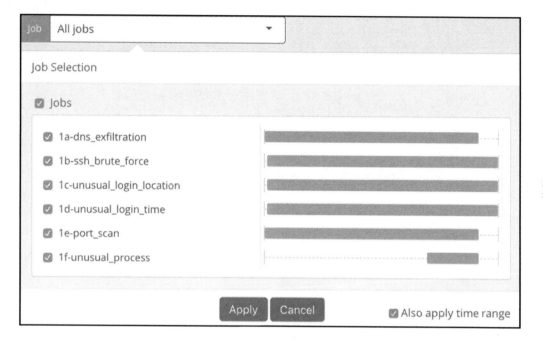

The other aspect we can notice in the previous Kibana dashboard is the processes that were executed on the **mikep** laptop, which might indicate that a piece of malware was responsible for the attack. The detection of unusual processes running on systems is also something we could automate with ML: we could build a job that looks for rare processes per machine (`rare by process_sig, partition_field_name="beat.name"`). If we created such a job, it would highlight that some intriguing processes have been executed on the machine:

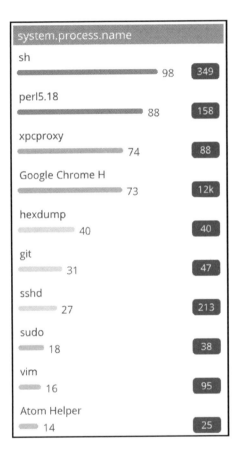

Now that we have pretty much the whole kill chain, we could investigate to find similar behavior to that attack, or maybe look at another machine that could potentially be infected.

For this, we can use an existing dashboard that contains a data table of the top domain that has been reached. It doesn't come as a surprise that we can see **vodkaroom.ru** at the top:

Security Analytics - Domains by Unique Subdomain Count			
Domains ⬍	**IP** ⬍	**Graph Analysis** ⬍	**# of Subdomains** ⬍
vodkaroom.ru.	5.101.152.77	Graph Analysis - 🔍 🔍 vodkaroom.ru	5,445
ubuntu.com.	54.195.20.85	Graph Analysis - ubuntu.com	1
ubuntu.com.	54.216.255.40	Graph Analysis - ubuntu.com	1
ubuntu.com.	54.217.129.123	Graph Analysis - ubuntu.com	1

The interesting bit here is the link that had been added as a column in the data table. This allows the user to jump into the Elastic Graph visualization, as shown in the following screenshot:

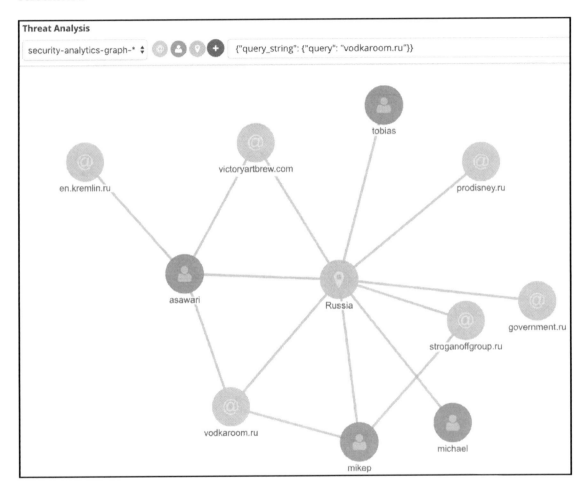

Elastic Graph allows you to reveal the connections between documents of the same index, which here is showing the connection between **mikep** and **vodkaroom.ru**. In addition, we can see that **mikep** is not the only laptop connected to that domain—**asawari** is another one—plus the fact that other domains are connected to them, which might be suspicious as well.

One of the default modes of Elastic Graph is to remove noisy or popular data and only establish connections between relevant data. The drawback in this use case, however, is that we actually want to reveal popular connections that would translate to highly interesting entities for our suspicious behavior.

Thus, the solution is to disable the **Significant links** option, as shown in the following screenshot:

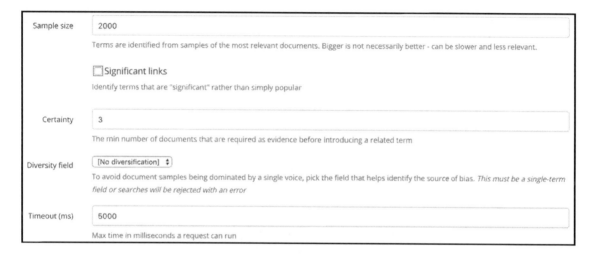

If a domain node is selected and expanded (here, this is happening on the **vodkaroom.ru** node), we'll see the connection to **server_101**, since there are many documents that share those terms in the DNS traffic index:

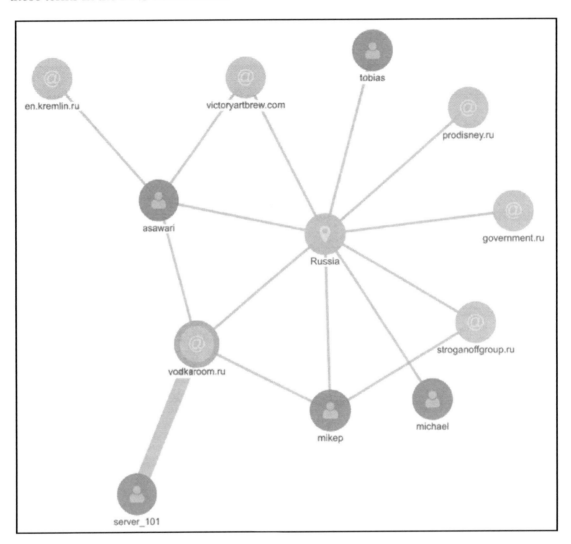

As we can see, this diagram in Elastic Graph corroborates our suspicions about the relationship between **server_101** and **vodkaroom.ru**. But are there any other interesting connections? Exploring further by clicking the link button in Elastic Graph yields yet more information:

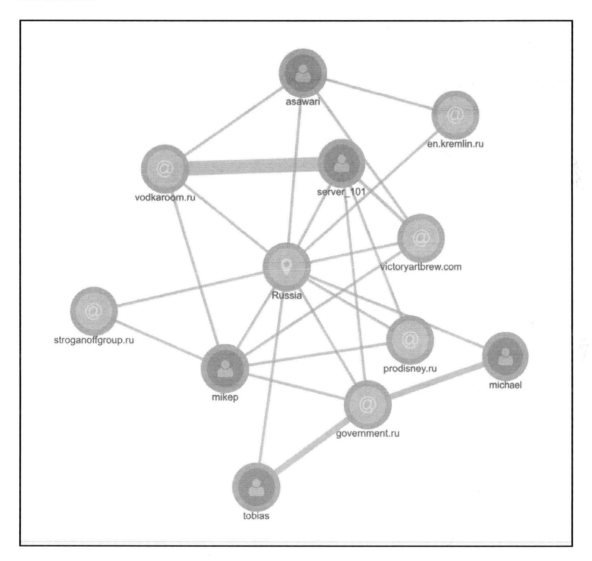

The preceding screenshot shows that, in addition to the **mikep** and **asawari** systems communicating with **vodkaroom.ru**, those two systems have also communicated with **victoryartbrew.com**. Perhaps this is a coincidence, but it's also a potentially important clue as to how the original malware was first acquired. Perhaps the **asawari** system is also currently infected but hasn't yet exhibited other malicious behavior. This gives us the opportunity to thwart future risky activity from that machine.

Summary

In this chapter, we have learned about the challenges that modern security teams face with legacy security solutions in keeping up with complex APT, and how Elastic ML allows analysts to have an iterative investigation approach by automating some of the forensic analysis and threat hunting steps.

In the next chapter, Chapter 6, *Alerting on ML Analysis*, we will put a particular focus on the alerting component that comes with commercial features and walk you through how to effectively make security insights actionable.

6
Alerting on ML Analysis

Throughout this book, we have seen that ML is very powerful, flexible, and useful for determining and highlighting unexpected events and entities that exist in massive datasets. However, the real value of the technology is often its ability to uncover these insights in near-real time, thus making those insights proactive and actionable. In this chapter, we'll discuss how to effectively integrate ML with Alerting (that is, Watcher). To do this, we will cover the following topics:

- Getting an understanding of how ML's results are published to the results indices
- Review how the default watch for an ML job works
- Learn how to create a custom watch for advanced functionality

This chapter, however, will not be an extensive overview of Alerting (Watcher). To find out more information about Watcher and its functionality and capabilities, please refer to the Alerting documentation at `https://www.elastic.co/guide/en/elastic-stack-overview/current/xpack-alerting.html`.

Results presentation

Before we get into the detail of where the results are stored and what they look like at a document level, we need to understand that the results from ML jobs are presented at three different levels of abstraction:

- **The bucket level**: This level summarizes the results of the entirety of the ML job per time bucket. Essentially, it is a representation of how unusual that time bucket is, given the configuration of your job. If your job has multiple detectors, or splits in the analysis resulting in results for possibly many entities simultaneously, then each bucket level result is an aggregated representation of all of those things.

- **The record level**: This is the most detailed information about each and every anomalous occurrence or anomalous entity within a time bucket. Again, depending on the job configuration (multiple detectors, splits, and so on), there can be many record-level documents per time bucket.
- **The influencer level**: This is used to better understand the most unusual entities (influencers) within a timespan.

In general, and as we will see through the examples that are given later in this chapter, leveraging these different levels of abstraction can be useful for different kinds of Alerting, such as summary alerts, detailed alerts, and so on.

Getting actual access to the results means having to implement one of two methods:

- Using the ML `/results` API
- Querying the results indices that ML creates in Elasticsearch

The method that's chosen is up to the user. In general, directly querying the results indices offers more flexibility and is more common than using the results API, so we will focus our discussions on understanding the results indices and the different kinds of documents therein.

The results index

As we mentioned previously, ML analyzes data and summarizes the results into a results index. By default, this index is called `.ml-anomalies-shared`, unless the job was configured to use a dedicated index via ticking the box in the configuration **user interface (UI)** or via setting the `results_index_name` field when using the API. If that was the case, then the results index will be called `.ml-anomalies-custom-myname`, where `myname` is either the declared value of the `results_index_name` field when using the API, or the name of the job itself when using the UI. In either case, the results index can be quite small compared to the size of data that was used to feed the ML analysis. In addition, an index alias is also created of the `.ml-anomalies-jobname` form, where `jobname` is the name of the job. The definition of this alias can be seen by hitting the following API call:

```
GET ml-anomalies-*/_alias
```

The results will include entries that look as follows:

```
".ml-anomalies-farequote": {
  "filter": {
    "term": {
      "job_id": {
        "value": "farequote",
        "boost": 1
      }
    }
  }
},
```

Here, `farequote` is the name of the ML job. It's obvious that the purpose of the alias is to only show results for a specific `job_id` via a `term` filter. Otherwise, querying the `.ml-anomalies-shared` index (or a greedier index pattern of `.ml-anomalies-*`) will return records for many jobs. If the user wants to query for the results of only one ML job, it is up to the user to either use this index alias or to do their own term filter on the proper `job_id`.

Inside the result index, there are a variety of different documents, each with their own usefulness with respect to Alerting. The ones we will discuss are the ones that directly relate to the three levels of abstraction that we discussed previously. They are aptly named as follows:

- `result_type:bucket`: To give bucket-level results
- `result_type:record`: To give record-level results
- `result_type:influencer`: To give influencer-level results

The distribution of these document types will depend on the ML job configuration and the characteristics of the dataset being analyzed. These document types are written with the following heuristic:

- `result_type:bucket`: One document is written for every bucket span's worth of time. In other words, if the bucket span is `15m`, then there will be one document of this type being written every 15 minutes. Its timestamp will be equal to the leading edge of the bucket. For example, for the time bucket that encompasses the range between 11:30 and 11:45, the result document of this type will have a timestamp of 11:30.

- `result_type:record`: One document is written for every occurrence of an anomaly within a time bucket. Therefore, with big datasets encompassing many entities (IP addresses, hostnames, and so on), a particular bucket of time could have hundreds or even thousands of anomaly records in a bucket during a major anomalous event or widespread outage. This document will also have a timestamp equal to the leading edge of the bucket.

- `result_type:influencer`: One document is written for every influencer that's found for each anomaly record. Because there can potentially be more than one influencer type found for each anomaly record, this type of document can be even more voluminous than record results. This document will also have a timestamp that's equal to the leading edge of the bucket.

The reason why understanding this is so important with respect to Alerting is because there will inevitably be a balance between alert detail (usually, more is preferable to less) with the number of individual alerts per unit time (usually, less is preferable to more). We will revisit this when we start writing actual alerts.

Bucket results

At the highest level of abstraction are the results at the bucket level. Essentially, this is the aggregated results for the entire job as a function of time and essentially answers the question "how unusual was this bucket of time?" To understand the structure and content of bucket-level results, let's query the results for a particular ML job. We will start by looking at the results for a simple, single metric job that has no defined influencers:

```
GET .ml-anomalies-*/_search
{
    "query": {
            "bool": {
              "filter": [
                    { "range" : { "timestamp" : { "gte": "now-2y" } } },
                    { "term" :  { "job_id" : "farequote_single" } },
                    { "term" :  { "result_type" : "bucket" } },
                    { "range" : { "anomaly_score" : {"gte" : "90"}}}
                ]
            }
        }
}
```

Here, the query is asking for any bucket results that have existed over the last two years where the `anomaly_score` is greater than or equal to `90`. The result looks as follows:

```
{
  ...
  "hits": {
    "total": 1,
    "max_score": 0,
    "hits": [
      {
        "_index": ".ml-anomalies-shared",
        "_type": "doc",
        "_id": "farequote_single_bucket_1486656600000_600",
        "_score": 0,
        "_source": {
          "job_id": "farequote_single",
          "timestamp": 1486656600000,
          "anomaly_score": 90.67726,
          "bucket_span": 600,
          "initial_anomaly_score": 85.04854039170988,
          "event_count": 277,
          "is_interim": false,
          "bucket_influencers": [
            {
              "job_id": "farequote_single",
              "result_type": "bucket_influencer",
              "influencer_field_name": "bucket_time",
              "initial_anomaly_score": 85.04854039170988,
              "anomaly_score": 90.67726,
              "raw_anomaly_score": 13.99180406849176,
              "probability": 6.362276028576088e-17,
              "timestamp": 1486656600000,
              "bucket_span": 600,
              "is_interim": false
            }
          ],
          "processing_time_ms": 7,
          "result_type": "bucket"
        }
      }
    ]
  }
}
```

You can see that just one result record is returned, a single anomalous time bucket (at timestamp `1486656600000`, or in my time zone, Thursday, February 9, 2017 11:10:00 A.M. GMT-05:00) that has an `anomaly_score` greater than `90`. In other words, there were no other time buckets with anomalies that big in this time range. Let's look at some key portions of the output to fully understand what this is telling us:

- `timestamp`: The timestamp of the leading edge of the time bucket (in epoch format).
- `anomaly_score`: The current normalized score of the bucket, based upon the range of the probabilities seen over the entirety of the job. The value of this score may fluctuate over time as new data is processed by the job and new anomalies are found.
- `initial_anomaly_score`: The normalized score of the bucket, that is, when that bucket was first analyzed by the analytics. This score, unlike the `anomaly_score`, will not change as more data is analyzed.
- `event_count`: The number of raw Elasticsearch documents seen by the ML algorithms during the bucket's span.
- `is_interim`: A flag that signifies whether or not the bucket is finalized or whether the bucket is still waiting for the all of the data within the bucket span to be received. This field is relevant for ongoing jobs that are operating in real time. For certain types of analysis, there could be interim results, despite the fact that not all of the data for the bucket has been seen.
- `bucket_influencers`: An array of influencers (and details on them) that have been identified for this current bucket. Even if no influencers have been chosen as part of the job configuration, or there are no influencers as part of the analysis, there will always be a default influencer of the `influencer_field_name:bucket_time` type, which is mostly an internal record-keeping device to allow for the ordering of bucket-level anomalies in cases where explicit influencers cannot be determined.

If a job does have named and identified influencers, then the `bucket_influencers` array may look like the following:

```
"bucket_influencers": [
  {
    "job_id": "farequote",
    "result_type": "bucket_influencer",
    "influencer_field_name": "airline",
    "initial_anomaly_score": 85.06429298617539,
    "anomaly_score": 99.7634,
    "raw_anomaly_score": 15.040566947916583,
    "probability": 6.5926436244031685e-18,
```

```
      "timestamp": 1486656000000,
      "bucket_span": 900,
      "is_interim": false
    },
    {
      "job_id": "farequote",
      "result_type": "bucket_influencer",
      "influencer_field_name": "bucket_time",
      "initial_anomaly_score": 85.06429298617539,
      "anomaly_score": 99.76353,
      "raw_anomaly_score": 15.040566947916583,
      "probability": 6.5926436244031685e-18,
      "timestamp": 1486656000000,
      "bucket_span": 900,
      "is_interim": false
    }
  ],
```

Notice that in addition to the default entry of
the `influencer_field_name:bucket_time` type, in this case, there is an entry for a field
name of an analytics-identified influencer for the `airline` field. This is a cue that `airline`
was a relevant influencer type that was discovered at the time of this anomaly. Since
multiple influencer candidates can be chosen in the job configuration, it should be noted
that in this case, `airline` is the only influencer field and no other fields were found to be
influential. It should also be noted that, at this level of detail, the particular instance of
`airline` (that is, which one) is not disclosed; that information will be disclosed when
querying at the lower levels of abstraction, which we will discuss next.

Now that we have knowledge of the bucket-level details, we can look at how we can
leverage this information for summary alerts. We will cover this later in this chapter.

Record results

At a lower level of abstraction, there are results at the record level. Giving the most amount
of detail, record results show specific instances of anomalies and essentially answers the
question "what entity was unusual and by how much?" To understand the structure and
content of record-level results, let's query the results for a particular ML job. We will start
by looking at the following results, which are for a simple, single metric job that has no
defined influencers:

```
GET .ml-anomalies-*/_search
{
    "query": {
            "bool": {
```

```
                    "filter": [
                        { "range" : { "timestamp" : { "gte": "now-2y" } } },
                        { "term"  :  { "job_id" : "farequote_single" } },
                        { "term"  :  { "result_type" : "record" } },
                        { "range" : { "record_score" : {"gte" : "90"}}}
                    ]
                }
            }
        }
```

Here, the query is asking for any record results that have existed over the last two years, where the `record_score` is greater than or equal to 90. The result looks as follows:

```
{
  ...
  "hits": {
    "total": 1,
    "max_score": 0,
   "hits": {
   "total": 1,
    "max_score": 0,
     "hits": [
       {
         "_index": ".ml-anomalies-shared",
         "_type": "doc",
         "_id": "farequote_single_record_1486656600000_600_0_29791_0",
         "_score": 0,
         "_source": {
           "job_id": "farequote_single",
           "result_type": "record",
           "probability": 3.3099524615371287e-20,
           "record_score": 90.67726,
           "initial_record_score": 85.04854039170988,
           "bucket_span": 600,
           "detector_index": 0,
           "is_interim": false,
           "timestamp": 1486656600000,
           "function": "count",
           "function_description": "count",
           "typical": [
             120.30986417315765
           ],
           "actual": [
             277
           ]
         }
       }
     }
   ]
```

```
    }
  }
```

Let's look at some key portions of the output:

- `timestamp`: The timestamp of the leading edge of the time bucket, inside of which this anomaly occurred.
- `record_score`: The current normalized score of the anomaly record, based upon the range of the probabilities seen over the entirety of the job. The value of this score may fluctuate over time as new data is processed by the job and new anomalies are found.
- `initial_record_score`: The normalized score of the anomaly record, that is, when that bucket was first analyzed by the analytics. This score, unlike the `record_score`, will not change as more data is analyzed.
- `detector_index`: An internal counter to keep track of which detector configuration that this anomaly belongs to. Obviously, with a single-detector job, this value will be zero, but it may be non-zero in jobs with multiple detectors.
- `function`: A reference to keep track of which `detector` function was used for the creation of this anomaly.
- `is_interim`: A flag the signifies whether or not the bucket is finalized or whether the bucket is still waiting for all of the data within the bucket span to be received. This field is relevant for ongoing jobs that are operating in real time. For certain types of analysis, there could be interim results, despite the fact that not all of the data for the bucket has been seen.
- `actual`: The actual observed value of the analyzed data in this bucket. For example, if the function is `count`, then this represents the number of documents that are encountered (and counted) in this time bucket.
- `typical`: A representation of the expected or predicted value based upon the ML model for this dataset.

If a job has splits defined (either with `by_field_name` and/or `partition_field_name`) and identified influencers, then the record results documents will have more information:

```
...
        "timestamp": 1486656000000,
        "partition_field_name": "airline",
        "partition_field_value": "AAL",
        "function": "count",
        "function_description": "count",
        "typical": [
          17.853294505163284
        ],
```

```
            "actual": [
              54
            ],
            "influencers": [
              {
                "influencer_field_name": "airline",
                "influencer_field_values": [
                  "AAL"
                ]
              }
            ],
            "airline": [
              "AAL"
            ]
        } ...
```

Here, we can not only see the addition of the `partition_field_name` and `partition_field_value` fields (which would have been `by_field_name` and `by_field_value` if a `by_field` were used), but we can also see that an array for the `partition_field_name` (`airline`) was constructed as well, with a value inside of the single instance of the field that was found to be the one that was anomalous. Also, like the bucket results, there is an `influencers` array with an articulation of which influencers (and the values of those influencers) are relevant to this anomaly record.

In some examples, some of the information in the results document seems redundant, especially in the case where the only influencer defined in the job is the same field that you are splitting the analysis on. While that's a recommended practice, it causes the output record results to seemingly contain superfluous information. Things will look more interesting (and less redundant) if your job configurations have more influencer candidates defined.

If your job is doing population analysis (via the use of `over_field_name`), then the record results document will be organized slightly differently as the reporting is done with an orientation as to the unusual members of the population. For example, let's say we have an example job of analyzing Apache web logs with a configuration of the following:

```
...
"analysis_config": {
    "bucket_span": "15m",
    "detectors": [
      {
        "detector_description": "count by status over clientip",
        "function": "count",
        "by_field_name": "status",
        "over_field_name": "clientip",
```

```
            "detector_index": 0
        }
    ],
    "influencers": [
      "clientip",
      "status",
      "uri"
    ]
  },
...
```

Here, an example anomaly record could look like this:

```
...
    {
      "_index": ".ml-anomalies-shared",
      "_type": "doc",
      "_id": "gallery_record_1487223000000_900_0_-628922254_13",
      "_score": 0,
      "_source": {
        "job_id": "gallery",
        "result_type": "record",
        "probability": 4.593248987780696e-31,
        "record_score": 99.71500910125427,
        "initial_record_score": 99.71500910125427,
        "bucket_span": 900,
        "detector_index": 0,
        "is_interim": false,
        "timestamp": 1487223000000,
        "by_field_name": "status",
        "function": "count",
        "function_description": "count",
        "over_field_name": "clientip",
        "over_field_value": "173.203.78.60",
        "causes": [
          {
            "probability": 4.593248987780688e-31,
            "by_field_name": "status",
            "by_field_value": "404",
            "function": "count",
            "function_description": "count",
            "typical": [
              1.1177332137173952
            ],
            "actual": [
              1215
            ],
            "over_field_name": "clientip",
```

```
            "over_field_value": "173.203.78.60"
          }
        ],
        "influencers": [
          {
            "influencer_field_name": "uri",
            "influencer_field_values": [
              "/wp-login.php"
            ]
          },
          {
            "influencer_field_name": "status",
            "influencer_field_values": [
              "404"
            ]
          },
          {
            "influencer_field_name": "clientip",
            "influencer_field_values": [
              "173.203.78.60"
            ]
          }
        ],
        "clientip": [
          "173.203.78.60"
        ],
        "uri": [
          "/wp-login.php"
        ],
        "status": [
          "404"
        ]
      }
    },...
```

 This example is the same brute-force authentication attempt against a non-existent WordPress login page that we saw in Chapter 3, *Event Change Detection*.

Notice that, first, the main orientation is around `over_field` (in this case, the IP address of the clients hitting the website), and that once an anomalous IP is found, an array of `causes` is built to compactly express all of the anomalous things that that IP did in that bucket. Again, many things seem redundant, but it is primarily because these different ways of recording information makes it easier to aggregate. It is also easier to display this information in different ways in the user interface of Kibana. With that being said, we will see that having access to this detailed information means that we can make very detailed alerts.

Influencer results

Yet another lens by which to view the results is via influencers. Viewing the results this way allows us to answer the question "what were the most unusual entities in my ML job and when were they unusual?" To understand the structure and content of influencer-level results, let's query the results for a particular ML job. We will start by looking at the results for a job split on a partition field. That field will also be the sole influencer that was chosen in the job configuration:

```
GET .ml-anomalies-*/_search
{
    "query": {
        "bool": {
          "filter": [
            { "range" : { "timestamp" : { "gte": "now-2y" } } },
            { "term" :  { "job_id" : "farequote" } },
            { "term" :  { "result_type" : "influencer" } },
            { "range" : { "influencer_score" : {"gte" : "98"}}}
          ]
        }
    }
}
```

Here, the query is asking for any influencer results that have existed over the last two years where the `influencer_score` is greater than or equal to 98. The result looks as follows:

```
{
    ...
    "hits": {
    "total": 1,
    "max_score": 0,
    "hits": [
      {
        "_index": ".ml-anomalies-shared",
        "_type": "doc",
```

```
          "_id": "farequote_influencer_1486656000000_900_airline_64556_3",
          "_score": 0,
          "_source": {
            "job_id": "farequote",
            "result_type": "influencer",
            "influencer_field_name": "airline",
            "influencer_field_value": "AAL",
            "airline": "AAL",
            "influencer_score": 98.56065708451416,
            "initial_influencer_score": 98.56065708451416,
            "probability": 6.252543460836487e-19,
            "bucket_span": 900,
            "is_interim": false,
            "timestamp": 1486656000000
          }
        }
      ]
    }
...
```

Let's look at some key portions of the output:

- `timestamp`: The timestamp of the leading edge of the time bucket, inside of which this entity was anomalous.
- `influencer_score`: The current normalized score of the influencer, based upon the range of the influencers seen over the entirety of the job. The value of this score may fluctuate over time as new data is processed by the job and new influencers are found.
- `initial_influencer_score`: The normalized score of the influencers from when that bucket was first analyzed by the analytics. This score, unlike the `influencer_score`, will not change as more data is analyzed.
- `influencer_field_name`: The name of the influencer field being described here, in case there are multiple influencers in this anomaly.
- `influencer_field_value`: The value of the influencer field being described here.
- `is_interim`: A flag the signifies whether or not the bucket is finalized or whether the bucket is still waiting for all of the data within the bucket span to be received. This field is relevant for ongoing jobs that are operating in real time. For certain types of analysis, there could be interim results, despite the fact that not all of the data for the bucket has been seen yet.

In this case, we can see that the data associated with a particular airline during this bucket significantly contributed to the formation of the anomaly, since the `influencer_score` is high.

In summary, there is a fair amount of detail, at different levels of abstraction, available in the ML results indices. This will obviously be useful when it comes to building alerts with different levels of detail.

Alerts from the Machine Learning UI in Kibana

In this section, we will go through several Alerting techniques, but we should first start with the simplest method and later move up in complexity. The first method of getting an alert tied to your ML job is to use the built-in alert wizard in the **Machine Learning** UI. There are two places to invoke this wizard:

- After clicking the **Create new job** button in one of the job creation wizards (**Single metric** job, **Multi metric** job, **Population** job, and so on)
- When starting a previously stopped datafeed in the ML job listing page, as shown in the following screenshot:

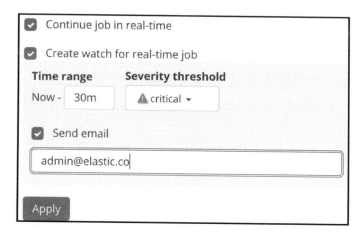

In either case, the option to create an alert (a watch) via the UI is only available when the ML job is set to run in **Continue job in real time**, meaning that the job will be scheduled to run continually (otherwise, Alerting really doesn't make sense). The UI only asks for a few inputs from the user:

- **Time range**: Defaulting to a range of *now-2 × bucket span*, although the UI will show the *2 × bucket span* as a numerical value based on the actual bucket span of the job. This is sensible under most circumstances. The true minimum of this range should be *now -(bucket span + query delay)*, as long as the query delay in the datafeed setting is no greater than the bucket span. Since the watch will have its own schedule and runs asynchronously from the ML job, it is important that this range of time does not miss any results in the .ml-anomalies indices, since we already know that results are written with a timestamp that is the leading edge of the bucket.
- **Severity threshold**: This gives the user the opportunity to alert on a minimum bucket anomaly score. For example, setting the value to **critical** means that the watch will only fire if the bucket anomaly score is greater than or equal to 75.
- **Send email**: If checked and your cluster has been configured to send emails, this will allow the watch action to email an alert to the recipient, in addition to logging the message to a file.

> Instructions for sending an email in Watcher can be found in the online documentation at https://www.elastic.co/guide/en/elasticsearch/ reference/current/notification-settings.html#email-notification- settings.

After creating the watch from the ML UI, the watch is viewable, editable, and can be tested/simulated via the **Watcher** UI (or via the API, of course). Let's take a moment to inspect the contents of the watch that ML creates. By doing so, we can understand the details of what the watch is doing, and also use this knowledge to create more detailed, complex watches.

Anatomy of the default watch from the ML UI in Kibana

Once created in the ML UI in Kibana, the contents of the watch definition will look something like the code in the following listing on the GitHub repository: https://github. com/PacktPublishing/Machine-Learning-with-the-Elastic-Stack/blob/master/ Chapter06/default_ML_watch.json.

Since this watch is quite lengthy, let's break it down into sections. First, let's look at the `trigger` section:

```
{
  "trigger": {
    "schedule": {
      "interval": "109s"
    }
  },
```

Here, we can see that the interval at which the watch will fire in real time is every `109s`. This will be a random value between 60 and 120 seconds so that if a node restarts, all of the watches will not be synchronized, and they will have their execution times more evenly spread out to reduce any potential load on the cluster. It is also important that this interval value be less than or equal to the bucket span of the job. Having it be larger than the bucket span may cause recently written anomaly records to be missed by the watch. With the `interval` being less (or even much less) than the bucket span of the job, you can also take advantage of the advanced notification that is available when there are interim results, anomalies that can still be determined despite not having seen all of the data within a bucket span.

The input section starts with the `query` section:

```
"query": {
  "bool": {
    "filter": [
      {
        "term": {
          "job_id": "farequote"
        }
      },
      {
        "range": {
          "timestamp": {
            "gte": "now-30m"
          }
        }
      },
      {
        "terms": {
          "result_type": [
            "bucket",
            "record",
            "influencer"
          ]
        }
```

```
                 }
               ]
             }
       },
```

Here, we are asking Watcher to query (in the `.ml-anomalies-*` index pattern) for bucket, record, and influencer result documents for a job called `farequote` in the last 30 minutes (again, the default window is twice the bucket span of the ML job, which was 15 minutes in this example). While all result types were asked for, we will later see that only the bucket-level results are used to evaluate whether or not to create an alert.

Next comes a series of three aggregations. When they're collapsed, they look as follows:

```
68 ▾    "aggs": {
69 ▸        "bucket_results": {▭},
139 ▸       "influencer_results": {▭},
180 ▸       "record_results": {▭}
224 ▴    }
```

The `bucket_results` aggregation first filters for buckets where the anomaly score is greater than or equal to 75:

```
"aggs": {
  "bucket_results": {
    "filter": {
      "range": {
        "anomaly_score": {
          "gte": 75
        }
      }
    },
```

Then, a subaggregation asks for the top 1 bucket sorted by `anomaly_score`:

```
"aggs": {
 "top_bucket_hits": {
    "top_hits": {
      "sort": [
        {
          "anomaly_score": {
            "order": "desc"
          }
        }
      ],
      "_source": {
        "includes": [
```

```
                              "job_id",
                              "result_type",
                              "timestamp",
                              "anomaly_score",
                              "is_interim"
                          ]
                      },
                      "size": 1,
```

Next, still within the `top_bucket_hits` subaggregation, there are a series of defined scripted fields:

```
                      "script_fields": {
                        "start": {
                          "script": {
                            "lang": "painless",
                            "inline":
"LocalDateTime.ofEpochSecond((doc[\"timestamp\"].date.getMillis()-
((doc[\"bucket_span\"].value * 1000)\n * params.padding)) / 1000, 0,
ZoneOffset.UTC).toString()+\":00.000Z\"",
                            "params": {
                              "padding": 10
                            }
                          }
                        },
                        "end": {
                          "script": {
                            "lang": "painless",
                            "inline":
"LocalDateTime.ofEpochSecond((doc[\"timestamp\"].date.getMillis()+((doc[\"b
ucket_span\"].value * 1000)\n * params.padding)) / 1000, 0,
ZoneOffset.UTC).toString()+\":00.000Z\"",
                            "params": {
                              "padding": 10
                            }
                          }
                        },
                        "timestamp_epoch": {
                          "script": {
                            "lang": "painless",
                            "inline":
"doc[\"timestamp\"].date.getMillis()/1000"
                          }
                        },
                        "timestamp_iso8601": {
                          "script": {
                            "lang": "painless",
                            "inline": "doc[\"timestamp\"].date"
```

```
          }
        },
        "score": {
          "script": {
            "lang": "painless",
            "inline":
"Math.round(doc[\"anomaly_score\"].value)"
          }
        }
      }
    }
```

These newly defined variables will be used by the watch to provide more functionality and context. Some of the variables are merely reformatting values (score is just a rounded version of anomaly_score), while start and end will later fill a functional role by defining a start and end time that is equal to +/- 10 bucket spans from the time of the anomalous bucket. This is later used by the UI to show an appropriate contextual time range before and after the anomalous bucket so that the user can see things more clearly.

The influencer_results and record_results aggregations ask for the top three influencer scores and record scores, but only the output of the record_results aggregation is used in subsequent parts of the watch (and only in the default email text).

The condition section of the watch is where the input is evaluated to see whether or not the action section is executed or not. In this case, the condition section is as follows:

```
"condition": {
  "compare": {
    "ctx.payload.aggregations.bucket_results.doc_count": {
      "gt": 0
    }
  }
},
```

We are using this to check whether the bucket_results aggregation returned any documents (where the doc_count is greater than 0). In other words, if the bucket_results aggregation did indeed return non-zero results, that indicates that there were indeed documents where the anomaly_score was greater than 75. If true, then the action section will be invoked.

The `action` section has two parts in our case: one action for logging information to a file and the other for sending an email. If the `action` section is executed because of `true` being returned from the `condition` section, then both the `log` action and the `email` action are invoked:

```
    "actions": {
      "log": {
        "logging": {
          "level": "info",
          "text": "Alert for job
[{{ctx.payload.aggregations.bucket_results.top_bucket_hits.hits.hits.0._sou
rce.job_id}}] at
[{{ctx.payload.aggregations.bucket_results.top_bucket_hits.hits.hits.0.fiel
ds.timestamp_iso8601.0}}] score
[{{ctx.payload.aggregations.bucket_results.top_bucket_hits.hits.hits.0.fiel
ds.score.0}}]"
        }
      },
      "send_email": {
        "throttle_period_in_millis": 900000,
        "email": {
          "profile": "standard",
          "to": [
            "ops@acme.co"
          ],
          "subject": "ML Watcher Alert",
          "body": {
            "html": "<html>\n  <body>\n    <strong>Elastic Stack Machine
Learning Alert</strong>\n    <br />\n    <br />\n\n
<strong>Job</strong>:
{{ctx.payload.aggregations.bucket_results.top_bucket_hits.hits.hits.0._sour
ce.job_id}}\n    <br />\n\n    <strong>Time</strong>:
{{ctx.payload.aggregations.bucket_results.top_bucket_hits.hits.hits.0.field
s.timestamp_iso8601.0}}\n    <br />\n\n    <strong>Anomaly score</strong>:
{{ctx.payload.aggregations.bucket_results.top_bucket_hits.hits.hits.0.field
s.score.0}}\n    <br />\n    <br />\n\n    <a
href=\"http://localhost:5601/app/ml#/explorer/?_g=(ml:(jobIds:!('{{ctx.payl
oad.aggregations.bucket_results.top_bucket_hits.hits.hits.0._source.job_id}
}')),refreshInterval:(display:Off,pause:!f,value:0),time:(from:'{{ctx.paylo
ad.aggregations.bucket_results.top_bucket_hits.hits.hits.0.fields.start.0}}
',mode:absolute,to:'{{ctx.payload.aggregations.bucket_results.top_bucket_hi
ts.hits.hits.0.fields.end.0}}'))&_a=(filters:!(),mlAnomaliesTable:(interval
Value:auto,thresholdValue:0),mlExplorerSwimlane:(selectedLane:Overall,selec
tedTime:{{ctx.payload.aggregations.bucket_results.top_bucket_hits.hits.hits
.0.fields.timestamp_epoch.0}},selectedType:overall),query:(query_string:(an
alyze_wildcard:!t,query:'*')))\">\n    Click here to open in Anomaly
Explorer</a>.\n    <br />\n    <br />\n\n    \n\n    <strong>Top
```

```
records:</strong>\n     <br />\n
{{#ctx.payload.aggregations.record_results.top_record_hits.hits.hits}}\n
{{_source.function}}({{{_source.field_name}}}) {{_source.by_field_value}}
{{_source.over_field_value}} {{_source.partition_field_value}}
[{{{fields.score.0}}}]\n     <br />\n
{{/ctx.payload.aggregations.record_results.top_record_hits.hits.hits}}\n\n
</body>\n</html>\n"
        }
      }
    }
  }
```

The `log` section will print a message to an output file, which by default is the Elasticsearch log file. Notice that the syntax of the message is using the templating language called Mustache (named because of its prolific usage of curly braces). Simply put, variables contained in Mustache's double curly braces will be substituted with their actual values. As a result, for an example job, the logging text written out to the file may look as follows:

```
Alert for job [farequote_alert] at [2017-02-12T00:00:00.000Z] score [91]
```

The email may look as follows:

```
Elastic Stack Machine Learning Alert

 Job: farequote_alert
 Time: 2017-02-09T16:15:00.000Z
 Anomaly score: 91
 Click here to open in Anomaly Explorer.

 Top records:
 count() [91]
```

It is obvious that the format of the alert HTML is really oriented around getting the user a summary of the information, but to entice the user to investigate further by clicking on the link within the email. The URL of this link contains context, and looking at the URL itself gives us those clues:

```
http://localhost:5601/app/ml#/explorer/?_g=(ml:(jobIds:!('farequote_alert')
),refreshInterval:(display:Off,pause:!f,value:0),time:(from:'2017-02-09T13:
45:00.000Z',mode:absolute,to:'2017-02-09T18:45:00.000Z'))&_a=(filters:!(),m
lAnomaliesTable:(intervalValue:auto,thresholdValue:0),mlExplorerSwimlane:(s
electedLane:Overall,selectedTime:1486656900,selectedType:overall),query:(qu
ery_string:(analyze_wildcard:!t,query:'*')))
```

The `job_id`, the `from` and `to` timestamps, and the `epoch` timestamp `selectedTime` correspond to the variables that are filled in via Mustache in the watch definition, with the actual values coming from the scripted fields mentioned in the `input` section we looked at previously.

Also, it is notable that the top three records are reported in the text of the email response. In our example case, there is only one record (a `count` detector with a score of 91). This section of information came from the `record_results` aggregation we described previously in the `input` section of the watch.

The default watch that was created by ML is a good, usable alert that provides summarized information about the unusualness of the dataset over time, but it is also good to understand the implications of using (without modification) the watch that's created by the ML user interface in Kibana:

- The main condition for Alerting is a bucket anomaly score above a certain value. Therefore, it would not alert on individual anomalous records within a bucket in the case where their score does not lift the overall bucket score above the stated threshold.
- By default, only a maximum of the top three record scores in the bucket are reported in the output, and only if the email action is chosen.
- The watch would still exist, even if the ML job was deleted. You would need to remember to also delete this watch.
- The watch's only actions are logging and email. Adding other actions (slack message, webhook, and so on) would require manually editing the watch.

Knowing this information, it may become necessary at some point to create a more full-featured, complex watch to fully customize the behavior and output of the watch. In the next section, we'll discuss some more examples of creating a watch from scratch.

Creating ML alerts manually

Now that we've seen the default bucket-level alert that you get automatically by using the ML UI in Kibana, let's look at a more complex watch that was created manually to solve a more interesting use case.

In this example, there is a desire to alert when a certain ML job has an elevated anomaly score at the bucket level, but it will only notify us (invoke the `action` clause) if there are also anomalies in two other supporting ML jobs within a 10 minute window (looking backwards in time). The main premise here is that the first job is an analysis of some important KPI that's worthy of Alerting upon, but only if there's supporting evidence of things that may have caused the KPI to deviate, some supporting, corroborating anomalies from other datasets analyzed in other ML jobs. If this is true, then give the user an alert that has all of the information consolidated together.

The full text of the example is shown at `https://github.com/PacktPublishing/Machine-Learning-with-the-Elastic-Stack/blob/master/Chapter06/custom_ML_watch.json`.

The scenario used in this example is the same one that we referenced at the end of `Chapter 4`, *IT Operational Analytics and Root Cause Analysis*. In this case, we want to proactively identify correlations across jobs instead of doing visual correlation in the **Anomaly Explorer**.

Breaking down only the unique sections of this watch, we can immediately see a new concept, the `metadata` section:

```
    "metadata": {
        "watch_timespan" : "10m",          //how far back watch looks each
invocation (should be > 2x bucket_span)
        "lookback_window" : "10m",         //how far back to look in other jobs
for related anomalies
        "job1_name" : "it_ops_kpi",
        "job1_min_anomaly_score": 75,      //minimum anomaly score (bucket
score) for job1
        "job2_name" : "it_ops_network",
        "job2_min_record_score" : 10,      //minimum record score for anomalies
in job2
        "job3_name" : "it_ops_sql",
        "job3_min_record_score" : 5        //minimum record score for anomalies
in job3
    },
```

This technique within **Watcher** allows variables to be used in subsequent sections of the watch definition, thus making the prototyping and modification of things easier. The gist of what is defined here includes the names of the three jobs to be involved in this watch, with the first job (`it_ops_kpi`) being the anchor for the whole Alerting condition. If this first job is never anomalous, then the watch will never fire. Correlated anomalies in the other two jobs (`it_ops_network` and `it_ops_sql`) will be looked for in the 10 minutes prior to the first job's anomaly, and each of these subsequent jobs have their own minimum record score thresholds.

The next section (the watch `input` section) leverages a special capability called input chains in which a sequence of inputs can be linked together and executed serially, with optional dependencies added between them. In our case, the collapsed view of this is as follows:

Each input within the chain employs parameters not only from the metadata section (to select specific data using query filters) but the second and third inputs leverage information that has been gathered in the first input chain. Specifically, this is the timestamp of the anomalous bucket. This information is passed on to the range filter of the second and third inputs explicitly in the following line (here, we're only showing this for the second input):

```
{ "range": { "timestamp": {"gte":
"{{ctx.payload.job1.hits.hits.0._source.timestamp}}||-
{{ctx.metadata.lookback_window}}", "lte":
"{{ctx.payload.job1.hits.hits.0._source.timestamp}}"}}},
```

The interpretation of this is as follows: look only in the range of the timestamp of the anomalous bucket in X, minus the lookback window. Notice the usage of job1's context payload `ctx.payload.job1` variable, which will yield the anomalous bucket's timestamp. The `||-` notation is used to perform the subtraction of the timestamps using date math.

Further on in the `condition` section of the watch, the following logic is employed:

```
"condition" : {
    "script" : {
        "source" : "return ctx.payload.job1.hits.total > 0 &&
ctx.payload.job2.hits.total > 0 && ctx.payload.job3.hits.total > 0"
    }
},
```

In other words, return `true`, but only if all three jobs have anomalies (the original KPI job in `job1`, plus the corroborating anomalies in `job2` and `job3`). The use of logical ANDs (`&&`) could be modified, of course, for different logic, such as (`job1` AND (`job2` OR `job3`)) if so desired. The key point here is that you can make this behave in any way you desire.

The most difficult section of the watch to explain is the `transform` of the `actions` section. In this case, we are leveraging the full power of the scripting language of Elasticsearch to reformat and organize the pieces of information that have been gathered from all three jobs:

```
        "transform": {
            "script": "return ['anomaly_score':
ctx.payload.job1.hits.hits.0._source.anomaly_score, 'bucket_time':
Instant.ofEpochMilli(ctx.payload.job1.hits.hits.0._source.timestamp).atZone
(ZoneOffset.UTC).format(DateTimeFormatter.ofPattern('yyyy-MM-dd
HH:mm:ss')),'job2_anomaly_details':ctx.payload.job2.hits.hits.stream().map(
p -> ['bucket_time':
Instant.ofEpochMilli(ctx.payload.job2.hits.hits.0._source.timestamp).atZone
(ZoneOffset.UTC).format(DateTimeFormatter.ofPattern('yyyy-MM-dd
HH:mm:ss')),'field_name':p._source.field_name,'score':p._source.record_scor
e,'actual':p._source.actual.0,'typical':p._source.typical.0]).collect(Colle
ctors.toList()),'job3_anomaly_details':ctx.payload.job3.hits.hits.stream().
map(p -> ['bucket_time':
Instant.ofEpochMilli(ctx.payload.job3.hits.hits.0._source.timestamp).atZone
(ZoneOffset.UTC).format(DateTimeFormatter.ofPattern('yyyy-MM-dd
HH:mm:ss')),'hostname':p._source.hostname.0,'field_name':p._source.field_na
me,'score':p._source.record_score,'actual':p._source.actual.0,'typical':p._
source.typical.0]).collect(Collectors.toList())]"
        },
```

The technique that's used here is to employ Java streams to assemble these disparate pieces of information into a concise list of JSON objects that can be easily iterated through later using the Mustache syntax. Despite the complicated-looking syntax, just realize that the purpose here is to create four things:

- `anomaly_score`: The `anomaly_score` of the first job in the input chain, that is, the KPI job that is anchoring this watch
- `bucket_time`: The time of the anomalous bucket from the first job in the input chain
- `job2_details`: An array of anomaly records that have been gathered from the second job in the 10 minutes prior to `bucket_time`
- `Job3_details`: An array of anomaly records that have been gathered from the third job in the 10 minutes prior to `bucket_time`

Once this transform is run (assuming that the condition section has been met), then an example of the output of this transform could look something like this:

```
"payload": {
  "anomaly_score": 85.4309,
  "job3_anomaly_details": [
    {
      "score": 6.023424,
      "actual": 846.0000000000005,
      "hostname": "dbserver.acme.com",
      "bucket_time": "2017-02-08 15:10:00",
      "typical": 12.609336298838242,
      "field_name":
"SQLServer_Buffer_Manager_Page_life_expectancy"
    },
    {
      "score": 8.337633,
      "actual": 96.93249340057375,
      "hostname": "dbserver.acme.com",
      "bucket_time": "2017-02-08 15:10:00",
      "typical": 98.93088463835487,
      "field_name":
"SQLServer_Buffer_Manager_Buffer_cache_hit_ratio"
    },
    {
      "score": 27.97728,
      "actual": 168.15000000000006,
      "hostname": "dbserver.acme.com",
      "bucket_time": "2017-02-08 15:10:00",
      "typical": 196.1486370757187,
      "field_name":
"SQLServer_General_Statistics_User_Connections"
    }
  ],
  "bucket_time": "2017-02-08 15:15:00",
  "job2_anomaly_details": [
    {
      "score": 11.217614808972602,
      "actual": 13610.62255859375,
      "bucket_time": "2017-02-08 15:15:00",
      "typical": 855553.8944717721,
      "field_name": "In_Octets"
    },
    {
      "score": 17.00518,
      "actual": 190795357.83333334,
      "bucket_time": "2017-02-08 15:15:00",
      "typical": 1116062.402864764,
```

```
          "field_name": "Out_Octets"
        },
        {
          "score": 72.99199,
          "actual": 137.04444376627606,
          "bucket_time": "2017-02-08 15:15:00",
          "typical": 0.012289061361553099,
          "field_name": "Out_Discards"
        }
      ]
    }
```

We can see that the `anomaly_score` of the first job was `85.4309`, which exceeds the defined threshold in the watch of `75`. The time of this bucket was `2017-02-08 15:15:00`, as seen in the `bucket_time`. The `job2_anomaly_details` and `job3_anomaly_details` arrays are filled with several anomalies that were found in their respective jobs in the 10 minutes between 15:05 and 15:15. For simplicity's sake, the `actual`, `typical`, and `score` values are not rounded to a reasonable number of significant figures, but that could also be done in the `transform` block.

The logging part of the `action` section simply iterates through these values using Mustache:

```
          "logging": {
            "text": "[CRITICAL] Anomaly Alert for job
{{ctx.metadata.job1_name}}: score={{ctx.payload.anomaly_score}} at
{{ctx.payload.bucket_time}} UTC \nPossibly influenced by these other
anomalous metrics (within the prior 10
minutes):\njob:{{ctx.metadata.job2_name}}: (anomalies with at least a
record score of
{{ctx.metadata.job2_min_record_score}}):\n{{#ctx.payload.job2_anomaly_detai
ls}}field={{field_name}}: score={{score}}, value={{actual}}
(typical={{typical}}) at {{bucket_time}}
UTC\n{{/ctx.payload.job2_anomaly_details}}\njob:{{ctx.metadata.job3_name}}:
(anomalies with at least a record score of
{{ctx.metadata.job3_min_record_score}}):\n{{#ctx.payload.job3_anomaly_detai
ls}}hostname={{hostname}} field={{field_name}}: score={{score}},
value={{actual}} (typical={{typical}}) at {{bucket_time}}
UTC\n{{/ctx.payload.job3_anomaly_details}}"
          }
```

This produces the following login output, given our sample output from the transform:

```
[CRITICAL] Anomaly Alert for job it_ops_kpi: score=85.4309 at 2017-02-08
15:15:00 UTC
 Possibly influenced by these other anomalous metrics (within the prior 10
minutes):
```

```
job:it_ops_network: (anomalies with at least a record score of 10):
field=In_Octets: score=11.217614808972602, value=13610.62255859375
(typical=855553.8944717721) at 2017-02-08 15:15:00 UTC
field=Out_Octets: score=17.00518, value=1.9079535783333334E8
(typical=1116062.402864764) at 2017-02-08 15:15:00 UTC
field=Out_Discards: score=72.99199, value=137.04444376627606
(typical=0.012289061361553099) at 2017-02-08 15:15:00 UTC
job:it_ops_sql: (anomalies with at least a record score of 5):
hostname=dbserver.acme.com
field=SQLServer_Buffer_Manager_Page_life_expectancy: score=6.023424,
 value=846.0000000000005 (typical=12.609336298838242) at 2017-02-08
15:10:00 UTC
hostname=dbserver.acme.com
field=SQLServer_Buffer_Manager_Buffer_cache_hit_ratio: score=8.337633,
value=96.93249340057375 (typical=98.93088463835487) at 2017-02-08 15:10:00
UTC
hostname=dbserver.acme.com
field=SQLServer_General_Statistics_User_Connections: score=27.97728,
value=168.15000000000006 (typical=196.1486370757187) at 2017-02-08 15:10:00
UTC
```

Summary

While this chapter was not intended to be a full demonstration of the powerful features of Watcher, it is important to see that alerts can be created with ML's detailed results—both using built-in mechanisms and via custom definitions. And, if Elastic chooses to provide a different or updated Alerting platform in lieu of Watcher in the future, the fundamentals of what ML provides are unlikely to change much over time. The ultimate key take-away is that Elastic ML provides detailed results, stored in an Elasticsearch index, that can be queried and reported upon for the purposes of Alerting.

In the next chapter, Chapter 7, *Using Elastic ML Data in Kibana Dashboards*, we will also learn how to leverage ML's detailed results for custom visualizations and dashboards in Kibana.

7

Using Elastic ML Data in Kibana Dashboards

At this point of the book, you have seen multiple use cases and multiple ways to leverage the output of Elastic ML, such as getting proactive alerts. Whether you are in a DevOps team or a security team, you will likely need to visualize your data. Visualizing lots of raw data can be a burden, as too many data sources overwhelm what our eyes can effectively capture. This is where the visualization capabilities of Kibana, combined with Elastic ML data, can be leveraged to highlight what really matters in dashboards.

This chapter will walk you through the creation of visualizations and dashboards that use Elastic ML data. In this manner, analysts who are not familiar with ML, but need to visualize the data, can be helped throughout their investigation.

First, we'll have a quick tour through Kibana and list the visualization options we'll use. Then, we'll prepare our data and create a couple of ML jobs, and finally we'll build our visualizations and dashboard.

The following are the topics that we'll cover in this chapter:

- Visualization options
- Preparing data for anomaly detection analysis
- Building visualizations

Visualization options in Kibana

Kibana has multiple options for visualizing data; all of them have distinct and similar options in terms of charting the data, whether that be line, bar, pie, data tables, or gauges.

What really differentiates them is either the user experience or the use case they are serving. First, we'll briefly introduce the different available visualizations and then use them later in this chapter to highlight some of Elastic ML's insights.

Visualization examples

In Kibana, if you click on the **Visualize** option in the left-hand side panel, you will be given the opportunity to create visualization panels for dashboards with different chart types. Clicking on the add (+) button shows the following set of visualization types:

We won't go through all of them here, but we encourage you to refer to the documentation at `https://www.elastic.co/guide/en/kibana/current/visualize.html` so that you can familiarize yourself with the different charts. We'll just focus on the **Data Table** and the **Heat Map**, which are the ones we'll use later on in this chapter to build our simple dashboard.

The **Data Table** is a pretty straightforward visualization that allows us to create an ordered list of fields. It is very practical for displaying string data types that could be used as filters, for example, a list of URIs (the path to the name of the web page being requested), alongside the number of hits each **URI** received on a web server:

URI ⌄	Hits ⇕
/shuttle/missions/sts-69/mission-sts-69.html	24,589
/shuttle/missions/missions.html	47,298
/shuttle/countdown/liftoff.html	29,860
/shuttle/countdown/	64,737
/ksc.html	83,874
/images/WORLD-logosmall.gif	125,928
/images/USA-logosmall.gif	127,076
/images/NASA-logosmall.gif	208,728
/images/MOSAIC-logosmall.gif	127,912
/images/launchmedium.gif	40,684

The other type of visualization we'll use in this chapter is a Heat Map. This will allow us to render two aspects of the data:

- The severity of an anomaly
- Multiple jobs on the same chart so that we can correlate the anomalies to each other

Our Heat Map, once built, will look as follows:

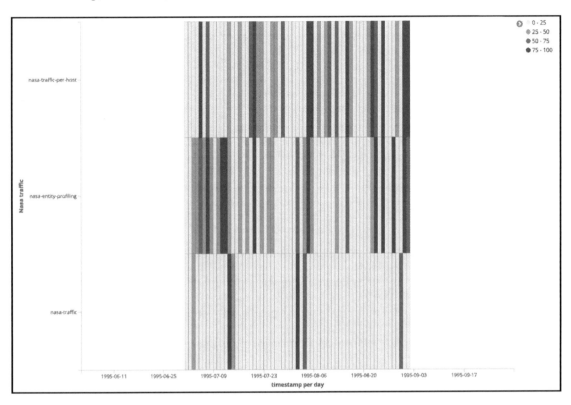

While these visualizations are click-driven, the next type of visualization, uses Timelion, is expression-based, which gives us the benefit of being able to combine data sources.

Timelion

Timelion, an expression-based visualization framework, allows the user to build charts by leveraging the Elasticsearch aggregation framework. Timelion is also very powerful in that it allows you to combine data from multiple sources in the same chart.

We'll learn how to use this visualization type to combine data sources later. Our final product will look as follows:

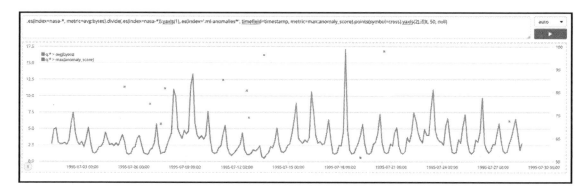

Time series visual builder

The **time series visual builder (TSVB)** is metric-driven and a perfect fit for time series-based metrics. It allows the use of aggregations, and pipeline aggregations, and offers multiple chart types in one comprehensive chart control:

We'll see that we can use pipeline aggregations, apply mathematical function to metrics, and even annotate the chart. The use of annotations is the main reason we'll use this visualization in our sample dashboard, as it will allow the analyst to capture where anomalies exist in a customizable chart at a glance, as shown here:

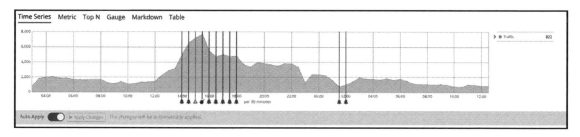

However, before we can assemble all of these visualization components into our dashboard, we need to download and prepare some data that we can feed into our ML jobs.

Preparing data for anomaly detection analysis

To make an effective, representative dashboard with different visualizations, we first need to download, ingest, and analyze a dataset that exists in the public domain.

We've chosen a very old dataset from NASA that you can obtain at `http://ita.ee.lbl.gov/html/contrib/NASA-HTTP.html`. The dataset contains HTTP access logs for the NASA website from between July 1, 1995 and August 31, 1995. It's almost a fossil dataset at the time of writing this book, it's nearly 24 years old!

However, the information in the logs is timeless and is perfect for what we want to achieve here. First, let's get an understanding of the dataset.

The dataset

In this dataset, each document represents a combined Apache log of the following structure:

```
128.159.122.45 - - [28/Jul/1995:13:31:57 -0400] "GET /ksc.html HTTP/1.0"
200 7280
```

The preceding log line contains the following information:

- The host making the request, that is, the IP address
- The timestamp of the request
- The request
- The HTTP response status
- The size of the reply in bytes

We'll use Logstash to transform this log file into JSON format, which we can then index into Elasticsearch.

Ingesting the data

We used this dataset to keep things simple for ingestion; Apache logs don't require a lot of configuration in Logstash to be parsed. The basic structure of our Logstash configuration will contain the following:

- A file input to consume the two files that are provided in the dataset; one for the month of July and one for the month of August
- **Two filters**: A `grok` filter to parse the log line and a `date` filter to transform the timestamp into a well-formatted timestamp
- One output to tell Logstash to send the data to our Elasticsearch cluster

Here is the complete Logstash pipeline configuration:

```
input {
  file {
    id => "nasa_file"
    path => "/Users/baha/Downloads/data/*.log"
    start_position => "beginning"
    sincedb_path => "/dev/null"
  }
}

filter {
  grok {
    id => "nasa_grok_filter"
    match => { "message" => "%{COMMONAPACHELOG}" }
  }
  date {
    match => ["timestamp", "dd/MMM/yyyy:HH:mm:ss Z"]
    target => "@timestamp"
    remove_field => [ "timestamp" ]
  }
}

output {
  elasticsearch {
    id => "nasa_elasticsearch_output"
    hosts => "localhost:9200"
    user => "elastic"
    password => "********"
    index => "nasa-%{+YYYY.MM}"
    template => "/Users/baha/Downloads/data/template.conf"
    template_name => "nasa"
```

```
        template_overwrite => "false"
    }
}
```

The file input consumes all of the log files that are contained in the specified directory (in my case, `NASA_access_log_Aug95.log` and `NASA_access_log_Jul95.log`). I've added a `.log` extension to the file compared to what is provided by default. For testing purposes, I've set the `start_position` parameter to start at the beginning of the file, so we combined this with `sincedb_path`, where the last position of ingestion is saved, pointing to `/dev/null`. The file is then consumed whenever I update the config or restart Logstash.

Notice that in the `filter` section, we are using the `COMMONAPACHELOG` grok pattern to parse the log contained in the input `message` field. Also, the `date` filter transforms the timestamp of the file into a date that we store in a `@timestamp` field.

Finally, we are using an output to index the data in Elasticsearch using the `template.conf` template file to set the index settings and mapping.

 See the `template.conf` file in the GitHub repository for this book at `https://github.com/PacktPublishing/Machine-Learning-with-the-Elastic-Stack/blob/master/Chapter07/template.conf` for more information.

The mapping is essential to have a proper mapping of field names to their desired type (bytes as `integer` and response as `keyword`, for example). Otherwise, the fields may not be available if we want to effectively use them in either Elasticsearch aggregations or ML job configurations.

In this example, Logstash has been configured to use centralized monitoring and management. The required configuration has been added at the end of the Logstash configuration's `logstash.yml` file, which is located in the `conf` directory, as shown here:

```
# X-Pack Monitoring
xpack.monitoring.enabled: true
xpack.monitoring.elasticsearch.username: elastic
xpack.monitoring.elasticsearch.password: ********
xpack.monitoring.elasticsearch.url: ["http://localhost:9200"]
# X-Pack Management
xpack.management.enabled: true
xpack.management.pipeline.id: ["nasa-apache-log"]
xpack.management.elasticsearch.username: elastic
xpack.management.elasticsearch.password: ********
xpack.management.elasticsearch.url: ["http://localhost:9200"]
```

Only supply username/password credentials if X-Pack Security is enabled.

In this manner, you will be able to add the Logstash pipeline in Kibana, and Logstash will connect and load it at bootstrap. To proceed, take note of the following steps:

1. Connect to Kibana and go to the **Management** | **Logstash** | **Pipelines** section.
2. Click on the **Create Pipeline** button.

This will display the following UI:

Description

NASA 90s HTTP Logs pipeline

Pipeline

```
1   input {
2     file {
3       id => "nasa_file"
4       path => "/Users/baha/Downloads/data/*.log"
5       start_position => "beginning"
6       sincedb_path => "/dev/null"
7     }
8   }
9
10  filter {
11    grok {
12      id => "nasa_grok_filter"
13      match => { "message" => "%{COMMONAPACHELOG}" }
14    }
15    date {
16      match => ["timestamp", "dd/MMM/yyyy:HH:mm:ss Z"]
17      target => "@timestamp"
18      remove_field => [ "timestamp" ]
19    }
20  }
21
22  output {
23    elasticsearch {
24      id => "nasa_elasticsearch_output"
25      hosts => "localhost:9200"
26      user => "elastic"
27      password => "*********"
28      index => "nasa-%{+YYYY.MM}"
29      template => "/Users/baha/Downloads/data/template.conf"
30      template_name => "nasa"
31      template_overwrite => "false"
32    }
33  }
34
35
36
```

3. From there, launch Logstash and you should see data coming through the pipeline that's been indexed in Elasticsearch, like in the following monitoring screenshot:

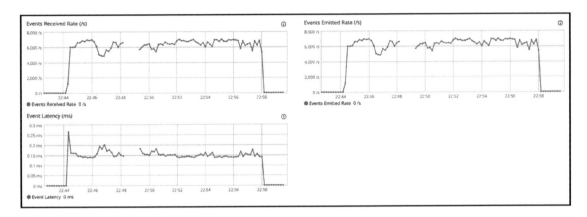

The relative index monitoring stats are as follows:

Nodes: **1** Indices: **73** Memory: **702.0 MB / 990.8 MB** Total Shards: **254** Unassigned Shards: **27** Documents: **30,508,248** Data: **11.4 GB**

🔍 nasa

Name	Status ↓	Document Count	Data	Index Rate
nasa-1995.07	● Yellow	1.9m	580.4 MB	0 /s
nasa-1995.08	● Yellow	1.6m	469.5 MB	0 /s
nasa-1995.09	● Yellow	10.6k	3.7 MB	0 /s

To summarize, we have ingested about 3.5 million documents, representing about 1 GB of data on disk. If you check the document structure by querying the Elasticsearch index, you should see something like the following:

```
{
        "host": "mbp-de-baha.lan",
        "ident": "-",
        "auth": "-",
        "@timestamp": "1995-09-01T03:59:53.000Z",
        "path": "/Users/baha/Downloads/data/NASA_access_log_Aug95.log",
        "bytes": "39017",
        "request": "/images/kscmap-small.gif",
        "@version": "1",
        "response": "200",
```

```
        "httpversion": "1.0",
        "message": "cindy.yamato.ibm.co.jp - - [31/Aug/1995:23:59:53
-0400] \"GET /images/kscmap-small.gif HTTP/1.0\" 200 39017",
        "verb": "GET",
        "clientip": "cindy.yamato.ibm.co.jp"
    }
```

At this stage, we are now ready to create some ML jobs.

Creating anomaly detection jobs

We are going to create three jobs so that we can use their results in the visualization. They are as follows:

- A traffic analysis job
- An HTTP response code profiling of the host making requests
- A traffic analysis of the host making requests

Global traffic analysis job

The first job is a simple traffic analysis of the access logs. Create it by following these steps:

1. Access the **Machine Learning** section in Kibana and create a new **Single metric** job on the NASA access logs index.
2. Configure the job so that it makes a distinct count on the `clientip` field, which allows us to count the distinct number of IPs making the traffic, as shown in the following screenshot:

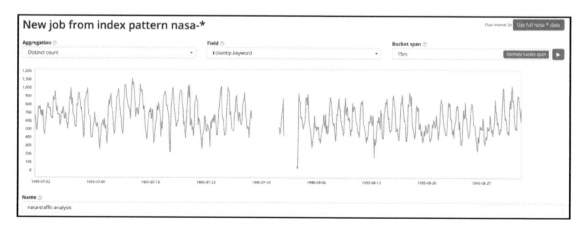

3. Running the job, you should get similar anomalies in the **Single Metric Viewer** to what's shown in the following screenshot. We'll use those anomalies in a TSVB visualization as annotations later:

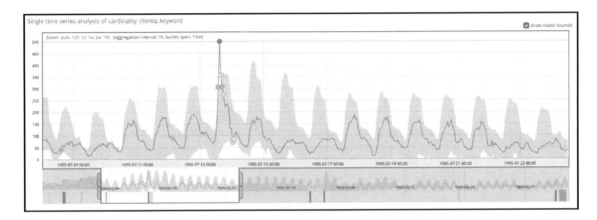

While the visualization that's built into ML's UI is useful to show when anomalies occur and what severity they have, many analysts already have a collection of their own visualizations in an operational dashboard. They may want to see these anomalies in their existing dashboard panels.

There may also be a situation in which the operations analysts may not have the permission or expertise to use the **Machine Learning** UI to look at anomalies. By externalizing the anomalies to standard dashboard visualizations, it allows the analysts to consume the information about the anomalies within a context they already know and understand.

A HTTP response code profiling of the host making requests

The second job will help the analysts detect suspicious client behaviors with respect to the volume of requests per response code. Here are the steps to configure this job:

1. Access the **Machine Learning** section in Kibana and create a new **Advanced** job on the NASA access logs index:

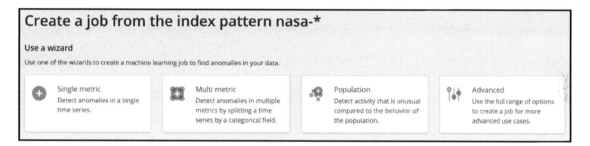

2. Name the job in the **Job Details** panel:

3. Finally, add the following detector in the **Analysis Configuration** panel, add `response.keyword` and `clientip.keyword` as influencers, and save the job:

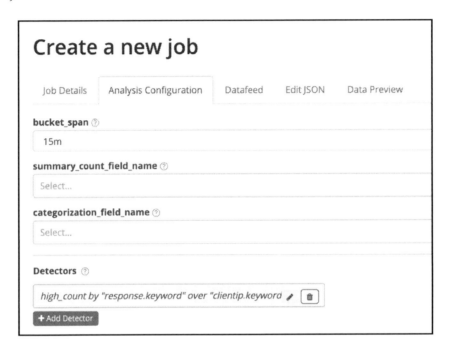

4. After running the job and accessing the **Anomaly Explorer** view, you should get results that are similar to the following ones:

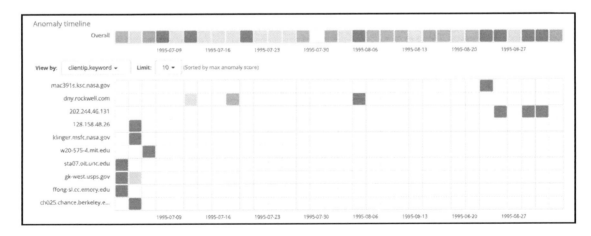

5. If you click on one of the red square anomalies, you will get the following details:

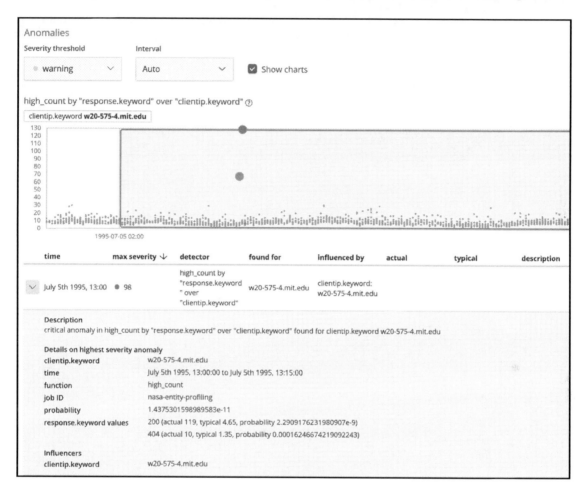

The preceding host has unusually high volumes of **200** and **404** response codes compared to the rest of the hosts.

Traffic per host analysis

The third job is a generalization of the previous one; it will also help us understand which host has abnormally high traffic. We'll proceed using the same steps as the previous job to create this, with the difference that we won't split the job (using **by_field_name**) like we did earlier. The steps for this are as follows:

1. Create the job in the **Advanced** job wizard:

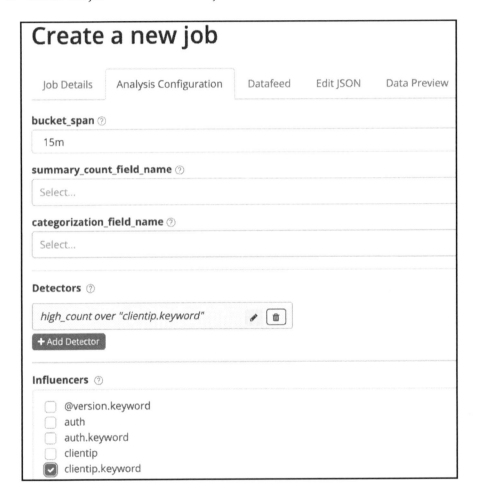

2. Running the job will give you a list of high traffic host anomalies, as shown in the following screenshot:

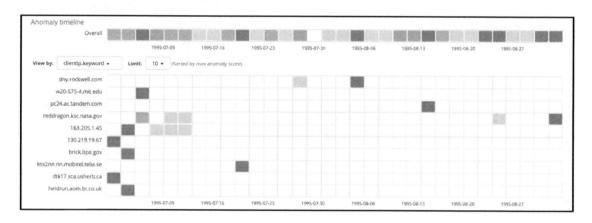

3. Clicking on one of the host anomalies will give you the following output:

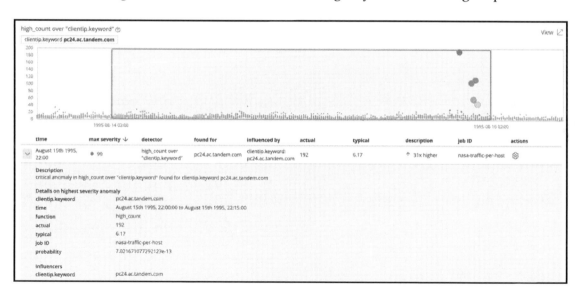

Here, the relative host has traffic that's 31 times higher than typical traffic.

Since we have our three jobs and some anomaly data to play with, we are ready to create a couple of visualizations and compose our dashboard.

Building the visualizations

Now that we have both raw data and some ML jobs completed on this data, let's begin the process of designing our own customized dashboard using a variety of standard Kibana visualization controls. But before we can do this, we need to let Kibana know that the ML results index exists, and that we want to plot data from this index.

Configuring the index pattern

To have Kibana recognize the data that's contained in the index that's storing the results of our ML jobs, we need to create an index pattern in the **Management** section of Kibana. Navigate to this part. Then, under the **Kibana** section, click on **Index Patterns** and then on **Create index pattern**.

In the **Create index pattern** UI, enable the **Include system indices** options and name your index `.ml-anomalies*` to include the index we need:

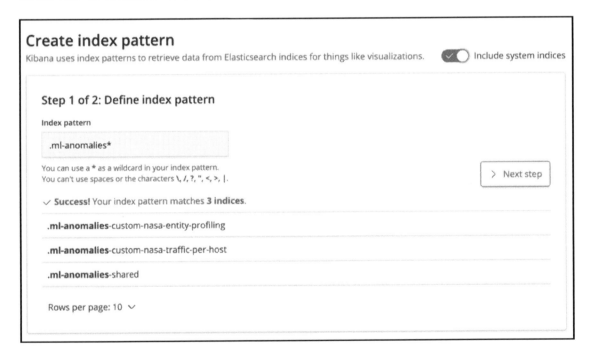

Click on **Next step** and choose **@timestamp** as the time field. Finally, click on **Create index pattern**.

We'll use this index pattern throughout our examples. Now, let's start building some visualizations.

Using ML data in TSVB

As we explained at the beginning of this chapter, the TSVB is a perfect fit for the metric analytics use case. It renders the chart using the Elasticsearch aggregation API, including the pipeline API, which allows us to process aggregation metric results with mathematical functions.

The example we'll go through will use the data from the first job, render the traffic in the NASA access logs, and annotate the traffic with three levels of anomalies: minor, major, and critical. We'll render them yellow, orange, and red, respectively.

Let's start and create a TSVB chart from the visualization palette (click **Visualize**, then the **Add** button, and then choose **Visual Builder** from the palette). The first thing you will see is the following empty chart:

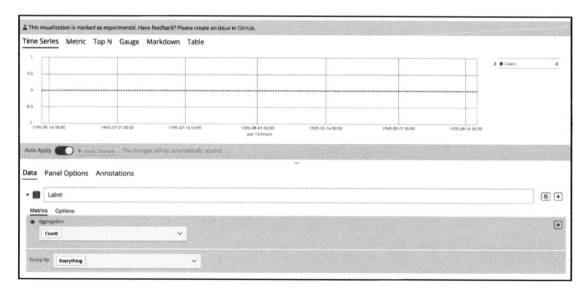

Take note of the following:

- The **Data** tab allows you to configure the aggregation and function to apply to the data.
- The **Panel Options** tab is where the data source is set.
- The **Annotations** tab is where we'll use a second, different data source. This will be where our ML data will be defined so that we can annotate the chart.

First, let's configure the data source in the **Panel Options**, like so:

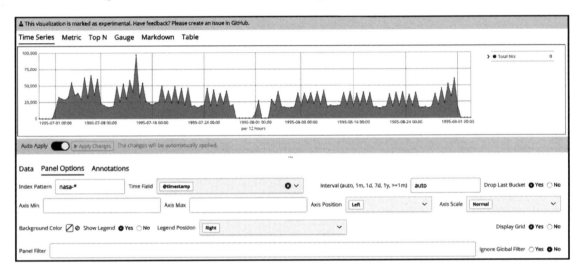

As you can see, the configuration is quite simple: we are just passing our index pattern name, that is, `nasa-*`, and the **Time Field @timestamp**. The rest of the options can be left as they are by default.

We need to leverage the anomaly detection job data to annotate the preceding chart and help users understand where (and when) to pay attention. First, let's add the critical (red) anomalies, as illustrated in the following screenshot:

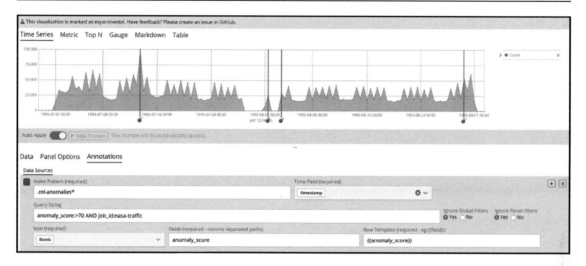

The annotations allow you to render the preceding vertical lines on top of the main data source. You can do this by choosing the following:

- A color, red, for critical.
- An index, such as `.ml-anomalies*`, which is the index pattern pointing to the results of anomaly detection jobs.
- The time field (here, this is **timestamp**).
- A query string to filter the data. We have set a condition where all anomalies with an `anomaly_score` above `70` are critical anomalies (as opposed to the standard value of `75` that the ML UI uses). In addition, since all of the results across jobs are stored in the same index, we only need to filter out the results of our job. This is why we have added `job_id:nasa-traffic`, where `nasa-traffic` is the name of our first ML job.
- An icon (here, this is a bomb) that characterizes a critical anomaly.
- Required fields; we just need the `anomaly_score` to render our annotation.
- A template to be rendered when hovering over an annotation. Here, this is the `anomaly_score` itself.

Just reproduce the same thing for a major anomaly by changing the query, the color to orange, and the icon:

The condition we have set for a major anomaly is an `anomaly_score` between 30 and 70. Do the same process for minor (blue) anomalies (for scores between 1 and 30), as shown in the following screenshot:

We haven't configured any particular aspect in the **Data** tab as the default count aggregation is what we are looking for. However, you can also edit the label to give a little more sense to the chart. With the label and annotations in place, here is how we are overlaying ML data on top of the traffic flow:

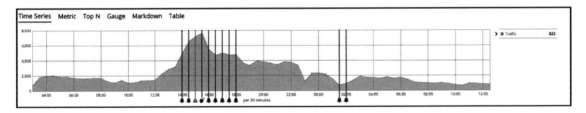

Creating a correlation Heat Map

With multiple jobs in our detection portfolio, an analyst might want to visualize all of a jobs' anomalies in a common time period. This is something equivalent to the **Anomaly Explorer** viewer in the **Machine Learning** Kibana application with all the jobs selected, as shown in the following screenshot:

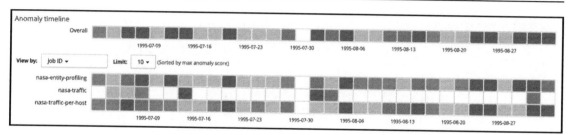

The Kibana visualization we are going to use to get an equivalent of the preceding screenshot is the **Heat Map**. Go into the visualization part to create a new **Heat Map** visualization:

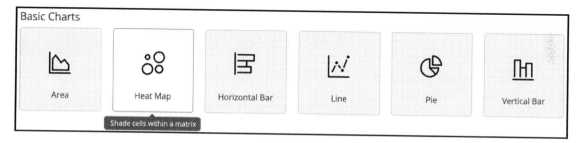

Pick the `.ml-anomalies*` index pattern, which contains all of the results that are relative to the jobs we have created so far:

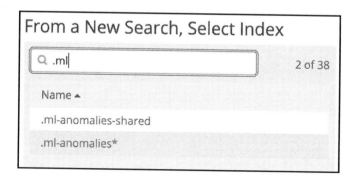

Now, let's configure the **Heat Map** by going into the left panel first and choosing **Buckets**. We want to represent the detected anomalies over time. Thus, for the **X-Axis**, we'll choose a **Date Histogram**:

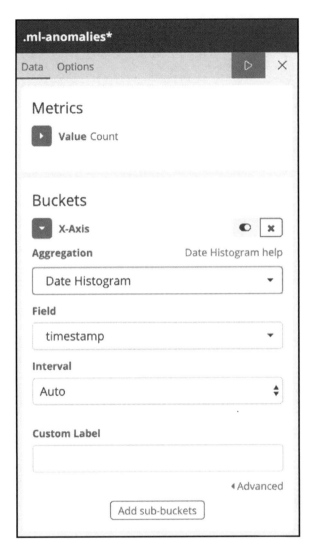

Now, let's add a sub-bucket so that we can split the vertical axis per job. Since we are focusing on the time period where our data exists (remember, the logs are from 1995!), we should decrease the possibility of causing collisions with results from other jobs. However, to make sure that you can still set filters on job names, click on **Add sub-buckets**, select **Y-Axis**, and choose a **Terms** aggregation to split on **job_id**, as shown in the following screenshot:

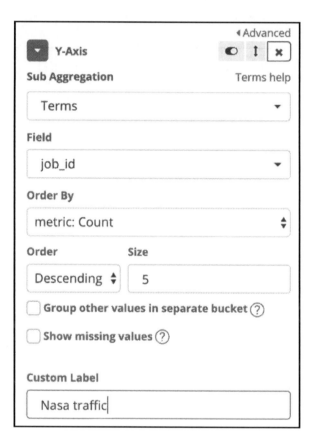

If you click on the **Play** button to render the chart, here is what you will get:

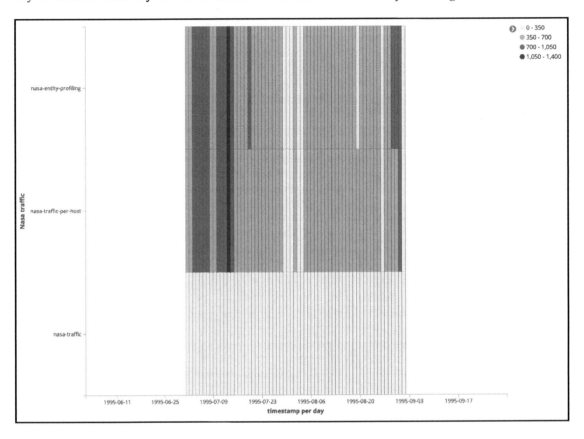

Now, let's configure the **Metrics** part so that we can emphasize every anomaly's severity over time on the Heat Map:

For the last touch on the Heat Map, we'll change the **Color Schema** to **Reds** in the **Options** panel:

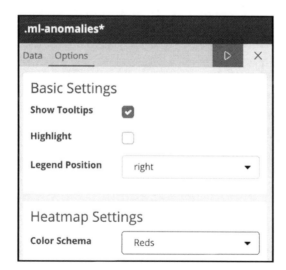

Finally, this is the rendering of our Heat Map:

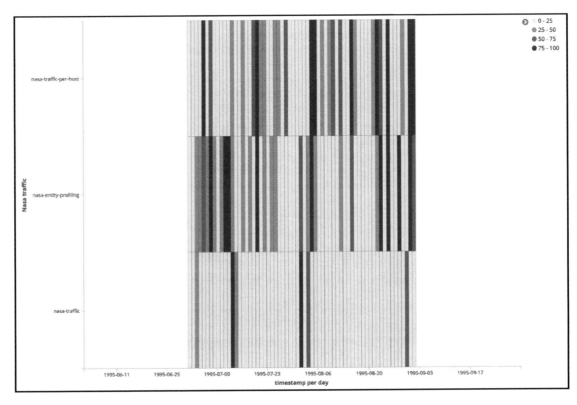

Using ML data in Timelion

Timelion is an expression-oriented visualization framework. It allows you to connect to Elasticsearch (but also to other data stores), as well as take multiple data series and combine them. In our case, we'll make a pretty simple operation, calculate the average bytes per request over time, and overlay the anomalies related to the traffic.

To do so, add a Timelion visualization from the palette, and start by adding the following expression:

```
.es(index=nasa-*)
```

Remember to configure the time picker to surround the temporal zone where our data exists. The preceding expression will just draw the traffic we've already seen so far:

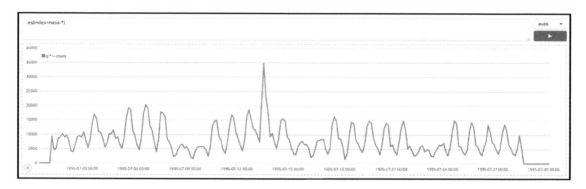

Now, let's calculate the bytes per request. Let's divide the two expressions. Here's the first one:

```
.es(index=nasa-*, metric=avg:bytes).divide(.es(index=nasa-*))
```

This will render the following line chart:

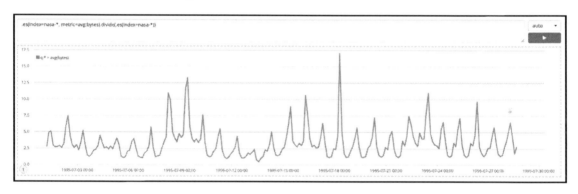

Now, we just need to add our ML results on top of it by completing the expression, like so:

```
.es(index=nasa-*, metric=avg:bytes)
  .divide(.es(index=nasa-*)).yaxis(1),
.es(index='.ml-anomalies*',
    timefield=timestamp,
    metric=max:anomaly_score)
  .points(symbol=cross).yaxis(2).if(lt, 50, null)
```

Take note of the following:

- The data sources are separated by a comma; the first data source is the ratio and the second is the anomaly detection results
- The anomalies are represented in the form of crosses, thanks to the `.points()` function
- Each data source has its own *y* axis to avoid different scales of data

The results will be as follows:

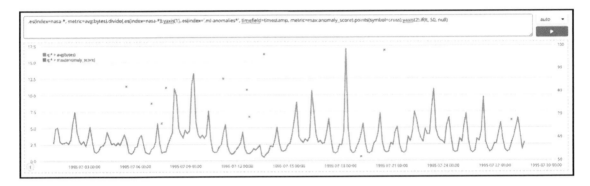

We finally have all of our visualizations created and we can now compose them as part of the same dashboard.

Don't forget to save and name your visualizations!

Building the dashboard

Now, we're on to the easiest part; picking all of our visualizations and adding them all in the same dashboard. Navigate to the **Dashboard** section in Kibana to create a new dashboard. You will get an empty dashboard. Simply click on the **Add** button to choose your visualizations. When you've done that, feel free to organize the visualization as you like. This is an example of what you can get, first with the top of the dashboard:

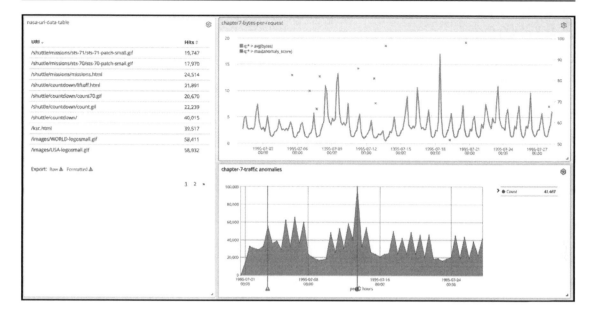

Here's the bottom of the dashboard:

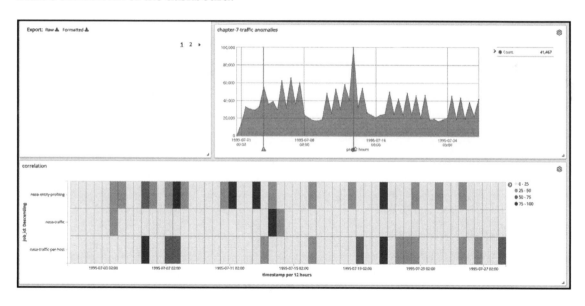

The dashboard highlights all of the visualizations we have built so far, which contain not only our raw NASA access logs, but also the results of the anomaly detection across multiple jobs. We have successfully integrated data coming from Elastic ML into our own custom dashboard directly.

Summary

In this chapter, we used different visualization capabilities of Kibana to render a dataset and leverage anomaly detection results to either annotate and correlate. This helps analysts who want to see anomaly detection results within the dashboard framework that they are familiar with and use every day.

In the next chapter, Chapter 8, *Using Elastic ML with Kibana Canvas*, we'll focus on users that don't necessarily want to go through a dashboard and need an infographic style of experience. This is where we'll introduce Canvas, a PowerPoint-like experience in Kibana that's connected to live data stored in Elasticsearch.

8
Using Elastic ML with Kibana Canvas

In the previous chapter, Chapter 7, *Using Elastic ML Data in Kibana Dashboards*, we saw how we can leverage Kibana visualizations to create dashboard analytics that are enhanced with Elastic ML results. In this way, users can detect at a glance where the anomalies sit in their data. Dashboards are great to present a set of KPIs in separate visualizations, all linked together through the filters users picked through their navigation. Going further, users often express the need to customize the look and feel of their reports. While standard Kibana dashboards do not offer that, Kibana Canvas, on the other hand, gives the user the flexibility to create fully custom, pixel-perfect reports that are powered by dynamic data.

Canvas is a workspace to build presentations, slides, or infographics out of live data. You can compose, extend, and customize your report as you wish. Think about it like *PowerPoint in Kibana on live data*.

This chapter doesn't intend to go into Canvas in depth, but we will go through a short introduction so that you get an understanding of the key building blocks of Canvas. Then, we'll focus on using it for Elastic ML data to present a highly customized report that leverages anomaly detection data.

In this chapter, we will use Canvas for Elastic ML in the following three ways:

- Through standard Canvas elements and expressions
- Using Elastic SQL
- Building a custom plugin for Canvas

Introduction to Canvas

This section presents the key aspects of Canvas by walking through some live examples using Canvas itself. Canvas is part of the default distribution of the Elastic Stack as of version 6.5.

What is Canvas?

As explained previously, Canvas is a place for you to build highly custom-tailored reports with a set a customizable elements. The experience in Canvas is very different from standard Kibana dashboards. Canvas presents you with a workspace where you can build sets of slides (similar in concept to Microsoft PowerPoint) called the workpad.

Here is a screenshot of an empty Canvas **Workpad**:

As we can see, the workspace has a blank page where you can place and position components called **elements**. Elements can be directly connected to data that's stored in Elasticsearch and can be configured in the sidebar, where all options relative to the elements can be customized, including defining your own CSS. The following screenshot shows just some of the elements at your disposal:

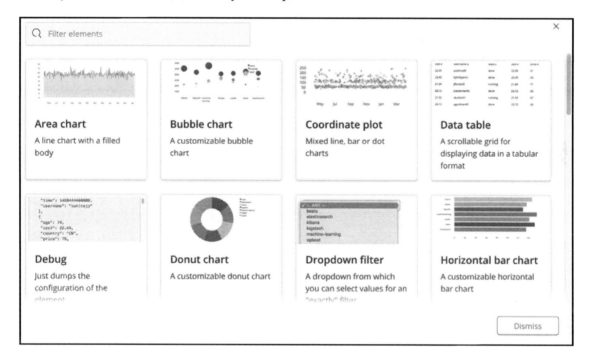

For example, in a blank Workpad, click on **Add element** and select **Donut Chart** from the list of elements. This will put a representative **Donut chart** (a pie chart with a hole) onto the workpad:

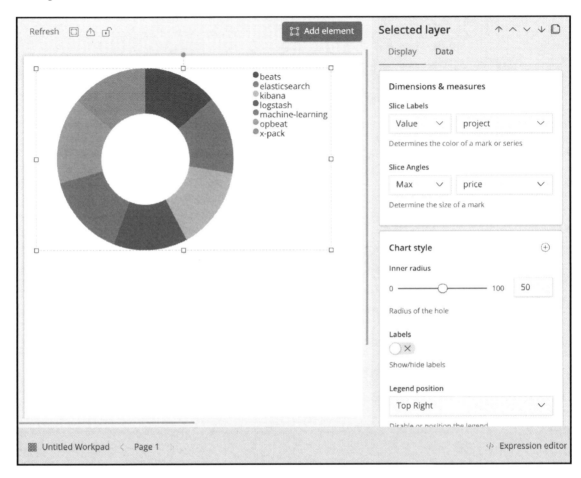

Notice that the chart has been pre-populated with demo data. This is done so that users can get a feel for what an element looks like, even before hooking that element up to a real data source. If you click on the **Data** tab, you will see the following message:

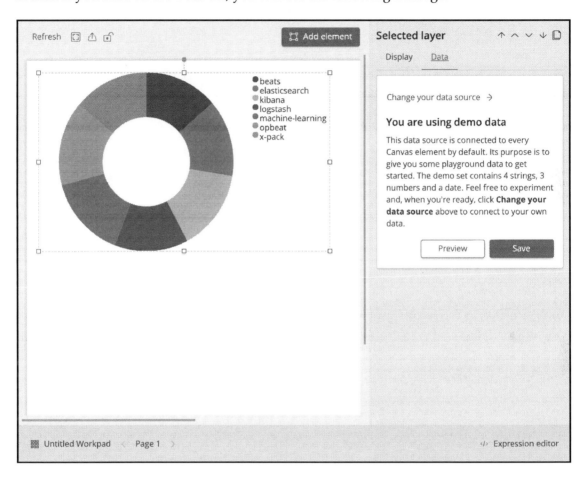

Later, we will attach some real data to our elements. But, for now, go back to the **Display** tab and play with a few of the options. For example, we can change the following:

- The **Slice Labels** to **state** (from the former setting of project)
- The **Inner radius** to a value of **25**
- The **Labels** slider to enable them
- Select **Hidden** for the **Legend position**

The resulting changes are immediately applied to the look and feel of the chart element. The new chart now looks as shown in the following screenshot:

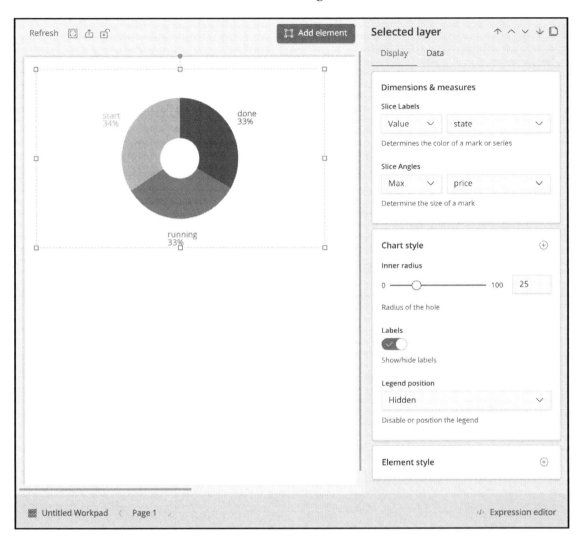

This demonstrates how easy it is to place and modify elements in the workpad. However, there are a lot more power and customization capabilities available at your disposal. One of the key ways to customize elements is to also understand the expression syntax that works behind the scenes of each element. Let's take a brief tour of that syntax.

The Canvas expression

Behind each element or component you use in the interface, there is a Canvas expression that defines how that component is constructed. If we take the donut chart we just created and click on the **Expression editor** button, we will see the expression syntax behind our element:

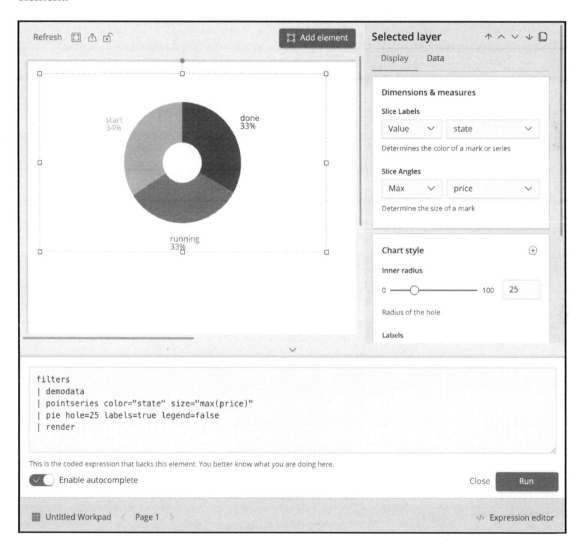

Notice that the expression is composed of multiple layers, separated by the | character, which chains functions together, just like Linux/Unix. Let's decompose it to understand how the expression syntax works:

- On the top, the opening function is `filters`, which collects element filters on the workpad, usually to provide them to a data source. An example element filter on the workpad is a time picker.
- The `demodata` function is the data source that's used in the pie chart. Again, because we haven't hooked up the element to any *real* data yet, the element defaults to using demo data. By the way, if you were remove the entire subsequent expression after `demodata` and click the **Run** button, you would get a data table of the raw demo data. You can then put it back if you did indeed remove it.
- The `pointseries` function prepares the data so that it can be passed to a charting element.
- The `pie` function uses the `pointseries` to build a pie chart (again, a pie with a hole is a donut).
- Finally, the `render` function renders the entire expression.

Not only is the expression automatically generated for you as you build your workpad with the UI, but you can also directly write your own. We will see how to do that later on in this chapter.

 The full documentation for Canvas can be found at https://www. elastic.co/guide/en/kibana/current/canvas.html.

Also, notice that, within the expression, there are attributes for some of the functions:

```
filters
| demodata
| pointseries color="state" size="max(price)"
| pie hole=25 labels=true legend=false
| render
```

These attributes directly correspond to the options that are set using the UI controls. So, for example, if the **Inner radius** control is changed to **50**, the value of the `hole` property in the expression would follow suit. Likewise, if you manually edited the value of `hole` in the expression, the value on the slider control would change as well (but only when you click the **Run** button). In other words, the expression and the UI controls are meant to be in sync.

We will now see how Canvas' UI elements and expressions will allow us to build a custom view from information in the ML results index.

Building Elastic ML Canvas slides

In this section, we are going to build examples of a Canvas slide by showcasing real-time results from an Elastic ML job so that we can showcase the results in a very customized way.

Preparing your data

Before starting our workpad, we need to do some preparation so that we can use ML data in Canvas. We actually just need two things:

- An Elastic ML job running and producing results
- An index pattern pointing to the job results data

For the Elastic ML job, I'm going to use a single metric job that analyzes the traffic on a nginx web server by looking at the distinct count of IP interacting with the server.

The following Elastic ML analysis screenshot will give you an idea of the general traffic behavior, thus revealing a couple of significant anomalies:

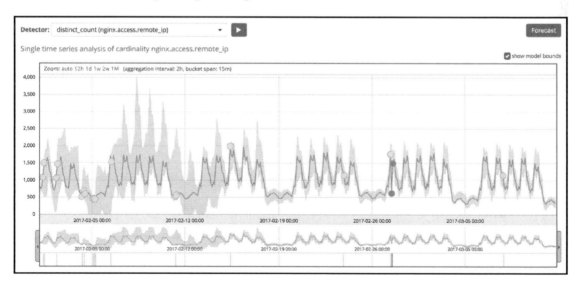

Elastic ML uses, by default, an index called `.ml-anomalies-shared` to store the detailed job results. However, dedicated result indices per job can also be defined. By creating an index pattern with a wildcard of `.ml-anomalies-*`, we can use a single index pattern to access results from all jobs. To do so, go into the **Kibana Management** section, click on **Index pattern**, and then click on **Create index pattern**. From here, enter `.ml-anomalies-*` into the box (and remember to select the **Include system indices** option to show internal indices that begin with the dot character):

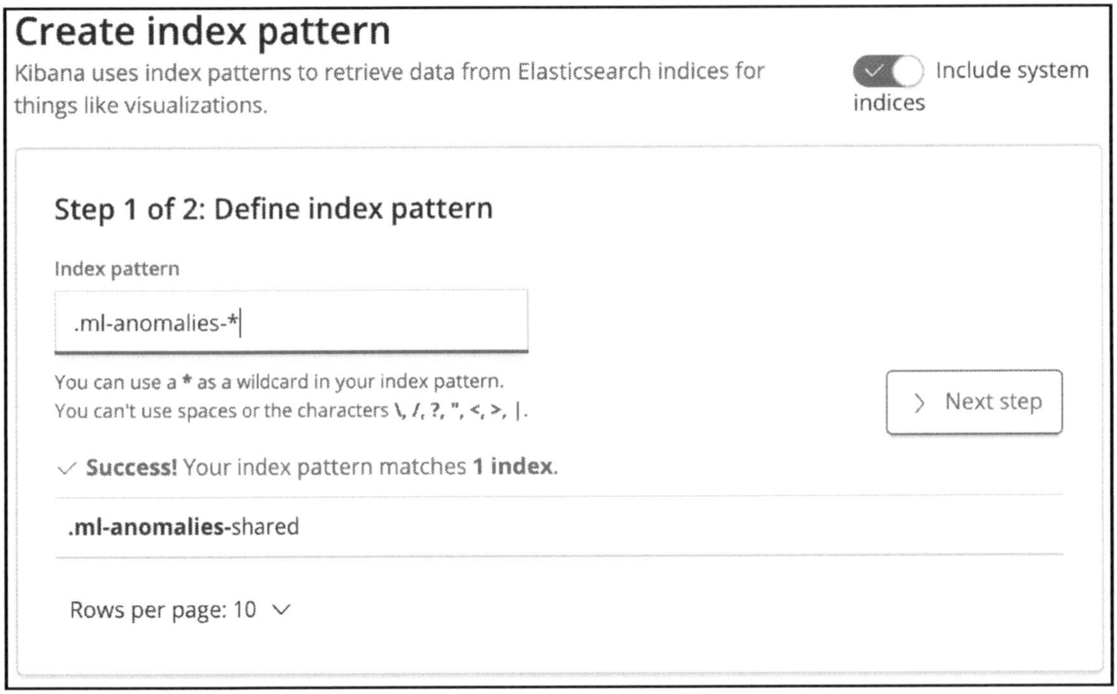

Create index pattern

Kibana uses index patterns to retrieve data from Elasticsearch indices for things like visualizations.

Include system indices

Step 1 of 2: Define index pattern

Index pattern

.ml-anomalies-*|

You can use a ***** as a wildcard in your index pattern.
You can't use spaces or the characters \, /, ?, ", <, >, |.

> Next step

✓ **Success!** Your index pattern matches **1 index**.

.ml-anomalies-shared

Rows per page: 10 ∨

The last step is to select the **Time Filter field name** in the index with the value of **timestamp**, as shown in the following screenshot:

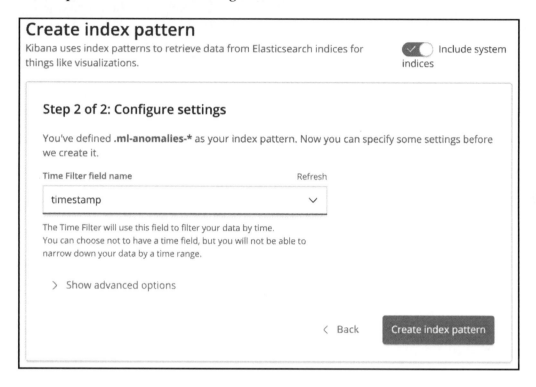

With this logistical step out of the way, we can now start to begin constructing our Canvas workpad.

Anomalies in a Canvas data table

We now want to obtain the anomaly results from our ML job and get them into Canvas. To start, let's create a blank, new workpad and add a data table element. As mentioned earlier, demo data populates the table to give us a feel for how it works:

time 🗓	cost #	username a	price #	age #	country a	state a	project a
2016-04-10T09:00:00+02:00	22.99	acollinsd9	51	30	GY	done	kibana
2016-04-10T09:00:00+02:00	23.43	kphillipsmv	54	18	CN	done	opbeat
2016-04-10T09:00:00+02:00	21.84	jfloresn0	71	35	NO	running	logstash
2016-04-11T09:00:00+02:00	23.12	jcarpenter6c	53	47	CU	done	machine-learning
2016-04-11T09:00:00+02:00	21.93	sbutlerb1	67	44	RU	running	kibana
2016-04-11T09:00:00+02:00	23.13	agardnerd0	60	49	ID	done	logstash
2016-04-11T09:00:00+02:00	22.73	preyesej	53	33	CN	done	machine-learning
2016-04-12T09:00:00+02:00	22.75	swhitejp	53	32	CN	done	opbeat
2016-04-13T09:00:00+02:00	22.69	rjackson2q	79	74	CN	done	opbeat
2016-04-13T09:00:00+02:00	23.63	sgraya7	64	70	ID	start	logstash

1 2 3 4 5 6 7 8 9 10 11 12 13 14 15 16 17 18 19 20 21 22 23 24 25 26 27 28 29 30 31 32 33 34 35 36 37 38 39 40 41 42 43 44 45 46 47 48 49 50 51 52 53 54 55 56 57 58 59 60 61 62 63 64 65 66 67 68 69 70 71 72 73 74 75 76 77 78 79 80 81 82 83 84 85 86 87 88 89 90 91 92 93 94 95 96 97 98 99 100 >

To get the results from our ML job into this table (instead of the demo data), we are going to need change the data table's data source. With the data table selected, click on the **Data** button and then click on the **Change your data source** link:

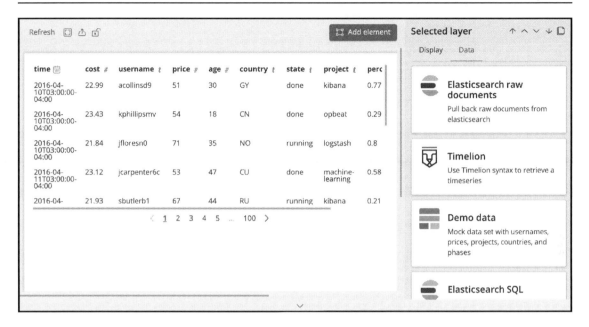

Now, select the **Elasticsearch raw documents** choice and enter the appropriate information to fetch the anomaly scores from the `result_type:bucket` documents of the `.ml-anomalies-*` index pattern for the `job_id` of interest (in this case, a job called `nginx-traffic`):

- **Index**: `.ml-anomalies-*`
- **Query**: `job_id:nginx-traffic AND result_type:bucket`
- **Sort Field**: `anomaly_score`
- **Sort Order**: **Descending**
- **Fields**: `job_id`, `timestamp`, and `anomaly_score`

This appears as follows:

Note that we are using Lucene query string syntax to filter our data; the preceding is a very simple Boolean AND expression using the `job_id` and the `result_type` field.

We have also selected the columns we want to display in the data table. Here, we will simply be using the `job_id`, `anomaly_score`, and `timestamp` fields.

The result when the **Save** button is clicked is as follows:

If we want to see the corresponding Canvas expression that is driving this data table, we can click the **Expression editor** button to see the following expression:

```
filters
| esdocs index=".ml-anomalies-*" fields="job_id, timestamp, anomaly_score"
query="job_id:nginx-traffic AND result_type:bucket" sort="anomaly_score,
DESC"
| table
| render
```

Again, the expression is a succession of components that has two main components:

- `esdocs`: The query to Elasticsearch, with the options we issued in the UI
- `table`: This just creates a data table

If you are not fully comfortable with Lucene query string syntax, and would like to use SQL, then you can also query the data that way as well.

Using the new SQL integration

Elasticsearch SQL was a feature that was introduced in version 6.3, and allows users to query Elasticsearch with SQL queries.

The API is available through the X-Pack API to query an index, like the one shown in the following example:

```
POST /_xpack/sql?format=txt
{
    "query": "SELECT * FROM my_index WHERE release_date < '2000-01-01'"
}
```

 If you want more details on this API, check out the documentation
at https://www.elastic.co/guide/en/elasticsearch/reference/
current/xpack-sql.html.

To switch and use Elasticsearch SQL as the preferred data source, simply click on the **Data** button when your data table is selected and choose **Change your data source**. Then, pick Elasticsearch SQL. In the text area, you can paste any Elasticsearch SQL-compliant query. For example:

```
SELECT job_id, timestamp, anomaly_score FROM ".ml-anomalies-*" WHERE
job_id='nginx-traffic' AND result_type='bucket' ORDER BY anomaly_score DESC
```

This appears as follows:

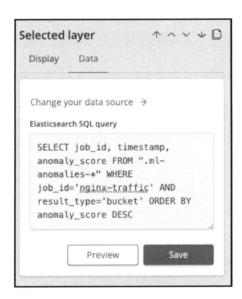

The result is exactly the same as in the previous example, where we queried using Elasticsearch's Lucene query string syntax:

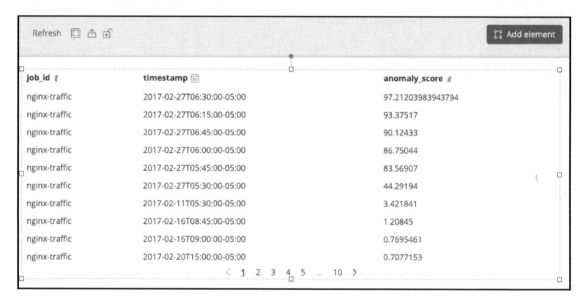

Notice in the request that we limited our query to only select `result_type:bucket`. However, as we described in `Chapter 6`, *Alerting on ML Analysis*, there are many other result types that can be queried. The full list of all result types can be easily retrieved, however, by making the following request in the **Dev Tools Console** of Kibana:

```
GET .ml-anomalies-*/_search
{
    "size":0,
    "aggs":{
        "result_type":{
            "terms":{
                "field":"result_type"
            }
        }
    }
}
```

This gives you the following list:

- `bucket`
- `model_plot`
- `bucket_influencer`
- `influencer`
- `record`
- `model_size_stats`
- `model_forecast`
- `model_forecast_request_stats`

 You can find the respective definitions in the documentation at `https://www.elastic.co/guide/en/elasticsearch/reference/current/ml-results-resource.html`.

As for the next step, let's customize our SQL query a little bit more and add a clause that will limit the results to only those where the `anomaly_score>10` to get rid of all anomalies with a very low score. Simply click on the **Expression editor** button and modify the Canvas expression to be as follows:

```
filters
| essql
 query="SELECT job_id, timestamp, anomaly_score FROM \".ml-anomalies-*\"
WHERE job_id='nginx-traffic' AND result_type='bucket' AND anomaly_score>10
ORDER BY anomaly_score DESC"
| table
| render
```

Now, let's change the raw data table into a horizontal bar chart by replacing the `table` part of the Canvas expression. In its entirety, this would now be as follows:

```
filters
| essql
  query="SELECT job_id, timestamp, anomaly_score FROM \".ml-anomalies-*\"
WHERE job_id='nginx-traffic' AND result_type='bucket' AND anomaly_score>10
ORDER BY anomaly_score DESC"
| pointseries x="anomaly_score" y="timestamp" color="job_id"
| plot defaultStyle={seriesStyle lines=0 bars="0.75" points=0
horizontalBars=true} legend=false
| render
```

In detail, here's what changed:

- We removed, between the `query` and the `render` functions, the `table` function as it's not needed to render the bar chart
- We added a `pointseries` function to build the data series that will be consumed by the bar chart
- We added a `plot` function to plot the series neither as a line chart (`lines=0`) nor a points chart (`points=0`), but as a horizontal (`horizontalBars=true`) bar chart (`bars="0.75"`)

This is what you should obtain:

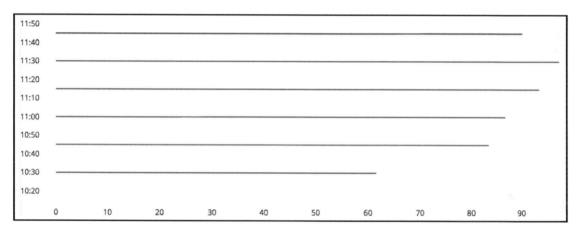

This gives us a bar chart representing top anomalies over time. This might be interesting, but we have yet to leverage the biggest advantage of Canvas over other visualizations in Kibana, the ability to create a pixel-perfect infographic.

So, let's be a little bit more creative and build a very customized slide to represent a fake network operation center. To do so, we can leverage online resources, such as the `https://www.freepik.com/` website, which provides a huge amount of vectorized pictures that can be then exported to a PNG file with Adobe Illustrator for use in Canvas. In addition to a few *eye candy* pictures, we can perhaps create another data element that shows a simple single metric value for the total number of anomalies seen for our ML job.

One way to accomplish this is with the Metric element. Another is with the Markdown element. Let's choose the latter and have the Markdown element display the number of rows that our SQL query returns (as in the total number of anomalies), as defined in the following expression:

```
filters
| essql
  query="SELECT timestamp, anomaly_score FROM \".ml-anomalies-shared\"
WHERE result_type = 'bucket' AND anomaly_score > 10 AND job_id = 'nginx-
traffic'"
| markdown
"#
#
# {{rows.length}}"
| render
```

For more information on Markdown or Handlebars, consult the following links:

- **Markdown**: https://daringfireball.net/projects/markdown/syntax
- **Handlebars**: http://handlebarsjs.com/expressions.html

Here, we're using the `rows` variable that was returned by the data source component in Canvas. The end result is a simple number in a transparent box:

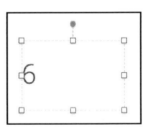

We need to add a bit of customization to our `markdown` object, such as the background color, the font, the color, and so on. Feel free to play with the different element style settings to make this element more visually appealing. You can even add your own CSS, for example:

```
filters
| essql
  query="SELECT timestamp, anomaly_score FROM \".ml-anomalies-*\" WHERE
result_type = 'bucket' AND anomaly_score > 10 AND job_id = 'nginx-traffic'"
| markdown "
```

```
#
#
# {{rows.length}}"
| render css="h1 {
text-align: center;
color: #ff1744;
}
"
  containerStyle={containerStyle backgroundColor="#444444" border="5px none
#FFFFFF" borderRadius="7px" padding="px"}
```

This will make the element look as follows:

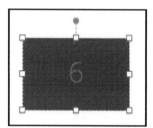

This gives us a lot of opportunities to create a look and feel that will suit any report, even if you want to match your corporate branding or color palette. You can even leverage the fact that markdown elements can be made clickable to allow the user to link to other Canvas workpads or other standard dashboards or visualizations.

The same type of customization that's applied to the bar chart gives me the following expression:

```
filters
| essql
  query="SELECT timestamp, anomaly_score FROM \".ml-anomalies-shared\"
WHERE result_type = 'bucket' AND anomaly_score > 10 AND job_id = 'nginx-
traffic'"
| pointseries x="anomaly_score" y="timestamp"
| plot
  defaultStyle={seriesStyle lines=0 bars="2" points=0 horizontalBars=true
color="#d32f2f"} legend=false xaxis=true yaxis=true
  font={font family="'Open Sans', Helvetica, Arial, sans-serif" size=12
align="left" color="#FFFFFF" weight="normal" underline=false italic=false}
| render containerStyle={containerStyle backgroundColor="#444444"}
```

This gives us the following rendering:

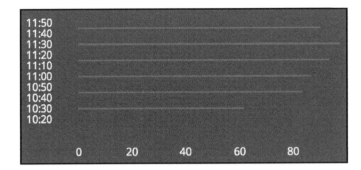

At this point, you can let your creativity do the rest of the work. We will add some static images of furniture and a silly portrait of one of our colleagues to round out our custom, data-driven infographic:

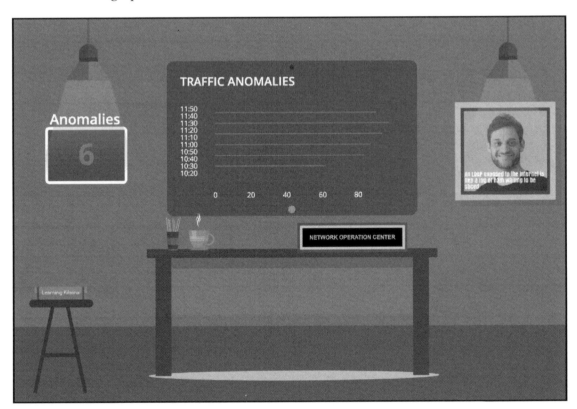

As you can see, we are probably not going to be hired for our graphic design capabilities! If you want to see a beautiful example of how interactive and visually stunning a Canvas dashboard can be, take a look at this particular example on the Elastic blog at `https://www.elastic.co/blog/monitoring-airport-security-operations-with-canvas-and-elasticsearch`.

Summary

In this chapter, we looked at how we can use Canvas to leverage the output of ML to build a customized report so that information can appeal to any audience. With the power of the full flexibility of Elasticsearch (and even the use of Elasticsearch SQL queries), we can make real-time data-driven infographics where your only limit is your creativity.

In the next chapter, `Chapter 9`, *Forecasting*, we will delve into the world of forecasting, where we can have ML extrapolate data trends into the future to satisfy a whole new set of use cases.

9
Forecasting

Forecasting is a natural extension of the time series modeling of Elastic ML. Since very expressive models are built behind the scenes and describe how data has behaved historically, it is therefore possible to project that information forward in time and predict how something should behave at a future time.

In this chapter, we will cover the following topics:

- Use cases for forecasting
- Theory of operation
- Single-metric forecasting
- Multiple-metric forecasting

First, however, we need to get an understanding of the caveats of predicting the future.

Forecasting versus prophesying

Past performance is not indicative of future results. This disclaimer is used by financial companies when they reference the performance of products such as mutual funds. But this disclaimer is a bit of an odd contradiction, because the past is all that we have to work with. If the companies that comprise the mutual fund have consistently had positive quarterly results for the last eight quarters straight, does that guarantee that they will also have a positive set of results for the next eight quarters and that their public valuation will continue to rise? Probability could be on the side of that being the case, but that might not be the whole story. And, before we get too wishful in thinking that Elastic ML's ability to forecast is our key to making a fortune in the stock market, we should be realistic about one key caveat.

The reason financial companies use this disclaimer is that there are often unknown, uncontrollable factors that emerge and can be very influential on the trajectory of something. For example, the government could change regulations or trade policies that greatly help or hinder the company's ability to operate and be profitable. There could be an internal fraudulent accounting scandal in which the executives conspired to falsify corporate performance, which becomes untenable to maintain and ultimately bankrupts the company.

These factors are deemed unknown and external because of the following reasons:

- They are outside of the control of the entity itself (as in the example of the government dictating policies independently of the company's activities)
- They are hidden from the available information about the system (an outside investor, in real time, only has access to publicly available performance reports, and not to the knowledge of the fraudulent activities that may be fabricating those performance reports)

As such, predictions are only as good as the information you have and your ability to eliminate or mitigate external unknown factors that will affect your prediction. The same is true in the world of IT data. It's not always possible to predict a trend or a failure if an unknown, external factor is at play (someone incorrectly making a configuration change, a failing piece of hardware, and so on). However, we can use probabilistic analysis to give us our best guess at the future, aside from those possible external factors. Understanding this caveat allows us to satisfy some good forecasting use cases without getting hung up on the expectation of prophecy.

Forecasting use cases

In the context of Elastic ML, there are really just two, somewhat similar, use cases in which someone would use forecasting. These are as follows:

- **Value-focused**: Extrapolating a time series into the future to understand a probable future value. This would be akin to answering questions such as: "how many widgets will I sell per day two months from now?"
- **Time-focused**: Understanding the likely time at which an expected value is to be reached. This would be answering questions similar to: "do I expect to reach 80% utilization in the next week?"

The differences between these two use cases might not just be how the question is asked (how the data is searched), but also how you interpret the output. However, before we delve into a few examples of how to use the forecasting feature, let's take a little time to discuss how it works logistically.

Forecasting – theory of operation

The first thing to realize is that the act of invoking a forecast on data is that it is an extension of an existing job. In other words, you need to have an ML job configured and that job needs to have analyzed historical data before you can forecast on that data. This is because the forecasting process uses the models that are created by the ML job; the same ones that are used for anomaly detection. To forecast, you need to follow the same steps to create an ML job that has been described in other chapters. If anomalies were generated by the execution of that job, you can disregard them if your only purpose is to execute forecasting. Once the ML job has learned on some historical data, the model or models (if the ML job contains more than one time series) associated with that job are current and up to date, as represented by the following diagram:

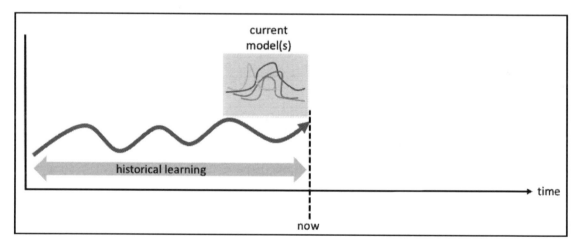

We'll consider the **time** before **now** as **historical learning**; the **time** over which the models have learned on actual data. When the user wishes to invoke a forecast at a particular time, a copy of the models is created, and a separate process is used to take those models and extrapolate them into the "**future**". This process is run in parallel to not interfere with the original models and their evolution. This is represented in the following diagram:

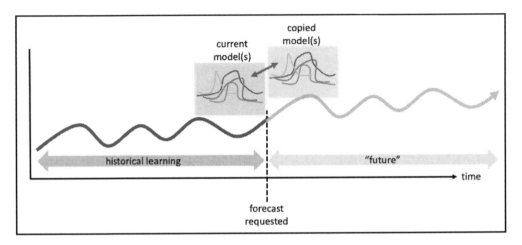

The forecast values are written to the results index as a special type of result (more detail on this later) and will be available for viewing in the UI or accessible via the API.

It's important to note that the normal path of the ML job analyzing the actual real data will continue (if it is running in real time) and therefore after an amount of time there could be a difference between the predicted value for a future time (made at the time of the forecast) and the actual value when that time arrives, as shown in the following diagram:

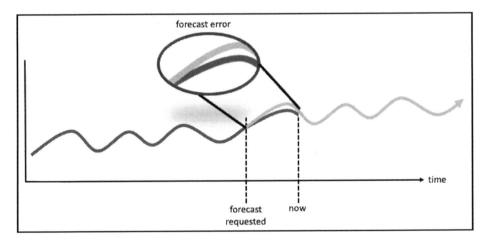

This forecasting error is to be expected, but hopefully it will be minimal. The differential between the two is not currently used by ML, but perhaps in the future it could inform the models about more accurate subsequent forecasts. Surely it is also possible that an unknown external factor (as described earlier) could lead to a certain amount of forecasting error. Another (perhaps simpler) way to think about uncertainty in predictions is to think about predicting the outcome of a coin toss. You could observe a sequence of prior coin flips, but if you are not taking into account the physics of the coin flip (speed, height, rotations, and so on) and are only relying on the outcome of past observations, then you'll never get better than a 50/50 prediction on the outcome. Additionally, it is likely the ML didn't see behaviorally perfectly consistent data during the learning period. As such, with a certain amount of noise in the data, we should also expect a certain amount of variation or uncertainty in the forecast.

There also can be multiple forecasts made by the user at other times. These will be stored separately, as represented by the following diagram:

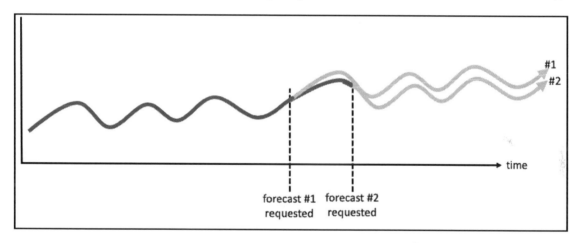

The distinction between **forecast #1** and **forecast #2** will be keyed off with an internal unique ID for each forecast instance. This will become apparent later when we look at how the forecast results are stored in the index.

Single time series forecasting

Now that we have a base understanding of the logistical operation of the forecasting process, let's walk through an example of how to use Elastic ML for forecasting. We will start with a dataset that is a single time series.

Dataset preparation

The dataset we will use in our example is available in the GitHub repository at `https://github.com/PacktPublishing/Machine-Learning-with-the-Elastic-Stack/tree/master/example_data`. This dataset, once downloaded, can be easily imported into your Kibana via ML's **Data Visualizer** (only in versions 6.5+). To upload the data, go to ML's **Data Visualizer** tab and select the **Upload file** button:

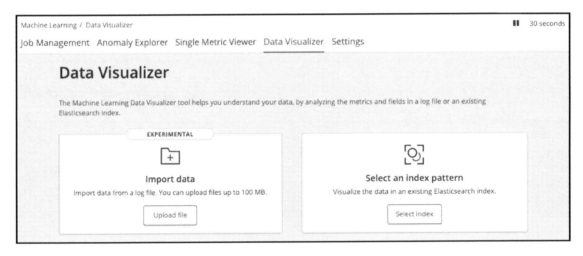

Choose the `forecast_example.json` file from your local machine. The **Data Visualizer** will then display the first **1000** lines of the file to give you a preview of what the file contains, as well as a breakdown of the different fields:

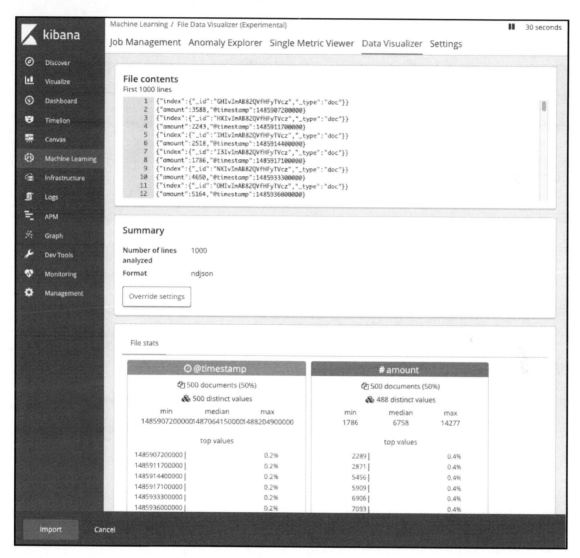

In this specific case, we do not need to override any of the settings that the **Data Visualizer** has made automatically, so we can proceed by clicking on the **Import** button. We can supply a name for the destination index (we can use `forecast_example` for this exercise):

Clicking on the **Import** button now will complete the import process:

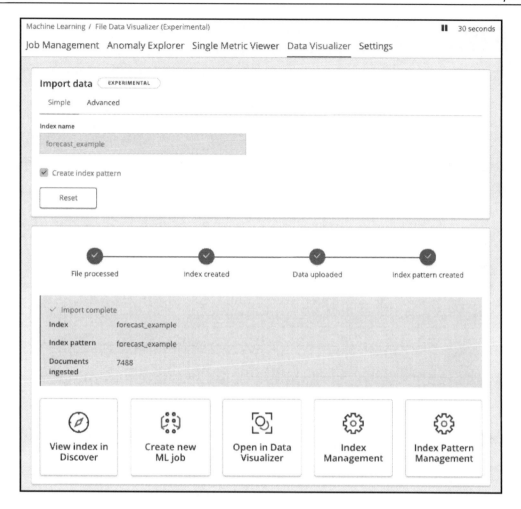

We can now create a new ML job so that we can do some forecasting on this dataset.

Creating the ML job for forecasting

This example dataset goes from **January 31st 2017** to **March 11th 2017**. Despite being from the past, we can contrive a scenario in which we are pretending to be in that time frame and say that today's date is March 1st, 2017. We therefore want to have an ML job analyze the data between January 31st and today, and then use ML to forecast that data ten days into the future.

If your Kibana time zone is set to your local time, the dates in this chapter may look slightly different as the screenshots were taken with a version of Kibana that's been set to the Eastern time zone of the United States.

We can then have the ML job analyze the rest of the data in the index (from March 1st through March 11th) and we can see how close the forecast tracked the actual dataset. Let's begin!

The first step is to create a **Single Metric job** that uses the **Sum** aggregation function on the **#amount** field with a **Bucket span** of 15m:

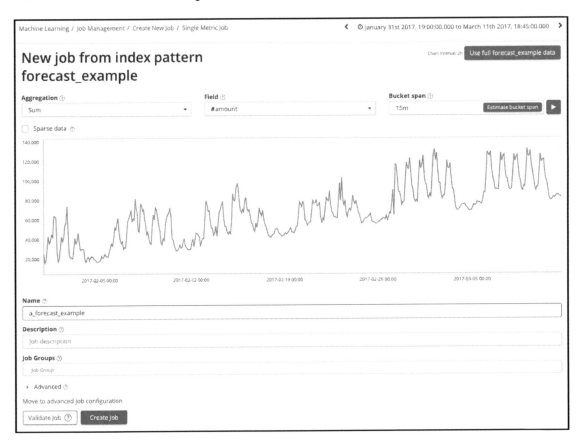

However, we don't want to analyze all of the data; we want to stop short on March 1st. Therefore, in the top right, change the end date of the Kibana date picker to be March 1st:

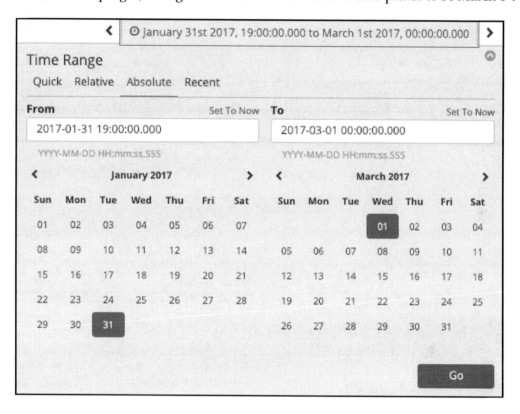

With that date modification made, you can name the job `a_forecast_example` and click the **Create Job** button:

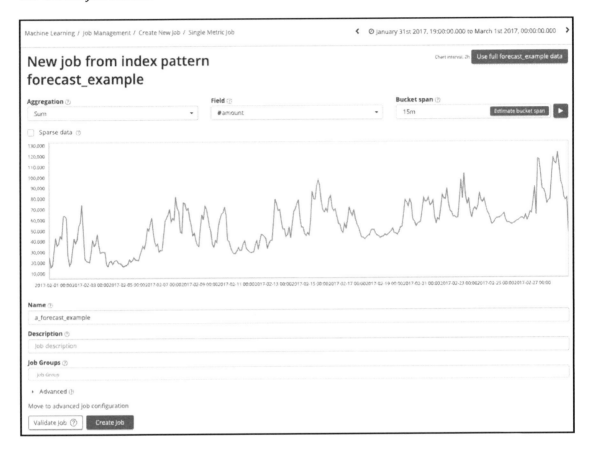

Once the job has run, we can see the results preview in the UI:

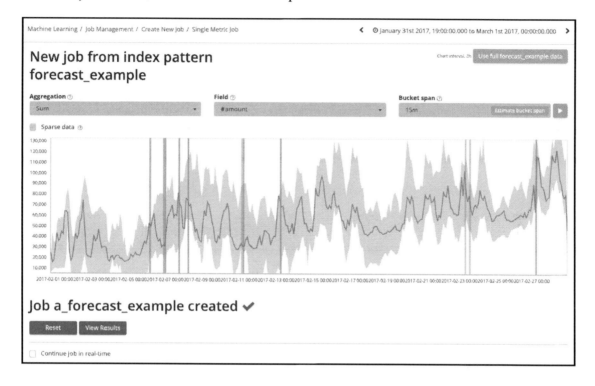

To access the ability to forecast, we need to click the **View Results** button, which will take us to the **Single Metric Viewer**. In the **Single Metric Viewer**, we can see the overall dataset and can appreciate the shape and complexity of the way this data behaves; there are both daily and weekly periodic components, as well as a gradual positive slope/trend that causes the data to drift up over time:

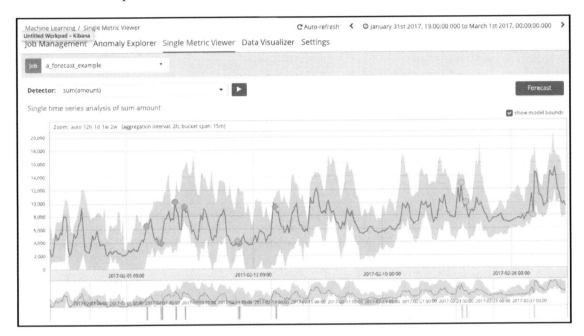

Remember, despite the fact that we may only be interested in forecasting on this data, the ML job will still point out anomalies throughout the data's history, but we can simply ignore them.

To invoke a forecast on this data, click the **Forecast** button and in the dialog box, enter a duration of 10 days (10d):

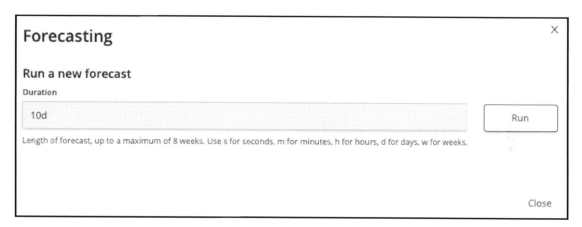

 There is currently a hard eight-week limit on the duration (this is likely to be extended in future versions of ML). Also, you should note that you should not attempt to ask for a forecasting duration that is longer than the duration of the data that the ML job has analyzed. In other words, don't ask for a two-week forecast if the ML job has only ever seen one week of data. Lastly, supply enough consistent data to learn about the principal patterns. For example, a minimum of three cycles of a periodic pattern is used to achieve the best possible predictions.

Clicking the **Run** button will invoke the forecast request, which will run in the background, but once finished will display the results of the forecast to extend over the time period of interest:

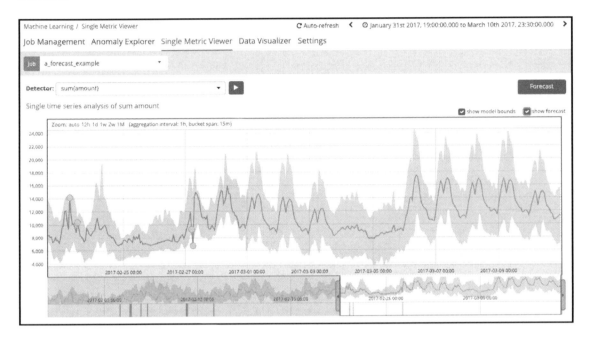

The shaded area around the forecast/predicted zone is the 95th percentile confidence interval. In other words, ML has estimated that there is a 95% chance that the future values will be within this range (and likewise, only a 2.5% chance that the future values will be either above or below the confidence interval). The 95th percentile range is currently a fixed value and is not yet settable by the user.

Now that we have the ability to create simple forecasts from the UI, let's explore the results of the forecast in more depth before moving to a more complicated example.

Forecast results

Now that we have run a forecast, we can look in more depth at the results that are generated by the forecasting process. By the way, we can view the results of a previously created forecast at any time in the UI via one of two methods. You can click the **Forecast** button in the **Single Metric Viewer** to reveal a list of **Previous Forecasts**, like so:

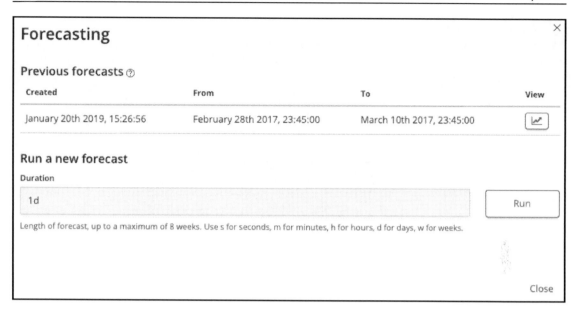

Alternatively, you can view them in the **Job Management** page under the **Forecasts** tab for that job:

 Forecast results built in Kibana have a default lifespan of 14 days. After that, the forecast results are deleted permanently. If a different expiration duration is desired, then the forecast will have to be invoked via the `_forecast` API endpoint, which will be discussed later, but is documented at `https://www.elastic.co/guide/en/elasticsearch/reference/current/ml-forecast.html`.

In either case, clicking on the **View** icon will bring the user to the **Single Metric Viewer**. Notice that when you mouse over the forecast data points in the UI, the popup display will list three key pieces of information about the data point, the prediction value, the upper bound, and the lower bound value:

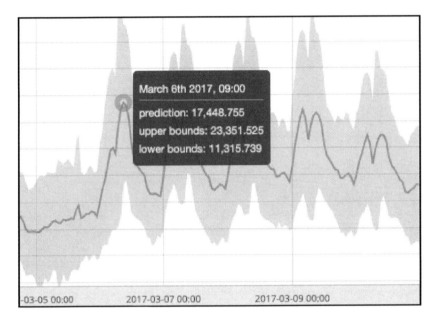

Recall that the upper and lower bounds define a range of 95th percentile confidence. The prediction value is the value with the highest likelihood (probability). These three key values are stored in the `.ml-anomalies-*` results indices with the following names:

- `forecast_prediction`
- `forecast_upper`
- `forecast_lower`

We can query the `.ml-anomalies-*` indices to locate this exact point in time (remembering that the dates are stored in epoch time). Therefore, let's say we are executing the following query in the **Dev Tools Console**:

```
GET .ml-anomalies-*/_search
{
  "query": {
    "bool": {
      "filter": [
        {"term": {"timestamp": "1488808800000"}},
        {"term": {"result_type": "model_forecast"}},
```

```
            {"term": {"job_id": "a_forecast_example"}}
        ]
    }
  }
}
```

The output would be as follows:

```
{
  "took" : 1,
  "timed_out" : false,
  "_shards" : {
    "total" : 20,
    "successful" : 20,
    "skipped" : 0,
    "failed" : 0
  },
  "hits" : {
    "total" : 1,
    "max_score" : 0.0,
    "hits" : [
      {
        "_index" : ".ml-anomalies-shared",
        "_type" : "doc",
        "_id" :
"a_forecast_example_model_forecast_i2DxbGgBITRq2rXM21p4_1488808800000_900_0
_961_0",
        "_score" : 0.0,
        "_source" : {
          "job_id" : "a_forecast_example",
          "forecast_id" : "i2DxbGgBITRq2rXM21p4",
          "result_type" : "model_forecast",
          "bucket_span" : 900,
          "detector_index" : 0,
          "timestamp" : 1488808800000,
          "model_feature" : "'bucket sum by person'",
          "forecast_lower" : 11315.739312779506,
          "forecast_upper" : 23080.83486433322,
          "forecast_prediction" : 17198.287088556364
        }
      }
    ]
  }
}
```

Note the unique `forecast_id`. If multiple forecasts were created spanning this time frame, there would be more than one result with different IDs.

These values match what we saw in the ML **Single Metric Viewer** in Kibana (with slight mathematical rounding). This type of query can be mapped to one of the use cases that we mentioned at the beginning of this chapter a *value-focused* inquiry (we give a date, and we ask for the value). Here, we asked for the most probable value of the time series for a particular time in the future.

To satisfy the *time-focused* inquiry, we need to re-orient the query a little to ask it to return the date (or dates) on which the predicted values meet certain criteria. To mix it up a little, we'll submit the query using Elastic SQL:

```
POST /_xpack/sql?format=txt
{
  "query": "SELECT timestamp FROM \".ml-anomalies-*\" WHERE
job_id='a_forecast_example' AND result_type='model_forecast' AND
forecast_prediction>'17700' ORDER BY timestamp DESC"
}
```

Here, we are asking if there are any times in which the predicted value exceeds our limit of the value of 17,700. The response is as follows:

```
        timestamp
----------------------
2017-03-06T14:45:00.000Z
```

In other words, we may breach the threshold of 17,700 on March 6th (5 days from now in our fictitious example of today being March 1st, 2017) at 2:45 P.M. GMT, which is 9:45 A.M. in the Eastern time zone of the United States. This matches what is seen in the Kibana UI (which is localized to the East Coast GMT-5 time zone):

Your results might vary slightly in your time zone (since we chose an end time of the analysis to be relative to our local time zone). Thus, you may have analyzed a few hours more or less data than what was done in this example. Your prediction model could be slightly different and therefore your highest predicted value might be slightly different.

This approach could be useful for capacity planning, where you could ask something like "within the next 10 days, will my capacity exceed 80%?"

If we want to see how well ML's forecasting did compared to the actual next ten days of the dataset (remember, the ML job's models haven't yet actually seen those days), we can return to the **Job Management** page and start the datafeed of the job to continue on and analyze the remainder of the data. To do so, click on the **Start datafeed** link from the menu on the right-hand side:

Once the dialog comes up, set the **Search start time** to **Continue from 2017-02-38 23:45:00** (or whatever it says it is for your local time zone) and specify the **Search end time** to be March 11th, 2017 at **12:00 AM**:

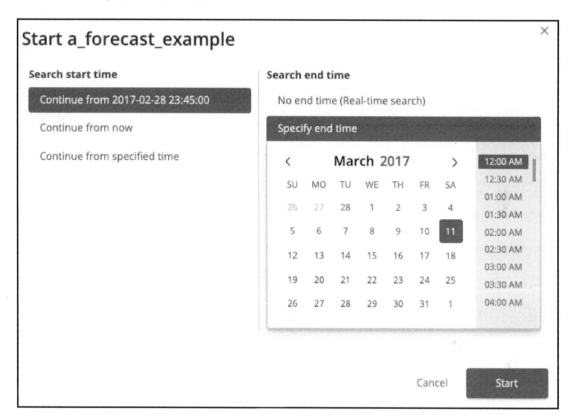

Once you have done this, return to the **Single Metric Viewer** for the job, ensure that you are viewing the correct range of time with the Kibana time picker, and click on the **Forecast** button to view the previously created forecast, as described earlier in this chapter. You will now be able to see the forecast values superimposed over the actual values from the data:

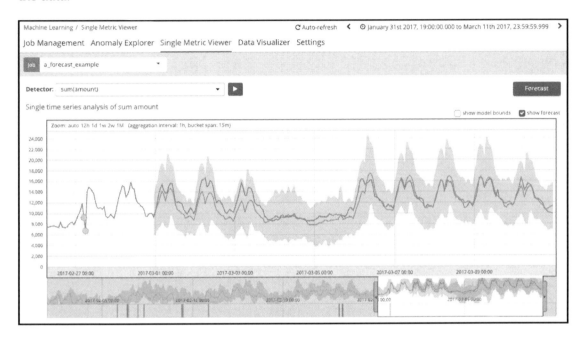

As described earlier in this chapter, there will be a slight discrepancy between the Elastic ML prediction of the data and the actual value that arrives in the future. This is because the predictions are probabilistic, and with probability comes a certain level of uncertainty. However, this does not diminish the usefulness of the forecasts. Combined with the proactive alerting of Watcher (as described in Chapter 6, *Alerting on ML Analysis*), we could have been alerted to the possibility of a breach. This proactive notification is especially useful when users cannot track hundreds or thousands of entities individually. Multi-metric forecasting will allow us to track those entities automatically.

Multiple time series forecasting

To invoke forecasting on multiple time series, you simply just need an ML job that is modeling multiple time series. Let's assume that we have an ML job that has analyzed web requests per country. We may have over 200 unique time series in our weblogs because of the diverse clientele that visit our website. In an ML job, in the logs that were collected by Filebeat, we have elected to configure a multi-metric job of the count of requests for every **tnginx.access.geoip.country_iso_code**:

When we click the **Forecast** button in the **Single Metric Viewer**, the forecast will automatically be run for all detectors and partitions (even if there are hundreds or more). Alternatively, you can use the `_forecast` API endpoint to invoke the forecast. To do so, in the **Dev Tools Console**, we could issue this request:

```
POST _xpack/ml/anomaly_detectors/web_traffic_per_country/_forecast
{
  "duration": "7d"
}
```

The immediate response from the API call is as follows:

```
{
  "acknowledged" : true,
  "forecast_id" : "DGT6bWgBITRq2rXMb1Rr"
}
```

 The ML job must be in the open state to invoke a forecast via the API.

The results of our forecast request will be available for viewing either in the **Single Metric Viewer** or programmatically by querying the results indices, as demonstrated earlier. For example, we can see that the forecast for the **US** (**nginx.access.geoip.country_iso_code**) appears as follows:

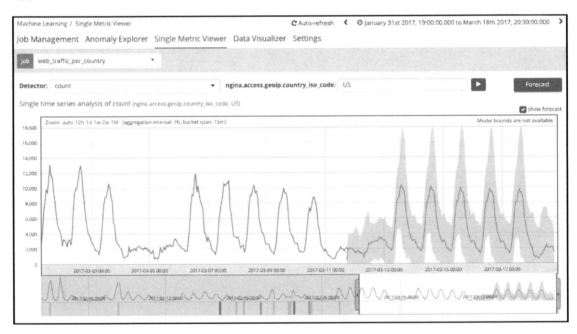

This is significantly different in volume than that of Vietnam
(**nginx.access.geoip.country_iso_code VN**):

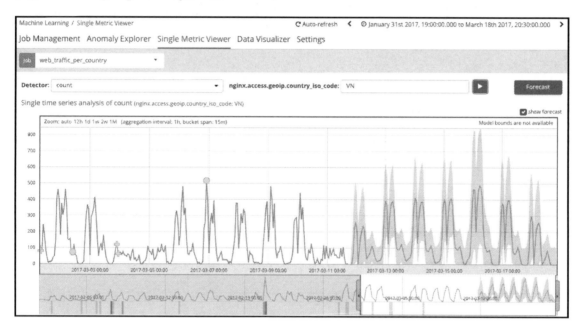

As you can see, the forecast is done per time series, automatically. Again, this could be extremely useful for capacity planning use cases where hundreds or possibly thousands of entities need to be analyzed and forecast to see if any pending breaches in the near future are possible.

Summary

Elastic ML has an additional feature over and above anomaly detection, the ability to take and extrapolate the time series models into the future for forecasting purposes. With use cases that include advanced breach detection and capacity planning, this feature alleviates the human burden of manually charting, tracking, and predicting where things are going in the future, based upon how they have behaved in the past.

In our next and final chapter, Chapter 10, *ML Tips and Tricks*, we'll run through a plethora of practical tips and tricks that didn't find a home in the other chapters.

10
ML Tips and Tricks

As we wind down the content for this book, it occurred to us that there's still a plethora of good, bite-sized explanations, examples, and pieces of advice that didn't quite fit into the other chapters. It therefore made sense to give them a chapter all to themselves. Enjoy this potpourri of tips and tricks!

The following topics will be covered in this chapter:

- Job groups
- Ignoring time periods
- Top-down alerting
- Sizing ML deployments

Job groups

We saw in Chapter 4, *IT Operational Analytics and Root Cause Analysis*, that there were good reasons to simultaneously view the results of several jobs against different kinds of data. Therefore, it makes sense that sometimes we need the ability to logically group jobs together around a common theme. To accomplish this, let's review the **Job groups** feature, which was introduced to ML in version 6.1.

Job groups allow the user to arbitrarily tag jobs with keywords for organizational purposes. You can, for example, determine that all jobs that are related to a specific application should be tagged with the application name. You can assign a job to a group at creation time, or you can edit the job after its creation; the process is simple. For example, the first time we assign a job to a Job group, the name will not be recognized and will create a new group name:

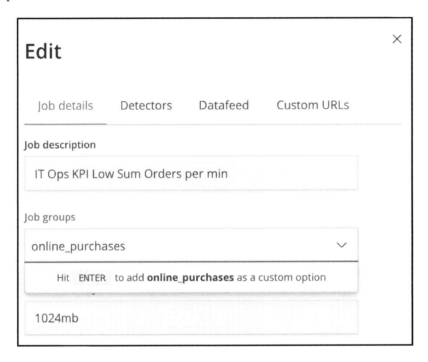

Subsequently, when additional jobs are edited to be assigned to a group, the UI will give you a clue about the existing groups:

Once we have assigned several jobs to a particular group, and when the **Anomaly Explorer** user interface is loaded and the job selector pulldown is clicked, you will be able to select, with a single click, to display all jobs belonging to a particular group:

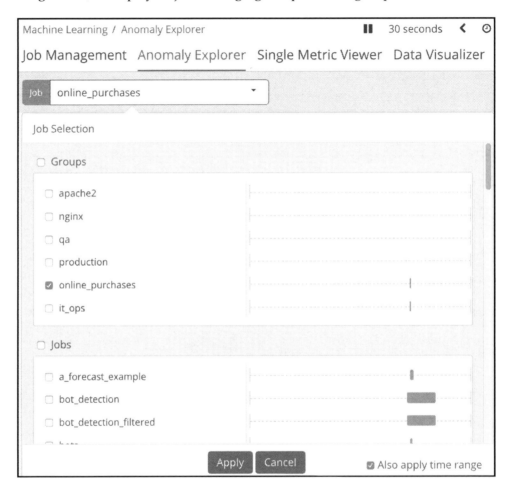

This very simple organizational tool will allow operators to orient their view of the results of ML jobs without having to remember which jobs are relevant to which applications that are being monitored.

Job groups can also be useful for organization and administrative tasks in the **Job Management** screen. Here, you can see that five jobs all belong to the **nginx** group, but some are tagged with **qa** and some are tagged with **production**:

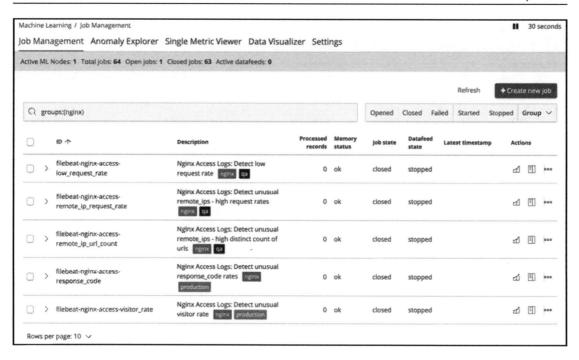

Jobs in the view can be filtered by keywords, and groups, and have bulk operations applied against them (start datafeed, delete job, and so on).

Influencers in split versus non-split jobs

You might question whether or not it is necessary to split the analysis by a field, or merely hope that the use of influencers will give the desired effect of identifying the offending entity.

Let's remind ourselves of the difference between the purpose of influencers and the purpose of splitting a job. An entity is identified by ML as an influencer if it has contributed significantly to the existence of the anomaly. This notion of deciding influential entities is completely independent of whether or not the job is split. An entity can be deemed influential on an anomaly only if an anomaly happens in the first place. If there is no anomaly detected, there is no need to figure out whether there is an influencer. However, the job may or may not find that something is anomalous, depending on whether or not the job is split into multiple time series. When splitting the job, you are modeling (creating separate analysis) for each entity of the field chosen for the split.

To illustrate this, let's look at one of my favorite demo datasets, called `farequote` (available in the GitHub repository for this book at `https://github.com/PacktPublishing/Machine-Learning-with-the-Elastic-Stack/tree/master/example_data`). This dataset is essentially an access log of the number of times a piece of middleware is called in a travel portal to reach out to third-party airlines for a quote of airline fares. The JSON documents look like this:

```
{
    "@timestamp": "2017-02-11T23:59:54.000Z",
    "responsetime": 251.573,
    "airline": "FFT"
}
```

The number of events per unit of time corresponds to the number of requests being made, and the `responsetime` field is the response time of that individual request to that airline's fare quoting web service.

Let's take a look at the following cases:

- **Case 1**: An analysis of count over time, not split on `airline`, but using `airline` as an influencer

  If we analyze the overall count of events (no split), we can see that the prominent anomaly (the spike) in the event volume was determined to be influenced by `airline=AAL`:

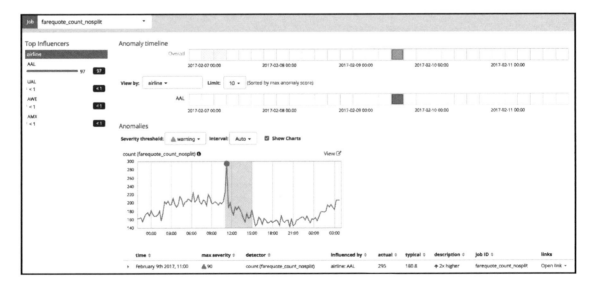

This is quite sensible because the increased occurrence of requests for `AAL` affects the overall event count (of all airlines together) very prominently.

- **Case 2**: An analysis of count over time, split on `airline`, and using `airline` as an influencer

If we set **partition_field_name**=`airline` to split the analysis so that each airline's count of documents is analyzed independently, then of course, we still properly see that `airline`=`AAL` is still the most unusual:

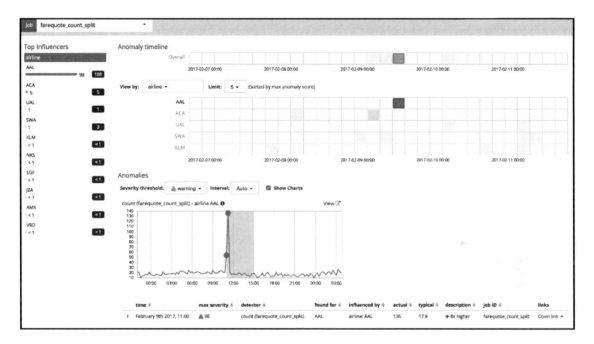

- **Case 3**: Analysis of **mean(responsetime)**, no split, but using `airline` as an influencer

In this case, the results are as follows:

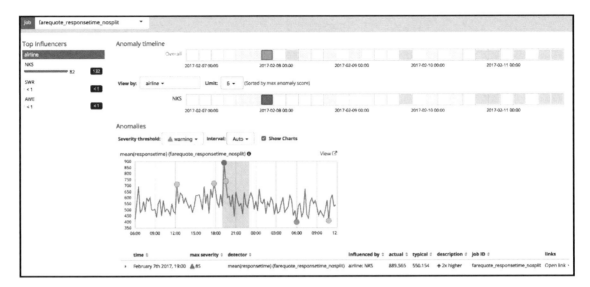

Here, remember that all of the airline's response times are getting averaged together each `bucket_span`, because the job is not split. In this case, the most prominent anomaly (even though it is a relatively minor variation above normal) is shown and is deemed to be influenced by `airline=NKS`. However, this may be misleading. You see, `airline=NKS` has a very stable response time during this period, but note that its normal operating range is much higher than the rest of the group:

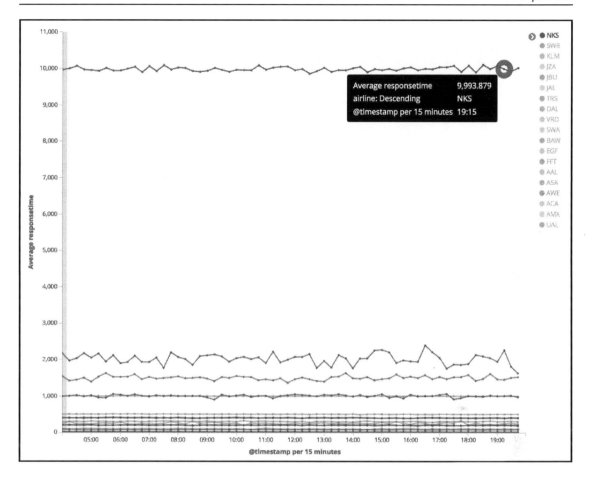

As such, the contribution of NKS to the total aggregate response times of all airlines is more significant than the others. So, of course, ML identifies NKS as the most prominent influencer.

But this anomaly is not the most significant anomaly of reponsetime in the dataset! That anomaly belongs to airline=AAL, but it isn't visible in the aggregate because data from all the airlines drowns out the detail. See the next case.

- **Case 4**: Analysis of **mean(responsetime)**, split on `airline`, and using `airline` as an influencer

In this case, the most prominent response time anomaly for `AAL` properly shows itself when we set **partition_field_name**=`airline` to split the analysis:

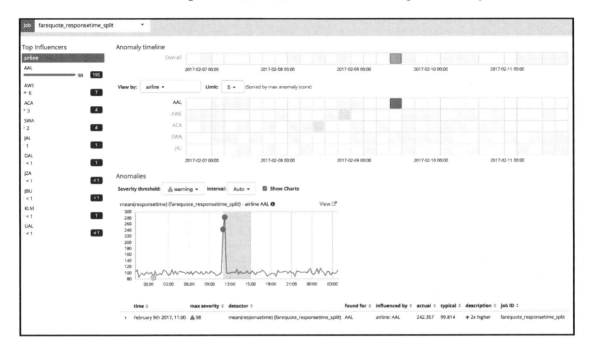

And there you have it: the moral here is that you should be thoughtful if you are simply relying on influencers to find unusual entities within a dataset of multiple entities. It might be more sensible to individually model each entity independently!

Using ML on scripted fields

In some cases, it might be necessary to analyze the relationship of fields within documents. Elasticsearch gives us the ability to create scripted fields (https://www.elastic.co/guide/en/elasticsearch/reference/current/search-request-script-fields.html) that allow us to programmatically combine individual fields into new fields; ML can then leverage that!

For example, let's say you have daily documents that summarize your product sales and that your documents have two fields, Amount and Count:

```
{
...
    "Count": 160,
    "Amount": 7200
...
}
```

We could easily define a use case in which we were interested in the per item cost (Amount/Count). To do so, we would define the ML job to focus on the new field (perhaps we'll call it per_item_cost and use the mean function on it):

```
PUT _xpack/ml/anomaly_detectors/my_job {
    "analysis_config": {
        "bucket_span": "1d",
        "detectors": [{
            "detector_description": "mean(per_item_cost)",
            "function": "mean",
            "field_name": "per_item_cost"
        }],
        "influencers": []
    },
    "data_description": {
        "time_field": "@timestamp"
    }
}
```

Then, we need to define the job's datafeed so that we can use Elasticsearch's scripted fields capability to create this new per_item_cost scripted field:

```
PUT _xpack/ml/datafeeds/datafeed-my_job/
{
  "job_id": "my_job",
  "indices": [
    "newapple"
  ],
    "query": {
      "match_all": {
      }
    },
    "script_fields": {
      "per_item_cost": {
        "script": {
          "source": "doc['Amount'].value / doc['Count'].value",
          "lang": "painless"
```

```
            },
            "ignore_failure": false
        }
    }

}
```

Then, we can preview the datafeed:

```
GET _xpack/ml/datafeeds/datafeed-my_job/_preview
```

By doing this, we can validate that the scripted field's output looks correct:

```
[
    {
        "@timestamp": 1529280000000,
        "per_item_cost": 7.190000057220459
    },
    {
        "@timestamp": 1529280000000,
        "per_item_cost": 7.190000057220459
    },
    {
        "@timestamp": 1529366400000,
        "per_item_cost": 21.56999969482422
    },
    {
        "@timestamp": 1529366400000,
        "per_item_cost": 21.56999969482422
    },
    {
        "@timestamp": 1529539200000,
        "per_item_cost": 159.5500030517578
    },
    . . .
```

When executing the job, we can find anomalies in this new field!

 Do not assume that if you've defined a scripted field in Kibana, the ML job will just use that instead. You can indeed have one defined in Kibana for use in visuals, but the ML job still needs you to define the scripted field in the datafeed's query to Elasticsearch. Also, this method only works if the fields to be combined are in the same document. If they are in different documents, you're out of luck for now.

Using one-sided ML functions to your advantage

Many people realize the usefulness of *one-sided* functions in ML, such as `low_count`, `high_mean`, and so on, to allow for the detection of anomalies only on the high side or on the low side. This is useful when you only care about a drop in revenue or a spike in response time.

However, when you care about deviations in both directions, you are often inclined to use just the regular function (such as `count` or `mean`). However, on some datasets, it is actually more optimal to use both the high and low version of the function as two separate detectors. Why is this the case and under what conditions, you might ask?

The condition where this makes sense is when the dynamic range of the possible deviations is asymmetrical. In other words, the magnitude of potential spikes in the data is far, far bigger than the magnitude of the potential drops, possibly because the count or sum of something cannot be less than zero. Let's look at the following screenshot:

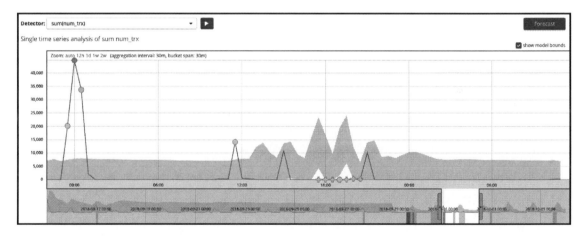

Here, the two-sided **sum** function properly identifies the large spike with a critical anomaly on the left, but the lack of expected *double bumps* in the middle is identified with only warning anomalies. Again, this is because with a double-sided function the normalization process ranks all anomalies together. The magnitude (and therefore the unlikeliness) of the spike is far bigger than the lack of data around **18:00**, so the anomaly scores are assigned relatively.

However, if the dataset was analyzed with two separate detectors, using an advanced job, that is, **low_sum(num_trx)** and **high_sum(num_trx)**, then the results would look very different. Here's the result of the high side:

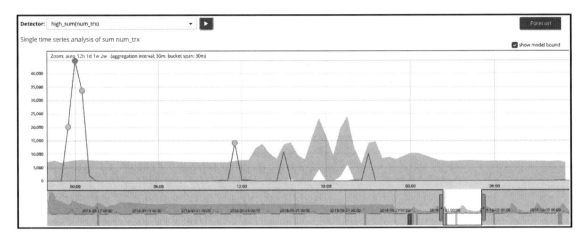

Here's the result of the low side:

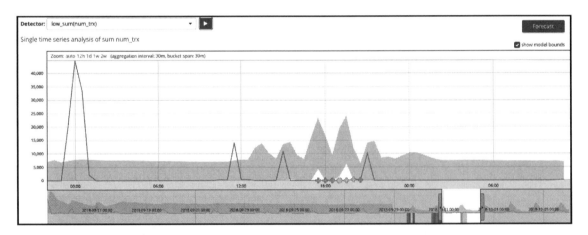

Notice that the anomalies in the middle are now scored much higher (in this case, with a max score of 47 yellow).

So now, when the two one-sided detectors are run together in the same job, you've optimized the dynamic range of each detector (since they have their own normalization table)!

Ignoring time periods

Often, people ask how they can get ML to ignore that a certain time period has occurred. Perhaps it was an expected maintenance window, or perhaps something was broken within the data ingest pipeline and data was lost for a few moments. There are a few ways that you can get ML to ignore time periods and, for distinction, we'll separate them into two groups:

- A known, upcoming window of time
- An unexpected window of time that is discovered after the fact

To illustrate things, we'll use a reference job and dataset that has an anomaly on the date of February 9th:

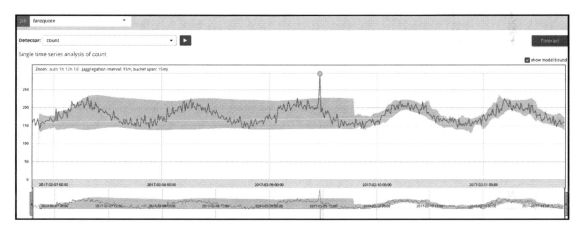

Ignoring an upcoming (known) window of time

Two methods can be used to ignore an upcoming window of time, as shown in the following sections.

Creating a calendar event

You can create an event by clicking on **Settings** I **Calendar Management** I **Edit Calendar**. Here, I've created a calendar entry for February 9th:

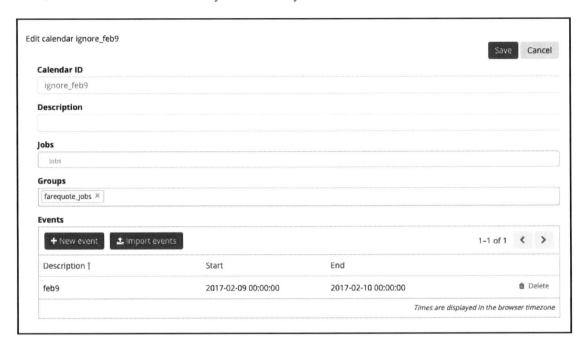

Now, when the job is run, that entire day is ignored:

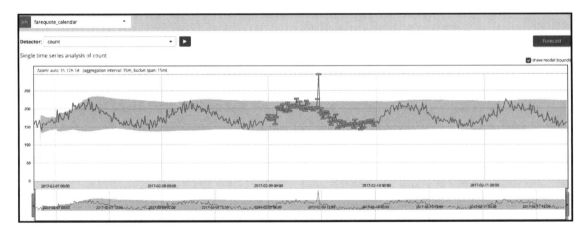

As you can see, the entire day was masked, including the time of the anomalous spike.

Stopping and starting a datafeed to ignore the desired timeframe

By simply stopping and restarting the datafeed of the ML job at the appropriate times, you can create a gap in the analysis. Here, the datafeed was stopped at midnight on February 9th and restarted at midnight on February 10th:

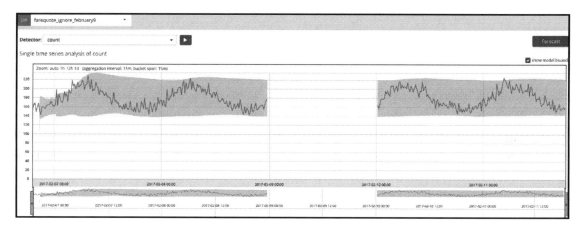

It was like February 9th never happened!

Ignoring an unexpected window of time, after the fact

To *go back in time* and *forget* that a window of time happened, we can use two methods, as we will discuss in the following sections.

Clone the job and re-run historical data

Similar to the previous section, on the new, cloned job, just have the datafeed ignore the window of time you wish to ignore. Stop it at the beginning of the window and resume it at the end of the window.

Revert the model snapshot

When cloning and retraining the job on existing historical data isn't desired or practical, you can effectively remove a window of time by using the `model_snapshots` API (`https://www.elastic.co/guide/en/elasticsearch/reference/6.5/ml-apis.html#ml-api-snapshot-endpoint`), as shown in the following steps:

1. Stop the datafeed
2. Find the last snapshot taken by using the `GET model_snapshots` API (and passing the desired end time)
3. Revert to that earlier snapshot ID using the `_revert` API call, but also pass the `delete_intervening_results` flag to erase any results/anomalies that were created after the time the snapshot was created
4. Start the datafeed at an appropriate time, that is, the end of the window of time that you want to ignore

Don't over-engineer the use case

I once worked with a user where we discussed different use cases for ML. In particular, this customer was building a hosted security operations center as part of their **managed security service provider (MSSP)** business, so they were keen to think about use cases in which ML could help.

A high-level theme to their use cases was to look at a user's behavior and find unexpected behavior. One example that was discussed was login activity from unusual/rare locations such as *Bob just logged in from Ukraine, but he doesn't normally log in from there.*

In the process of thinking the implementation through, there was talk of them having multiple clients, each of which had multiple users. Therefore, they were thinking of ways to split/partition the data so that they could execute "rare" by country for each and every user of every client.

I asked them to take a step back and said "Is it worthy of an anomaly if *anyone* logs in from Ukraine, not just Bob?" to which the answer was "Yes."

So, in this case, there is no point in splitting the analysis out per user, perhaps just keep the partitioning at the client level and simply lump all of the user's locations from each client into a single pool of observed countries. This is actually a better scenario; there's more overall data, and as we know, the `rare` function works best when there's lots of routine data to contrast a novel observation against.

Likewise, they were also interested in detecting excessive failed login attempts. Again, their original idea was to track the expected/normal number of logins for every user of every client. Again, this is not really necessary. Simply tracking the typical rate of login activity for the *population* of users within a client is good enough. It again solves the sparse data issue, and ultimately allows for a more scalable ML job since it is not expected to maintain baseline models for every single user.

The moral of the story here is as follows: don't over-engineer the use case if it isn't necessary.

ML job throughput considerations

ML is awesome, and is no doubt very fast and scalable, but there will still be a practical upper bound of events/second processed to any ML job, depending on a couple of different factors:

- The speed at which data can be delivered to the ML algorithms (that is, query performance)
- The speed at which the ML algorithms can chew through the data, given the desired analysis

For the latter, much of the performance is based upon the following:

- The function(s) chosen for the analysis, that is, `count` is faster than `lat_long`
- The chosen `bucket_span` (longer bucket spans are *faster* than smaller bucket spans because more buckets analyzed per unit of time compound the per-bucket processing overhead that's writing results and so on)

However, if you have a defined analysis setup and can't really change it for other reasons, then there's not really much that you can do unless you get creative and split the data up into multiple jobs. This is because the ML jobs (at least for now) are currently tied to a single CPU for the analysis bit (running the C++ process called `autodetect`). So, splitting the data into a few separate ML jobs to at least take advantage of multiple CPUs might be an option. But, before that, let's focus on the former, the query's performance, as there are a variety of possibilities here:

- Avoid doing a cross-cluster search to limit data transmission across the network.
- Tweak datafeed parameters to optimize performance.
- Use Elasticsearch query aggregations to distribute the task of distilling the data to a smaller set of ML algorithms.

The first one is sort of obvious. You're only going to improve performance if you move the analysis closer to the raw data.

The second one may take some experimentation. There are parameters, such as `scroll_size`, which control the size of each scroll. The default is 1,000 and for decent sized clusters, this could be safely increased to 10,000. Run some tests at different scroll sizes and see how it affects query and cluster performance.

The last one should make the biggest impact on performance, in my opinion, but obviously it is a little tricky and error-prone to get the ES aggregation correct for it to work properly with ML, but it's not so bad. See the documentation at `https://www.elastic.co/guide/en/ elastic-stack-overview/current/ml-configuring-aggregation.html` for more information. The downside of using aggregations with ML, in general, is that you lose access to the other fields in the data that might be good as influencers.

All in all, there are a few things to consider when optimizing the ML job's performance.

Top-down alerting by leveraging custom rules

In `Chapter 4`, *IT Operational Analytics and Root Cause Analysis*, we asked "what percentage of the data that you collect is being paid attention to?" Often, a realistic answer is likely <10% and maybe even <1%. The reason why this is the case is that the traditional approach to making data proactive is to start from scratch and then build up thresholds or rules-based alerts over time. This can be a daunting and/or tedious task that requires upfront knowledge (or at least a guess) as to what the expected behavior of each time series should be. Then, once the alerts have been configured, there can be an extended tuning process that balances alert sensitivity with annoying false positives. Additionally, there could also be metrics whose unusual behaviors could never be caught with a static threshold.

Combine this challenge with scale; if I have 10 metrics per server and 100 servers, there are 1,000 individual metrics. Creating individual alerts for each of these is impractical.

However, a single ML job could be created against this data in less than 1 minute. ML's self-learning on historical data, which also takes very little time, will minimize false positives by adapting to the natural characteristics of each time series independently.

Once the ML job has created results, the user can then easily inspect the anomalies that ML finds, and can judge them for their usefulness (or wait for downstream consumers of the anomalies to judge their usefulness). If any of the anomalies are deemed to be not useful, custom rules (`https://www.elastic.co/guide/en/elastic-stack-overview/6.4/ml-rules.html`) allow the user to inject their own domain knowledge, and allow for the customization of how anomalies are determined (that is, never alert on an anomaly on CPU if the value is still less than 90%):

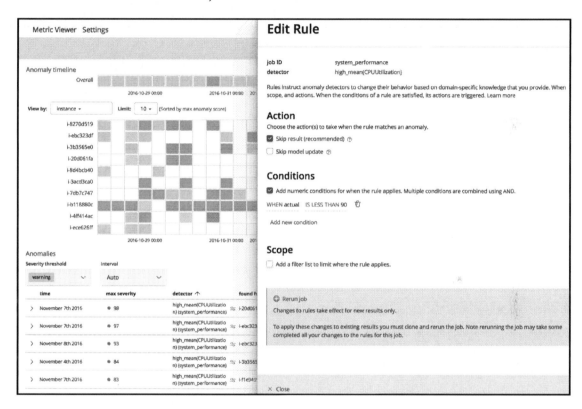

This top-down, rather than bottom-up, approach is much faster and provides more proactive coverage of the data.

Sizing ML deployments

People often ask how they should appropriately size their cluster if they plan on using Elastic ML. Other than the obvious *it depends* answer, it is useful to have an empirical approach to the process. As seen on the Elastic blog *Sizing for Machine Learning with Elasticsearch* (`https://www.elastic.co/blog/sizing-machine-learning-with-elasticsearch`), there is a key recommendation: use dedicated nodes for ML so that you don't have ML jobs interfere with the other tasks of the data nodes of a cluster (indexing, searching, and so on). To scope how many dedicated nodes are necessary, follow this approach:

- If there are no representative jobs created yet, use generic rules of thumb based on the overall cluster size from the blog. These rules of thumb are as follows:
  - Recommend 1 dedicated ML node (2 for HA) for cluster sizes < 10 data nodes
  - Definitely at least 2 ML nodes for clusters up to 25 nodes
  - Add additional ML nodes for every additional 25 data nodes

  Example: 60 data nodes should have 3 (aggressive) or 4 (conservative) ML nodes

- Representative jobs already created for a **proof of concept** (**PoC**) or some already in production:
  - Empirically analyze current jobs and extrapolate
  - Run a script (`https://github.com/PacktPublishing/Machine-Learning-with-the-Elastic-Stack/blob/master/Chapter10/get_all_job_model_bytes.sh`) to dump all of the job's memory usage from the ML API (this also uses the free, open source utility jq (`https://stedolan.github.io/jq/`)
  - Use the spreadsheet in the GitHub repository (`ml_job_sizing.xlsx https://github.com/PacktPublishing/Machine-Learning-with-the-Elastic-Stack/blob/master/Chapter10/ml_job_sizing.xlsx`) to do the extrapolation for you, as follows:

```
#!/bin/bash
HOST='localhost'
PORT=9200
#CURL_AUTH="-u elastic:changeme"
list=`curl $CURL_AUTH -s
http://$HOST:$PORT/_xpack/ml/anomaly_detectors?pretty
| awk -F" : " '/job_id/{print $2}' | sed 's/\",//g' |
```

```
sed 's/\"//g'`
while read -r JOB_ID; do
    curl $CURL_AUTH -s -XPOST
$HOST:$PORT/_xpack/ml/anomaly_detectors/${JOB_ID}/mode
l_snapshots?pretty |  jq '{job_id:
.model_snapshots[0].job_id, size:
.model_snapshots[0].model_size_stats.model_bytes}' |
jq --raw-output '"\(.job_id),\(.size)"'
done <<< "$list"
```

There are several assumptions being made in the sizing spreadsheet:

- CPU and query load are not going to be a limiting factor
- Future jobs will be similar to existing jobs, so extrapolation is a legitimate approach
- This approach does not exclude test jobs that may be configured, but unused
- The user will set `xpack.ml.max_open_jobs` to the appropriate number after the sizing
- The user sets `xpack.ml.max_machine_memory_percent` appropriately (the default is 30%)
- The user will not try to run the analysis over lots of historical data on all jobs at the same time, as this is the most intensive part of ML's operation

Here are some tips:

- ML jobs run outside of the JVM, so if there is a dedicated ML node, the JVM isn't used for much and you can reduce the heap size (from the typical size for a data node) to gain more room for ML jobs
- You can increase `xpack.ml.max_machine_memory_percent` on larger RAM machines, especially if the JVM heap has been reduced
- See other settings in the docs at `https://www.elastic.co/guide/en/ elasticsearch/reference/current/ml-settings.html`

Summary

Elastic ML is a powerful, flexible, yet easy-to-use feature that gives the power of data science to non-data scientists so that they can gain insight into massive amounts of data. Throughout this chapter and this book, there are many different ways that users can take advantage of technology to solve real-world challenges in IT. We hope that you will take the knowledge that you have gained in this book and implement some great use cases of your own. Don't worry about solving all possible problems on day 1; start small, get some tangible wins, and grow your usage as you gain more confidence. Success will breed success!

Other Books You May Enjoy

If you enjoyed this book, you may be interested in these other books by Packt:

Mastering Elastic Stack

Yuvraj Gupta, Ravi Kumar Gupta

ISBN: 978-1-78646-001-1

- Build a pipeline with help of Logstash and Beats to visualize Elasticsearch data in Kibana
- Use Beats to ship any type of data to the Elastic stack
- Understand Elasticsearch APIs, modules, and other advanced concepts
- Explore Logstash and it's plugins
- Discover how to utilize the new Kibana UI for advanced analytics
- See how to work with the Elastic Stack using other advanced configurations
- Customize the Elastic Stack and plugin development for each of the component
- Work with the Elastic Stack in a production environment
- Explore the various components of X-Pack in detail.

Learning Elastic Stack 6.0

Pranav Shukla, Sharath Kumar

ISBN: 978-1-78728-186-8

- Familiarize yourself with the different components of the Elastic Stack
- Get to know the new functionalities introduced in Elastic Stack 6.0
- Effectively build your data pipeline to get data from terabytes or petabytes of data into Elasticsearch and Logstash for searching and logging
- Use Kibana to visualize data and tell data stories in real-time
- Secure, monitor, and use the alerting and reporting capabilities of Elastic Stack
- Take your Elastic application to an on-premise or cloud-based production environment

Leave a review - let other readers know what you think

Please share your thoughts on this book with others by leaving a review on the site that you bought it from. If you purchased the book from Amazon, please leave us an honest review on this book's Amazon page. This is vital so that other potential readers can see and use your unbiased opinion to make purchasing decisions, we can understand what our customers think about our products, and our authors can see your feedback on the title that they have worked with Packt to create. It will only take a few minutes of your time, but is valuable to other potential customers, our authors, and Packt. Thank you!

Index

population job 52, 53, 54
probability models 14, 15
proof of concept (PoC) 282
prophesy
    versus forecasting 233, 234

R

rarity analysis 77
record level 148
record results 153, 155, 159
results index
    about 148, 149, 150
    bucket results 150, 152, 153
    influencer results 159, 160
    record results 153, 155, 159
results presentation
    about 147
    levels 147
root cause analysis, ML jobs
    outage background 101, 103
    shared influencers 103, 104, 107
    visual correlation 103, 104, 107

S

scripted fields
    ML, using 270, 272
Security Information and Event Management
    (SIEM) 111
Single metric job 42, 44, 45, 47
single time series forecasting
    about 238
    dataset preparation 238, 240, 241
    ML job, creating for forecasting 241, 243, 245, 248
split jobs influencers
    versus non-split jobs influencers 265, 267, 268, 270
SQL integration
    using 224, 225, 227, 228, 230, 231
statistical influencers 98, 100
stress process 53
summarized counts 65, 66

T

threat hunting architecture
    about 115
    layer-based ingestion 116, 117, 120
    threat intelligence 120, 122
threat intelligence 120, 122
time periods
    ignoring 275
    unexpected window of time, ignoring 277
    upcoming window of time, ignoring 275
time series visual builder (TSVB) 181
Timelion
    about 180
    ML data, using 204, 206
top-down alerting
    by leveraging custom rules 280, 281
TSVB
    ML data, using 195, 197

U

unexpected window of time
    historical data, re-running 277
    ignoring 277
    job, cloning 277
    model snapshot, reverting 278
unsupervised learning
    about 14
    models, learning 15, 17
    pattern de-trending 18
    probability models 14, 15
    unusualness, scoring 18, 19
unusual
    defining 12, 13
upcoming window of time
    calendar event, creating 276
    datafeed, starting to ignore desired timeframe 277
    datafeed, stopping to ignore desired timeframe 277
    ignoring 275
use cases, forecasting
    time-focused 234
    value-focused 234
user interface (UI) 148